Praise for *American Autopsy*

• • •

"In this book, Dr. Michael Baden exposes that the truth is always the objective no matter how much the powers that be try to ignore it. His autopsies in some of the most high-profile cases in the history of America spoke truth to power and exposed the implicit bias and racism as had never been done before in such a manner."

—Ben Crump, civil rights attorney

"Dr. Michael Baden is the person you call for hard truths, and he spares no one in his story of six decades as a medical examiner. A powerful narrative on its own, *American Autopsy* acts as a mirror in America's ongoing reform of its justice system. There isn't a more important book in 2023."

—Kevin Maurer, *New York Times* bestselling author of *No Easy Day* and *American Radical*

"*American Autopsy* is the revealing history of a medical examiner's journey in the fight for social justice. Dr. Michael Baden has been involved in some of the most high-profile civil rights and police brutality cases in US history—from the investigation into the assassination of Medgar Evers to the death of George Floyd, whose case sparked nationwide protests in 2020. A powerful narrative, *American Autopsy* helps explain the deep divisions in our nation related to race, class, policing, and the criminal justice system."

—Chris Wallace, broadcast journalist

"Dr. Michael Baden, a leader and soldier in the social and justice movement, in writing this personal, riveting, moving book, takes the reader for a journey into the world of a forensic pathologist seeking justice. I could not put this book down once I started reading. A fantastic read."

—Ted Williams, FOX News contributor and criminal and civil attorney

AMERICAN
AUTOPSY

Also by Michael M. Baden, MD

Alcohol, Other Drugs, and Violent Death (with Paul W. Haberman)
Unnatural Death: Confessions of a Medical Examiner
Dead Reckoning: The New Science of Catching Killers
Remains Silent (with Linda Kenney Baden)
Skeleton Justice (with Linda Kenney Baden)

AMERICAN AUTOPSY

• • •

One Medical Examiner's Decades-Long Fight
for Racial Justice in a Broken Legal System

MICHAEL M. BADEN, MD

BenBella Books, Inc.
Dallas, TX

The events, locations, and conversations in this book, while true, are recreated from the author's memory. However, the essence of the story, and the feelings and emotions evoked, are intended to be accurate representations. In certain instances, names of persons, organizations, and places, and other identifying details, have been changed to protect the privacy interests of individuals.

American Autopsy copyright © 2023 by Michael Baden and Linda Kenney Baden, LLC

BenBella Books, Inc.
10440 N. Central Expressway
Suite 800
Dallas, TX 75231
benbellabooks.com
Send feedback to feedback@benbellabooks.com

BenBella is a federally registered trademark.

Printed in the United States of America
10 9 8 7 6 5 4 3 2 1

Library of Congress Control Number: 2022031854
ISBN 9781637740460 (hardcover)
ISBN 9781637740477 (electronic)

Editing by Leah Wilson
Copyediting by James Fraleigh
Proofreading by Isabelle Rubio and Madeline Grigg
Indexing by Elise Hess
Text design and composition by Jordan Koluch
Cover design by Pete Garceau
Printed by Lake Book Manufacturing

Special discounts for bulk sales are available.
Please contact bulkorders@benbellabooks.com.

This book is dedicated to my wife, attorney Linda Kenney Baden,
and my children, Dr. Trissa Baden, Dr. Lindsey Baden,
and Dr. Sarah Baden, who struggle every day
to improve our criminal justice and healthcare systems.

Contents

◆ ◆ ◆

Prologue

...

MEDICAL EXAMINER ON THE ROAD

The midday sun was rising over the Catskill Mountains. I peeked out the front window and spotted a deer at the edge of my driveway. *Not what I was expecting, but a good omen,* I thought. I glanced at my watch. The car was five minutes late. I was a little impatient. Would I make it to the airport on time? My black Standard Poodle, Valjean, waited with me by the front door, wagging his tail. He hadn't seen the deer yet, but he hoped we were headed outside to play. He'd be disappointed when he realized I was leaving without him again.

My wife and children were concerned about my trip. We were in the middle of a once-in-a-century pandemic. Each day, thousands of people across America were being infected with the coronavirus, and more than a thousand were dying from COVID-19. Hospitals were at capacity, and there was no end in sight.

New York City was the epicenter of the pandemic, but my wife Linda and I had left Manhattan early on for a cabin in the Catskill Mountains, about ninety miles north of the city. We believed we'd be safer there than in New York, and so far, so good.

Then I received the call.

It came about noon on May 29, 2020. I was at my desk reviewing new evidence in a case involving a man on death row in a Texas prison. The caller was Benjamin Crump, a prominent civil rights attorney whom I had worked with in the past.

"Doctor Baden, I need your help," he said.

"Okay. What's happening?"

"Have you been following the George Floyd case?"

I took a deep breath. Yes, I knew the details. For days it had been the lead story in the national news. On the evening of Monday, May 25, 2020, Minneapolis police responded to a call about a man who allegedly used a counterfeit $20 bill to buy cigarettes at a grocery store. When officers arrived, they found Floyd sitting in a blue Mercedes-Benz SUV. The cops briefly questioned Floyd, then pulled the forty-six-year-old Black man from the vehicle.

What happened next was captured on bystanders' cellphones. After cuffing his hands behind his back, the officers wrestled and pinned Floyd to the ground. The videos showed Floyd lying on his stomach, the left side of his face pressed against the pavement. Even though he wasn't resisting, a white police officer dug his knee into Floyd's neck to restrain him.

Floyd begged the officer to stop. Unable to get oxygen into his lungs, he could be heard pleading repeatedly: "I can't breathe. I can't breathe." As the minutes ticked by, the officer continued to hold him down. Then, Floyd fell silent and motionless.

Nine minutes after putting his knee on Floyd's neck, the officer got up. But it was too late. By the time paramedics lifted a limp Floyd onto a stretcher, he was already in cardiac arrest—not breathing and lifeless. The videos of the altercation went viral, sparking national protests against police brutality.

A day after Floyd's death, Hennepin County medical examiner Andrew Baker conducted an autopsy. But the prosecutor's office didn't release Baker's preliminary findings until four days later, May 29. In a news release that morning, Hennepin County attorney Mike Freeman said the autopsy showed the police restraint had nothing to do with Floyd's death—there were "no physical findings that support a diagnosis of traumatic asphyxiation."

Instead, Freeman highlighted other factors. He said Floyd's underlying health problems, including preexisting cardiovascular disease and "potential intoxicants" in his system had "likely contributed to his death." He noted it could be months before they had the results of the toxicology tests, which were needed to complete the autopsy report.

Floyd's family was furious. That's why Crump called me. I had been New

York City's chief medical examiner and then the lead forensic pathologist for the New York State Police. I also had my own private practice, focusing on civil rights cases. During my five decades as a forensic pathologist, I had investigated many high-profile cases, including several with Crump. My findings have resulted in criminal charges being filed or dismissed, or judgments for victim's families in fatal police encounters.

I had been working with Crump since 2006 when he reached out to me about a Black teenager who had died in a Florida juvenile boot camp. A medical examiner had blamed the teenager's death on a benign blood disorder—not the excessive force law enforcement personnel had used to restrain him.

Now, in 2020, Crump sought my help again. "This is an outrage," Crump said. "The family wants you to do a second autopsy."

"When?"

"Now. Today if possible."

Most second autopsies are performed because the decedent's family believes the medical examiner or coroner could have made a mistake or missed something important, or because the survivors are biased against the police. And they know it could take months before a medical examiner releases a final autopsy report and issues the death certificate because the ME has to examine the toxicology tests. (The autopsy itself is an external and internal visual examination of the body to determine the cause of death. The toxicology report is an examination of body fluids to determine if drugs are present. Sometimes both are needed to make a determination.) They want a second opinion. But families don't have much time to decide whether to hire a forensic pathologist to conduct a second autopsy, because they need to bury or cremate the body. If the family has any doubts or misgivings, it may make sense to them to proceed with the second autopsy.

Crump was concerned about something else. Medical examiners are supposed to be independent scientists. But he knew that wasn't always the case. They work so closely with law enforcement that they often consider themselves part of the prosecution team—the so-called good guys. They are therefore supposed to help police and prosecutors defeat the "bad guys"—the defendants and their lawyers. In cases where police may have caused the death of a bad guy, Crump had seen how medical examiners often found ways to shift blame away from law enforcement and onto the victim.

That's why he pressed me: "We need you right away."

Silence. Yes, I wanted to do it. But the pandemic complicated everything. I promised Crump I'd talk to my family and call him right back.

When I broached the subject with my wife, who's an attorney, she didn't hesitate: "You've got to go." She reminded me how I'd been fighting for social justice for years. "This is for all you've tried to do. This death clearly exposes what you've been saying for decades."

My three children, all doctors, expressed concern about the trip. They and Linda wanted to make sure I was properly protected from the virus, for which we didn't yet have a vaccine. That meant double masks and safe distances from others at all times—even while I was in meetings.

If I contracted the coronavirus, I knew the outcome wouldn't be good. It would probably kill me. Yes, I was in good health, but the virus seemed to be hitting seniors the hardest. My children had warned me about overcrowded hospitals and the glaring shortage of personal protective equipment. Still, I had to go.

I phoned Crump to let him know. "I'll call you as soon as I make flight arrangements," I said.

I hung up and scrambled. I had a lot of work to do. My wife helped me make the reservations. With so many airlines grounded because of the pandemic, it was hard finding a flight. I managed to book a direct flight to Minneapolis, but it was for late afternoon the next day, and I'd have to fly out of Newark Liberty International Airport, more than a hundred miles south of Bethel.

I called Crump back and told him my travel plans. I asked him for the telephone number of the funeral home. I wanted to see if I could perform the autopsy there, and to ask if they had any of the equipment that I'd need but couldn't bring on the airplane, such as a scalpel, a knife, scissors, and a bone saw. Crump said he'd handle that and would arrange for someone to transport me from the airport to the hotel where he and other lawyers were staying. There, they'd update me on the case.

I didn't sleep much that night. I stepped mentally through the upcoming autopsy, careful not to miss anything. This death had profound implications. The video had captured the horror of what happened outside the grocery store.

Bystanders had shouted at the officers, saying they were killing Floyd. Yet the cop whose knee was on Floyd's neck appeared to be enjoying the situation. He looked directly into the phone camera of one of the bystanders with an imperious smirk that seemed to say: *I'm a police officer. I'm in charge here, and there's nothing you can do about it.*

I knew from experience that medical examiners, prosecutors, and officers often used preliminary autopsy results to spin fatal police encounters in favor of the police. After releasing their version of an incident, law enforcement might refuse to disclose further important information for months, hoping public interest would fade.

The following morning, I packed my small rolling suitcase with a green "scrub" autopsy outfit, my magnifying glass to better evaluate small abnormalities and injuries, an old gray ruler with inch and centimeter markings, and my cell phone and charger to take autopsy photographs. I included folders with information about the Texas death row case I'd been working on when Crump called.

Delta flight 4677 would depart at 4:47 PM. Now, as I bent to pet Valjean, it was already noon. I was cutting it close.

I looked at Linda. "I'll be careful."

She smiled. "I know."

A horn beeped. Valjean barked. The deer scampered away. It was time to go. I kissed Linda and Valjean goodbye.

"Be safe," she whispered.

"I will," I promised.

Linda had to hold back the dog as I opened the door. I put on my facemask, wheeled the suitcase to the car, and tossed it in the trunk. I knew the driver, Robert Schwartz, who was born and bred in the Catskills. He had driven me to airports many times before.

"Where ya going, Doc?"

"Minneapolis," I said.

He smiled. I think he knew why but didn't ask. We headed east on New York State Route 17, then south on the Garden State Parkway. I stared out the window at the countryside. Everything was in bloom—the flowers, the trees. It was May 30, 2020. Usually the roads would be crowded with families headed to the beaches along the Jersey Shore. But today there was no traffic because of COVID. It felt ominous.

The airport likewise was a ghost town. Schwartz dropped me off at the Delta terminal. Very few people were at security or the boarding gates. Everyone was wearing masks.

Early for my flight, I sat down at my gate, making sure I was at least six feet away from anyone else. I was antsy. I just wanted to board the plane and get there. The airport televisions were turned to the cable news stations, and the stories rolled over and over: COVID, George Floyd, protests in city after city. I wondered if the large crowds of shouting protesters would lead to more coronavirus cases. At least many of them were wearing masks.

Finally, my flight was ready to board. I watched the other passengers head to the gate. There weren't many. Onboard, many of the seats were covered with yellow tape to prevent passengers from sitting next to each other. We prepared for takeoff. Only a third of the seats were full, but people still felt too close. No one was flying unless they had to.

The engines whined. In a few minutes, we would be airborne. In a few hours, I would be there. I was anxious to see Floyd's body, to see what was done—and wasn't done—at the first autopsy. In my opinion, all autopsies begin at the scene of the death. I saw on the video that this death could have been due to neck compression and positional asphyxia, which happens when too much pressure is placed on a person's neck, face, or back when they're prone. That kind of restraint prevents a person from breathing but leaves no visible marks discoverable at autopsy. The news release from the prosecutor's office said there were no abnormal autopsy findings—nothing that was consistent with positional asphyxia. "No abnormal findings," however, *is* consistent with positional asphyxia. Pressure on the body by itself leaves no marks. I wondered, would the public even understand the term *positional asphyxia*? I shook my head. I felt that I was going to Minneapolis to simply confirm the obvious—to add the weight of expertise to what everyone could clearly see for themselves in the video.

If it wasn't for that video, it would have been the word of policemen against the word of civilian witnesses—and prosecutors and grand juries almost always believe law enforcement.

I thought about taking out my paperwork, but I was tired. The day was catching up with me, and the next few days would be hectic. As the plane taxied down the runway, I closed my eyes. Hopefully, my findings would be able to independently determine how Floyd died. And if they confirmed that the officers who held him down were responsible for his death, then maybe this time, the police would be held accountable.

Chapter 1

• • •

MOONLIGHTING

Another night, another eight hours of broken limbs and stopped hearts. I was exhausted. It was the autumn of 1960 and I had spent a long day at the Bellevue Hospital Emergency Room in New York City. Now I was headed uptown, ready for a quiet evening with my then-wife, Judianne, and our one-year-old daughter, Trissa. I was hoping I could provide some relief for Judianne, who was juggling medical school, a toddler, and a difficult pregnancy.

When I walked into our apartment, something in the kitchen smelled delicious. Spaghetti and meat sauce with garlic bread. But then, the phone on the wall started to ring. Judianne answered.

"It's for you," she said, handing me the phone.

It was a clerk at the medical examiner's office, rattling off a name and address. "Hold on," I said. I found a pen and a scrap of paper by the sink. "Okay. I'm ready."

I scribbled it down. "I'm on my way," I said. I hung up and turned to face my wife.

"I have to go."

"What is it tonight?"

"Dead baby."

She grimaced. "Where?"

"Harlem."

My wife knew the drill. I stuffed the paper in my pocket, grabbed my briefcase, kissed her goodbye, and headed out the door. I probably wouldn't be back until after midnight.

I hurried down two flights of stairs and into the street. I stopped for a moment to catch my breath. It was a crisp autumn night and the stars stretched across the slice of sky above the buildings. I flipped up my coat collar, then bounded down the block to my blue 1958 Nash Rambler. I started it up and headed east, then north on Franklin Delano Roosevelt (FDR) Drive.

As always, I was in a rush. I had two jobs. During the day I worked at Bellevue Hospital, where I was an intern in internal medicine. Then, three nights a week I worked as an assistant medical examiner "tour doctor"—the physician who goes to a death scene. It was ironic. At one job, I saved lives. At the other, I figured out how they'd been lost.

I knew I couldn't maintain this pace forever. At some point I'd have to decide between internal medicine and forensic pathology. It should have been an easy decision, but I was struggling with it.

Internists, specially trained physicians who diagnose and treat a wide range of complicated medical problems, were respected specialists. Forensic pathologists, specially trained physicians who examined and dissected the bodies of people who died suddenly, unexpectedly, or violently, were looked down on by the medical establishment. Before World War II, some physicians saw the field as a dumping ground for alcoholic and incompetent doctors who couldn't make it in the life-saving business. Instead, they ended up doing autopsies, analyzing others' failures.

I certainly didn't see it that way. For me, forensic pathologists were medical detectives. They looked for microscopic clues as they put together complex puzzles. When all the pieces were in place, they could tell if someone had died of natural causes or by accident, suicide, or foul play.

My path had seemed so clear when I began medical school in the fall of 1955. I wanted to follow in the footsteps of Dickinson Richards and André Cournand, well-known internists at Bellevue Hospital who would later be awarded the Nobel Prize in Medicine for their groundbreaking work in heart and lung disease using cardiac catheterization, a procedure that measures how well the heart is working.

But then, my ambitions began to change. During my first year at New

York University School of Medicine, I dissected, as all medical students did in those days, a formalin-fixed, dried-out human cadaver. We knew nothing about the corpse other than it had been donated for medical students to perform anatomical dissection and learn how the body functions.

The professor, an old Viennese anatomist, suggested that if we wanted to learn more about the human body, we could go across the street to the New York City Medical Examiner's Office at Bellevue Hospital.

"That's where autopsies are done on fresh bodies every day," he said.

I loved anatomy. So I took his advice and quickly discovered that I liked everything about medical examiner autopsies—the entire experience. I'd watch in awe as doctors holding scalpels, scissors, and bone saws or other tools of the trade carefully dissected the bodies lying atop steel tables. The building itself added a strange ambiance to the process.

At the time, the New York City Medical Examiner's Office was in Bellevue's pathology building on the hospital's sprawling campus, near the infamous Psychiatric Hospital. The morgue was on the second floor of a four-story Victorian building, a cavernous room with tall windows and a twenty-foot ceiling. Bodies were stored in the basement and hoisted by rope by the doctor or diener (a morgue assistant) to the second floor via a small, early-1900s freight elevator.

There was no air conditioning. It was brutally hot there in the summer. Opening the rooftop windows provided a welcome draft, but it also created a pathway for huge flies attracted by the dead. The room always had a strong odor of formaldehyde. You'd almost expect to see Dr. Victor Frankenstein in his white lab coat, hovering over a corpse, knife in hand.

The room was not a place for the squeamish. Yet, during my first visit, I was strangely drawn to it. All the elements that excited me about pathology were there: the mystery, the thrill of solving a puzzle, the rigor of research, and the connection with public health. It helped that during my first visit I met a man who would take me under his wing: Milton Helpern, the chief medical examiner, who I'd first encountered a few years before, when he gave a talk to the Pre-Medical Society of the City College of New York—his alma mater. When I stepped into the autopsy room, a group of white-coated doctors remained in the hallway, far from the autopsy table, where Helpern worked alone on the remains of a thirty-five-year-old man.

I walked over to Helpern and reminded him of that talk at the City College, when he had invited us to visit him at the city morgue.

"Well, here I am, a first-year medical student," I added.

Helpern smiled at me and said he was trying to determine if the man in front of him—whose body was spotted with red blisters, some containing pus—had died of smallpox.

Smallpox? I shook my head. That highly contagious, disfiguring, and often deadly disease had been nearly eradicated by a global vaccination campaign. It was rare to find the disease anywhere in the world, let alone the United States.

If it were smallpox, it could have a profound effect on the city's public health. Everyone in New York would have to be vaccinated again. Eight years before, in 1947, I had stood in a long line around Brooklyn's Cumberland Hospital waiting to be revaccinated against smallpox, along with six million other New Yorkers throughout the city, because a businessman had returned to Manhattan from Mexico with smallpox. Twelve people were infected, two died. All of us already had the easily recognizable circular smallpox vaccination scar on our shoulders from childhood. But the health commissioner wanted to revaccinate everyone just to be safe. It worked. New York City's vaccination effort—the most massive vaccination program in a US city at that time—stopped the spread.

"Bring over those lights," he said, pointing to lights on two green three-legged stools used for autopsy photography. He then took a lot of 35 mm photographs with an old medical examiner's camera.

He also sent me to the NYU medical school library across the street to search journals from the 1880s that compared smallpox to similar diseases and explained how to tell them apart. For instance, certain forms of chicken pox can look like smallpox. I pored over the papers, pulling as much information as possible. But I wasn't done. I also talked to the chairman of the pediatrics department, who had done work on fatal chicken pox cases in children. I was like a sponge, soaking in as much information as possible.

When I returned, I gave Helpern my report. He nodded as he listened. I could tell he was impressed that I had put together so much information in such a short time. He said the microscopic slides would be finished tomorrow and he'd know whether it was smallpox or chickenpox by the appearance of the nucleus in the white blood cells.

When I returned the next day, he had a big smile. "Hemorrhagic chicken-pox," he said.

That was my first exposure to a medical examiner case. It involved public health and autopsies. I was hooked. With training in both internal medicine and forensic pathology, I'd be able to correlate the autopsy findings with the clinical disease, which appealed to me very much.

I volunteered in Helpern's office throughout medical school, and when I started my internal medicine residency at Bellevue, I began moonlighting there as a second job. Because I had a license to practice medicine, Helpern hired me as an assistant medical examiner. That meant I had more responsibility: I could go to death scenes by myself and sign death certificates—things I couldn't do as a student. I was paid $25 for an eight-hour shift.

Issuing accurate death certificates is the most important part of a medical examiner's work. At that time, ninety thousand people died each year in New York City. About thirty thousand were reported to the medical examiner's office, and about eight thousand required autopsies. All deaths have to be certi-fied, either by a treating doctor or medical examiner. Family members need the document to settle estates, claim life insurance, or collect government benefits. Public health officials used them to compile data and statistics on why, where, and how people die.

That's why I went out to Harlem that night. I had to investigate and help find the baby's cause of death. This could mean not only examining the body at the scene, but also interviewing family and neighbors for valuable informa-tion about medical history and what had happened to the girl that day.

As I drove, I prepared myself. Seeing the body of a child is always a shock, and I couldn't let my emotions interfere. I reminded myself that my job was about science, gathering facts and evidence, seeing what had happened. At a scene, the tour doctor has to decide whether to issue a death certificate right away, allowing the family to make funeral arrangements, or send the body to the morgue for possible autopsy. Babies and children were always sent to the morgue because the cause of death was more likely to be unnatural. Maybe that's why I was still considering my career choices. As an internist, I wouldn't have to subject myself to these awful sights.

I got off the FDR Drive and headed west on 125th Street, cutting through one of the toughest sections of New York. When I went to death scenes at night, a police officer was supposed to meet me at the location. I sure hoped one would be waiting there tonight.

Yet, I didn't see any cops when I parked in front of the building. Even though it was late, there were still some people hanging out on both sides of the block. I took a deep breath and grabbed my briefcase, filled with papers and a camera. As usual, I'd take detailed notes of the scene and body.

Entering the building, I saw the place was a walk-up—no elevator. I'd have to trudge up the stairs. And of course, the apartment was on the top floor. When I got there, the police officer was standing outside a door, a "what the fuck am I doing here?" look on his face.

"Inside," he muttered.

I nodded and walked into the apartment. The parents were seated in the living room, crying. The place was filthy: dishes piled up in the sink, a few empty liquor bottles on the floor.

I entered the bathroom and there she was. Not a baby. A nude seven-year-old Black girl, face up in the bathtub, water drained out. Her parents said she had drowned, but I noticed that she had bruises on her body. Her skin was cool to the touch; early rigor mortis was present, early lividity on her back. These postmortem changes indicated that she had been dead for a few hours before someone called police.

"Abuse," I wrote in my pad. I took a few pictures. I told the police officer that he should notify the precinct that this was a possible homicide. I returned to the living room and asked the parents a few basic questions. Any prior illnesses? Seizures or disorders? Did they hear anything? How long had she been left alone in the tub? Then I stopped. I knew that arriving officers would take over that part of the investigation. Before leaving I went into the kitchen and checked the refrigerator: lots of beer bottles, no milk, little that a child could eat.

As I prepared to leave, one of the officers approached me. Dispatch wanted me to go to another case, he said. They'd gotten a call about an elderly woman on the Upper East Side, on Park Avenue. She had died, and her doctor was in Europe. They needed someone to sign a death certificate before the body could be released to the funeral home.

I sighed and wrote down the address. When I left the building, well after midnight, many people were still out in the street. Life went on, no matter what became of little girls in bathtubs on the floors above. I tried not to think about it as I drove to my next assignment.

I had seen poverty while growing up in a Brooklyn housing project, but nothing like some of the places I went to on these calls. Whatever little money the people I met there had was sometimes spent on the wrong things: alcohol and drugs. Often, the electricity had been turned off for nonpayment. There was no food in the refrigerators, even when the house was filled with children. Most of the cases I went to were in poor neighborhoods. Going to Park Avenue was unusual.

I parked outside the elderly woman's building. I didn't need protection here. This was an upscale neighborhood of well-maintained high-rises. A fully uniformed doorman greeted me when I walked to the front of the building. The lobby was immaculate, from the shiny marble floors to the chandelier.

I took the elevator to the sixth floor. The doors rolled open on a scene with nearly a dozen police officers, chatting, laughing. *A party*, I thought.

When I walked inside, the apartment looked like a spread from *Esquire*. There was a gold-colored couch and matching settee, red drapes, and area rugs that covered the hardwood floor. One of the officers filled me in: the woman had been battling cancer.

"She probably died of natural causes," he said.

I nodded and walked into the bedroom. Her body was in the bed. She looked peaceful, like she was sleeping. I was taken by the sharp contrast between this scene and the one I had just left. No one paid much attention when a Black child was beaten to death in Harlem. But when a rich, elderly white woman died in her sleep in a tony Manhattan co-op, half the police department turned out.

Death investigations mirror society. Money and power play the same role in death as they do in life. Rudolf Virchow, the father of pathology, wrote in the 1850s that "physicians are the natural attorneys of the poor" and that "social problems largely fall within their scope." If that was true, I reasoned, maybe I could make a bigger difference as a forensic pathologist than an internist. At least as a forensic pathologist I could help identify and find ways to address societal problems.

What I didn't know, as I wrestled that night with the choice I knew I had to make between my two possible career paths, was that a young drug addict would soon help me decide.

Chapter 2

. . .

THE NEEDLE AND THE DAMAGE DONE

Jose Maldonado was sick. Real sick. You didn't have to be a doctor to see that. He was gaunt, his cheeks sallow. The right side of his body was almost fully paralyzed; he could barely hold his head up. Maldonado was twenty-six years old but looked much older. I didn't have a diagnosis yet, but his forearms gave me a big clue.

I'd been finishing my patient rounds at Bellevue when a nurse approached me in the hallway. She said a young man had just been admitted and was on his way up. He was in bad shape.

"He may have had a stroke," she said.

"A stroke? How old is he?"

"In his twenties."

I sighed. It was a late afternoon in February 1961, and I was the receiving resident on the medicine ward. I had already been working twelve hours. I was on duty for thirty-six hours, followed by twelve off and another thirty-six on. As all the internal medicine house staff did, I had a small room in the hospital with a bed to use whenever I was able to get rest.

Bellevue was America's first free public hospital, founded in 1736. Ever since, it had followed a policy of treating every patient who showed up at its door. The hospital was on the forefront of dozens of advances in American medicine. Countless people had been treated there over the years, and thousands of great doctors and nurses had trained there, too. A half-dozen Nobel laureates were among the hundreds of attending doctors doing research, treating indigent patients, and teaching medical students and house staff. But New Yorkers knew Bellevue mainly as a psychiatric lockup for the insane. As a kid, I remember moms warning us to "stop acting crazy, or the men in white coats will haul you off to Bellevue." It didn't help that Bellevue's nine-story red-brick Psychiatric Hospital building was surrounded by a spiky wrought-iron fence, only adding to its creepy image.

A nurse's aide had changed our newest arrival into a hospital gown before bringing him to my twenty-bed ward and had already rolled two privacy screens around his bed. I picked up the chart attached to the foot of the bed as I approached. Temperature was 103°, high, and pulse 105, also high. And there was the clue to the reason for his admission: obvious old and fresh linear needle puncture marks and scars over veins on his forearms.

Whenever I saw a new patient, I thought of the words written 150 years earlier by Sir William Osler, the father of modern medicine and founder of Johns Hopkins School of Medicine: "Listen to the patient. He is telling you the diagnosis. The good physician treats the disease; the great physician treats the patient who has the disease." I found that in too many instances, doctors didn't have the time or desire to interact with patients. Instead of asking questions about a patient's lifestyle, which could have offered clues about their illness, the doctors preferred to run tests. Yet by doing tests alone, they could miss important clinical information.

"When was the last time you shot up?" I asked Maldonado.

He looked surprised that I was being so direct. "Why?"

I was blunt: "I think you have an infection from using dirty needles."

He grimaced. He said he had injected heroin about four hours earlier. He hadn't been feeling good for a few days. But after he shot up, he passed out in the lobby of his building. Someone called the police. In the ambulance, he discovered that he couldn't move his right arm and leg. He said he had no other medical conditions. Yes, he was a heroin addict, but before this episode he was healthy. Now, he was worried. "What's wrong with me?" he asked.

I didn't want to scare him, but when I inspected his hands, I saw thin, linear red hemorrhages under his fingernails. They were a sign that he probably had bacteria growing on his mitral or aortic heart valve and that small blood clots containing those bacteria were breaking off and causing the so-called splinter hemorrhages. I suspected that a small clot had traveled to the left side of his brain, blocking blood flow and paralyzing the right side of his body. If I was right, he'd probably die. I needed to get more information—not only to help Maldonado, but other addicts, too.

At that time, heroin addicts usually carried a pouch with "the works"— the drugs plus tools they'd need to get high. They would remove the white heroin powder from a small plastic envelope, place it in a bottlecap or spoon, add water, and heat it with a match. With a hypodermic needle attached to an eyedropper as a makeshift syringe, they would inject the dissolved heroin directly into a vein. It was the quickest way to get high. The drug swiftly traveled straight to the brain, causing euphoria, disorientation, and pain relief. Addicts didn't use a new needle or syringe every time they shot up; instead they used the same ones over and over. Nothing was sterile. Whatever bacteria were living on the dirty needle were injected into the addict's bloodstream along with the heroin. And if they shared their needles, they transferred the bacteria to other addicts.

Once in the bloodstream, the bacteria would look for places to nestle in and grow, forming colonies and clusters. Heart valves are among their favorite spots. If bacteria settle on the right side of the heart, clusters can move to the lungs and cause abscesses. If they settle on the left side, where the aortic and mitral valves are, clusters can break off as the valves continuously open and shut, then be carried to the brain or other organs. I believed that was what had happened to Maldonado. However, to save his life, I first had to confirm my suspicion.

I had been seeing more and more heroin addicts over the previous year— live ones at Bellevue, and dead ones at scenes and on examination tables at the morgue. Both my jobs involved conducting studies and research to diagnose injury and death. I had learned that if we could figure out the pathology of a disease, we could get a better handle on treating it effectively.

I told Maldonado I needed to draw some blood and get the samples down to the bacteriology lab right away. But when I came over with a rubber tourniquet, syringe, and test tubes to fill, Maldonado stopped me. "It's a pain in the ass for doctors to get blood from drug addicts," he said, adding that doctors only further scar their veins.

He was right. Collapsed, scarred veins were a common problem among intravenous drug users, making it difficult for doctors and nurses to find good ones.

"Let me do it. I know where the open veins are," he said.

I handed him the needle and watched. He slowly and methodically tapped his finger against a vein in his arm. I swabbed the area with an iodine mixture to sterilize it. Then he stuck the needle into the vein near the fold of his elbow. He drew blood into the syringe as skillfully as any doctor at Bellevue.

He handed me the filled syringe and I squeezed the blood into the four glass tubes to bring to the lab. When I returned, I did a full physical examination. Then I sat with Maldonado in the chair next to his bed. We talked for an hour about his symptoms, drug use, prior treatments, the significance of his tattoos, and how he got money to support his habit.

Maldonado was articulate and sometimes self-deprecating. He looked haggard, but he was still handsome, a tall, light-skinned Puerto Rican from East Harlem.

As he told me his story, I discovered that we had a few things in common. He grew up with a single mother in a housing project in East Harlem, a tough neighborhood in upper Manhattan. I was raised in the Fort Greene Projects in Brooklyn. My parents divorced when I was twelve. My mother worked as a sewing machine operator in Manhattan's Garment District, and my father was rarely there for my mother or me and my younger brother, Robert. Maldonado came from a broken home, too, but whereas I had my mother's love and support, he had no one. At home there was only violence. His father was in and out of his life. His mother didn't have time for him, burdened with working several jobs and caring for his six younger siblings. So, Maldonado found his "family" in a street gang.

By the time Maldonado was twelve, he'd stopped going to school and started living in abandoned buildings, sleeping on friends' sofas or in cars. Heroin helped him get through life. It helped ease the emotional pain. Soon the pleasure faded, but by then he couldn't stop. Heroin withdrawal is harrowingly painful, he said, especially in the joints.

"It's so bad it makes you want to keep using," he told me.

His life soon revolved around getting money not so much to get high, but to prevent withdrawal. From the time he got up in the morning, he'd steal whatever he could get his hands on. He'd rip off people he cared about. Nothing was more important than feeding his addiction. I knew he wasn't alone. The city's jails were filled with addicts like Maldonado.

Early-1960s New York City was in the middle of a heroin crisis. The city was undergoing dramatic cultural and socioeconomic changes. Tourists still flocked to admire the Empire State Building, the Statue of Liberty, and Central Park. They came for the restaurants, shows, and museums, or maybe to watch a ball game. But beneath the surface, the city had changed. After World War II, families who could afford it fled to the suburbs. They left behind working-class and poor families who struggled to make a living. Some turned to drugs to lighten their burdens. At the same time, landlords stopped making costly repairs to older buildings, and abandoned thousands of tenements, warehouses, and factory buildings. Those vacant structures became homes to feral children—and hangouts for addicts whose drug of choice was heroin.

City leaders struggled to downplay it, but I'd seen the bodies. I believed heroin abuse was an epidemic. New York's daily newspapers were filled with stories about "junkies" breaking into homes and businesses or mugging citizens in the streets.

Police officials claimed illicit drug abuse was a problem of Black and Hispanic people—not whites. I knew they were wrong. Whites were just as likely to shoot up, although I found that the hardest-hit neighborhoods in New York were in Manhattan: Harlem, which was predominantly Black, and East Harlem, which was overwhelmingly Puerto Rican. But cops used their narrative to justify aggressive policing tactics in minority communities, including stopping and searching Black and Hispanic people on the street or in their cars without justification.

The irony was heroin wasn't a new drug. It was the unfortunate result of the medical search for an effective painkiller.

As far back as six thousand years ago, Neolithic and Bronze Age peoples knew that the sap of the poppy seed capsule—opium—killed pain. In the nineteenth century, scientists extracted morphine—named after Morpheus, the Greek god of sleep and dreams—from the opium. The principal drug obtained from opium, morphine relieves pain while producing a very pleasant if brief euphoric feeling. But it is highly addictive: users would need to increase the dosage to continue to receive pain relief, and if they stopped using it, they developed a severe, painful withdrawal syndrome.

During the Civil War, physicians widely administered morphine injections to treat the agony of battle wounds. Troops also had free access to morphine and opium, which they carried with them to assist wounded fellow soldiers. But then as now, morphine caused more suffering and death than it relieved. By the end of the war, thousands of troops were addicted to the opiate painkiller. It was called "soldiers' disease." For many veterans, as Maldonado found, it was easier to keep taking the drugs than to quit and endure the terrible withdrawal symptoms. Morphine and opium were also legal for civilians, sold openly in drug stores in wildly popular tonics and elixirs.

By the 1890s, however, public sentiment began to turn. Newspapers ran stories about the dangers of morphine and opium addiction. The articles said some people were seen on the streets, walking like stoned-out zombies, while others became violent as they searched for the next fix. By 1895, an estimated 1 in 200 Americans were addicted to the drugs.

Enter the Bayer Company, a German pharmaceutical giant then and now. In 1898, Bayer marketed a new drug to cure morphine and opium addiction and the pain of cancer, too, by combining morphine with acetic acid, forming diacetylmorphine. Bayer called this miracle drug heroin. But the downside soon became apparent: heroin, while much more potent than morphine in relieving pain, was also more addictive and more likely to kill users.

In 1924, heroin was banned completely in the United States, creating thousands of addicts like Maldonado, who then struggled to get enough money to buy it illegally.

During World War II, limited access to Turkish poppy fields led to shortages in the morphine needed for medical and surgical use. So, the United States developed artificially made meperidine (Demerol) and Germany made methadone (Dolophine).

In the 1950s, heroin began making a comeback in the United States—thanks to organized crime. The "French Connection," a collaboration between Corsican gangsters in Marseille, France, and the Sicilian Mafia, smuggled heroin into the ready New York market. People in low-income neighborhoods were the prime victims. They took heroin for the same reasons their grand-parents used opiates in the late 1800s—as a momentary escape from dire circumstances.

By the time Maldonado turned up in my hospital ward, there were an estimated 100,000 addicts in the New York area alone.

Maldonado yawned; he was "talked out." As his eyes were closing, he asked, "Am I going to make it?"

I took a deep breath. "Let me get the test results back, and we'll figure it out. We'll take good care of you here," I said.

I stood up, closed my notepad, and stuffed my pen into my shirt pocket. The results would come soon. I was pretty sure it was subacute bacterial en-docarditis. *Streptococcus* was the most common bacteria present in these infec-tions, as they have a proclivity for the mitral valve.

The blood work and other tests confirmed my suspicion. Maldonado was infected with one of the viridans-group streptococci, and they were most likely growing on a heart valve. Now, I had to come up with a plan to save the man's life.

In theory, antibiotics should have knocked out the infection. It was sus-ceptible to penicillin. But for Maldonado to have any chance of survival, he'd have to be on the antibiotic intravenously for . . . weeks? Months? I just didn't know. He'd need a lot of penicillin and a lot of luck. The treatment had not succeeded in a drug addict in Bellevue before. Addicts didn't usually come in until the infection had become untreatable. Still, I saw this as his only hope. I'd treat Maldonado with massive doses of penicillin.

When I walked into the ward the following day to share our plan, Maldo-nado was still feeling weak. He could tell from my face that his situation was serious: "You don't look so good, Doc."

I didn't sugarcoat it. "Jose, I'm going to give it to you straight. You have a heart infection. For most people, it's a death sentence."

I could see the panic in his eyes, but before he had a chance to speak, I explained what I wanted to do. He'd have to be in the hospital for a long time, during which he'd be hooked up to an IV with penicillin. He couldn't leave Bellevue. He couldn't do heroin. He couldn't do much of anything. And maybe, just maybe, it would work.

"I'll oversee your treatment. I'll be here every step of the way," I promised. He nodded weakly. "Okay, Doc."

"One more thing. During this period, I'd like to ask you more questions about your life. I want to know everything about you. Everything about heroin."

"It's a deal."

And so, we began. Maldonado was the first person I saw at the beginning of my shifts, and the last person I saw before I left. Every day Maldonado lived was a small victory. Our conversations became an enjoyable part of my working days.

"You know, I wish I would have had more goals growing up," he told me one day. "My only goal was staying alive for the next day."

I asked how he got his heroin. He laughed.

"Do you think I went to a doctor?"

"No."

"When you're on the streets, you know where to score," he said.

Drug addicts usually hang out with one another, he said. They hide in plain sight. Any time of day, he could walk into an abandoned building and find other drug users shooting up. Sometimes, they'd share their stash and their needles.

I had noticed that when I was called to the scene of a fatal overdose, the body often was isolated: in a vacant apartment, an alley, a park, a staircase, on a rooftop, or by the curb. "It seems like heroin addicts always die alone. Why is that?"

"They don't die alone," he said. "We usually shoot up with others. If someone dies, we move the bodies." It had nothing to do with foul play. If someone died in your house, you didn't want the cops coming there. It could mean trouble. You didn't want the body in your hideout, either. That's like your home. So you moved them. But there was another reason, too. The addicts wanted the bodies to be found, so they could be buried—so their families would know what happened and could say goodbye.

I had never thought of it like that. I wrote it down in my notebook.

Maldonado began to trust me, and he opened up more about his life. He described unscrupulous behavior by some police officers. No one in his neighborhood trusted cops.

Then he told me about how police framed him when he was a teenager. He was walking in his neighborhood when a couple of cops stopped him.

"We got a call that someone stole some fruit from a grocery store and we just want to check you," a police officer told Maldonado.

Maldonado shrugged. "Go ahead," he said.

Just before they frisked him, another police officer pointed to a plastic bag containing a white substance by Maldonado's feet.

"Is that yours?" the cop asked.

"No," Maldonado said. "I don't know where that came from."

After examining the bag, the officer slapped handcuffs on Maldonado. "It's heroin."

Maldonado said his heart was racing, but there was nothing he could do. "It wasn't mine, but I couldn't protest too much because I knew what would happen if I did," he said. He'd seen police use excessive force on his friends. "They'd beat the shit out of me, and they'd push for a long prison sentence."

Racial injustice had built mistrust in minority neighborhoods. Police acted more like an occupying army than community protectors. Residents resented their presence.

But it was more than that, Maldonado said. "This wasn't the first time that cops had planted drugs on someone in my neighborhood. It went on all the time."

When he went to court, he pleaded guilty. "I knew I couldn't fight the system. It was my word against theirs." Since it was his first offense, Maldonado got a suspended sentence. But the damage was done. He now had a criminal record.

I believed Maldonado. Sometimes, police officers would hang out in the autopsy room while I dissected homicide victims. They considered me "part of the team," so they'd chat and crack jokes with me. A couple of times, they'd laughed about a medical condition they said afflicted drug addicts.

"What is it?" I asked.

"*Dropsy*," one cop said.

"Huh?" I only knew dropsy as an obsolete medical term used to refer to the accumulation of fluid in the body caused by heart, kidney, or liver disease.

The officer said if they suspected someone was a drug addict, they couldn't search him without probable cause. So, they'd stop him and surreptitiously place a plastic bag with heroin on the street near his feet. Then the cops would say they saw him drop it.

At the time, I wasn't sure if they were bullshitting me. But if it was true, there had to be a good reason, right? Police officers were the good guys. Now, after listening to Maldonado, I realized they were really doing it, and I was embarrassed. I hadn't thought about the consequences for the victim—the person who was wrongly arrested. The person who now had a criminal record because of police misconduct. The victims were usually poor and Black or Hispanic. They knew judges were unlikely to believe them if they said police planted evidence. So, the only thing Maldonado and others like him could do was plead guilty and hope for a light sentence—for a crime they didn't commit.

"I'm sorry about what happened," I told him.

He just shook his head. "Life on the streets," he said quietly.

Maldonado admitted that he had a prison record, but he said it was for minor crimes to feed his drug habit. "I never killed anybody. I never raped anybody. I'm not proud of what I did."

He paused. "I guess I'm paying for everything now, right?"

I tried to encourage him. "Listen, if you beat this, you'll be getting a second chance. You can turn around your life. I'll be here to help."

He smiled. "Okay, Doc. Can I ask you something?"

"Sure."

"Why isn't there a medical treatment for heroin addiction?"

I knew the city was starting to open methadone clinics to help wean people off heroin. When I told him that, he threw it back at me. "That's just going from the illegal addiction of heroin to the legal addiction of methadone. Why not just treat heroin addicts with heroin legally?"

I didn't know the answer. I later discovered that New York City had tried that in the early 1900s, with a free heroin clinic at the city's Health Department building in lower Manhattan. But when Congress passed the Harrison Narcotics Act of 1914, New York's heroin maintenance program—and similar clinics throughout the United States—were outlawed.

As Maldonado's treatment continued, I updated my colleagues on his progress at our weekly staff meetings. Back then, we'd gather in a small, crowded room with an X-ray view box to examine patients' cases. We'd look at whether the patient was improving or if we should change the treatment. If a patient died, Marvin Kuschner, the hospital's director of pathology, would be there to explain what the autopsy revealed.

Autopsies could tell us if our diagnosis was correct, what we overlooked, whether we made any mistakes in our treatment, and what we could have done better. The postmortem examination served as quality control for how we practiced medicine. It educated us on how to improve patient care—on how to become better doctors. If the pathologist was the master of natural diseases, the forensic pathologist was the master of unnatural deaths: homicides, accidents, suicides, drug overdoses.

A lot of knowledge was passed around the table in those sessions. And I discovered that finding the roots of a disease—what caused someone's death—was more exciting and satisfying than just treating disease as an internist.

I was still on the fence then on whether to become an internist or forensic pathologist. But every time I thought about it, I could hear Kuschner's voice in my head, pushing me toward pathology. "As a pathologist, you'll study how to prolong life for thousands of people, rather than treating patients just one at a time," he'd say to me.

Kuschner was a brilliant man who used autopsy findings to save lives. He was one of the world's first researchers to study the effects of pollutants, including tobacco, on the lungs. How could I not consider forensic pathology?

Meanwhile, my colleagues were impressed by Maldonado's progress. He didn't die. In fact, he made a dramatic recovery. In four months, he graduated from a hospital bed to a wheelchair to a cane. By summer, he was well enough to be discharged.

He was ready, clean, and sober. He looked healthy. He was going to stay with a friend while he looked for a job. He had gotten a second chance.

"This is it, Jose," I said. "Are you ready?"

"Yes."

"You have my number. You call me if you need anything."

He looked at me and smiled. "Thanks, Doc."

With that, he walked out the front doors. He had beaten the odds. I felt great. We had saved Maldonado, and he had taught me a lot.

I couldn't wait to see him again in the clinic, to hear how things were going and gauge his progress.

It took only two days before he showed up again—lying lifeless on the cold steel table in the new medical examiner's morgue across the street from Bellevue's psychiatric building. I was stunned. I fought to hold back the tears.

"Where did they find him?" I asked one of the assistant medical examiners.

"On a roof."

I recognized the location, a place where Maldonado and his friends used to shoot up. It had been a warm, clear night, so probably they were all up there and fell asleep under the stars. But Maldonado didn't wake up.

I didn't know for sure, but I suspected that he had injected the same amount of heroin that he had been taking before he was hospitalized. What he didn't realize was he'd lost his tolerance for the drug and didn't need as much to get high. His previous dose was now too much for his system to handle.

I needed time to think. I wheeled around, heading up the staircase and out into the street. I walked over a block to the East River. I had to clear my head. It was an early summer afternoon. The trees and flowers were in bloom. And the streets were alive with sound—children playing, people talking, hot dog vendors shouting, car horns honking. Standing by the river's edge, I tuned out the noise. This really hurt.

I blamed myself for Maldonado's death. I had only treated his heart infection, the secondary illness. I'd paid little attention to the primary cause, the reason he was so sick in the first place. I treated the disease successfully, but not the patient. I didn't address that he was returning to the same environment that had made him an addict in the first place.

My mind wandered. Was there anything else I could have done to save him? I was ashamed that he had been set up by police so many years ago. I wondered if that had somehow changed the trajectory of his life. How many others had been similarly mistreated by cops? How many of them would eventually end up in the morgue?

A few months earlier, President John F. Kennedy's election had conveyed a spirit of optimism and hope about the country's future, reinforced in his inaugural address when he said, "Ask not what your country can do for you . . . ask what you can do for your country."

But working in Bellevue Hospital and the medical examiner's office, I was finding it harder and harder to be upbeat. Living in the shadow of some of the world's tallest buildings in an amazing, magnificent city, I was witness to the outcome of many of America's social problems: drugs, poverty, racial discrimination, class disparity. It was overwhelming. Sometimes, it was hard not to feel helpless, to feel like things would never change. *It's just the way it is. Don't think about it. Just do your job.*

Then, by the edge of the river, something strange happened. I recalled a phrase from Joseph Campbell, an American educator and writer who had studied the myths and legends of cultures in the world: *Follow your bliss.* Campbell had used those words to advise his students and others to identify the parts of life they were truly passionate about and pursue them wholeheartedly. He viewed this as a crucial part of living life to the fullest.

That day, I decided to follow my bliss. Yes, I was heartbroken about Maldonado. But I knew if I truly wanted to make a difference, I could do more as a forensic pathologist than an internist. Maybe I could use autopsy findings to tackle social issues. Expose problems. Save lives.

I took a deep breath, then turned around and headed back to Bellevue. I didn't have a second to waste.

Chapter 3

. . .

THE CONFESSION

s soon as I walked outside, a gust of wind blew paper and other debris in my direction. I flipped up the collar of my winter coat against the cold.

A few minutes earlier, I had been nice and warm in my small office in Bellevue Hospital's pathology building, my eyes fixed on slides under a microscope from the autopsy of a woman who had died of tuberculosis. As I peered into the lenses, my phone rang.

"Michael, can you stop by?" asked George Weinstein, the chief psychiatrist of the prison ward at Bellevue. "I want to share something with you."

"Okay. I'll be right over," I said.

It was 1964 and I was chief resident in pathology at Bellevue Hospital. I didn't ask why Weinstein wanted to see me. But I knew it would probably be a "teaching moment," as he liked to say. He knew I was training for forensic pathology. So he'd often share findings in psychiatry related to forensic pathology, which both imparted knowledge and kindled my enthusiasm.

I didn't have to walk far. Once I left the Pathology Building, I crossed a small roadway on the hospital campus to get there. Still, it was cold outside. It was two weeks before Christmas and New York was immersed in the holiday spirit. You couldn't escape it. Storefronts and windows in apartment buildings were draped with holiday decorations—lights, trees, wreaths, and nativity scenes along with menorahs and dreidels.

My colleagues were talking about holiday parties. But I couldn't go to any of them. I simply had no spare time. I was finishing up my pathology residency—a necessary step toward becoming a forensic pathologist—and still working part time at the medical examiner's office. My wife had started her psychiatric residency at Metropolitan Hospital. If that wasn't enough, we had two young children at home; Trissa, four years old, and Judson, one.

As the wind blew, I scurried across the roadway. Just before I walked into the psychiatry building, a scowling, middle-aged white man exited hurriedly. He bumped into me but didn't stop. He didn't apologize. He just kept moving toward a police car parked at the curb. Jumping inside when he reached it, he sped away.

"Merry Christmas," I mumbled.

He was in street clothes, so he had to be a detective. I turned around and walked into the psychiatric hospital.

Over the years, the hospital has seen its fair share of notable patients. Writer William Burroughs was admitted after he chopped off his own finger to impress someone. Playwright Eugene O'Neill had several stays in the alcoholic ward. The third floor was home to the prison ward. Author Norman Mailer was sent there in 1960 after stabbing his wife in a drunken rage. Mark David Chapman was held there after he fatally shot John Lennon in 1980. When mentally ill inmates in New York City's detention centers became too sick, violent, delusional, or suicidal for the jails to handle, Bellevue Hospital's prison ward was where they were sent. And that's where I was going.

I walked into an elevator and pressed a black button marked 3. The elevator lifted, and when the doors opened, I turned left. After a few steps, I stopped and knocked on the door of Weinstein's office.

"Come in," he said.

There he was in the small room, sitting behind his desk, which was covered with papers and beige file folders. He rose and shook my hand.

"Good to see you, Michael," he said, smiling warmly. He pointed to a nearby chair. "Take a seat."

Weinstein was a stocky, middle-aged man with short gray hair. He was wearing a neatly pressed suit and tie. I knew Weinstein was highly regarded by forensic psychiatrists. In murder cases, judges often sent defendants to him so he could evaluate whether they were competent to stand trial. He was also a good friend of Helpern, who had introduced us.

I shifted in the seat, trying to get comfortable. "Someone bumped into me on the way in," I mentioned. "He didn't look too happy. I think he was a detective or something."

"I think I know who you're talking about. He was just in my office," Weinstein said.

"Why was he so angry?"

He sighed. "Well . . . I told him something he didn't want to hear."

"What was it?"

He smiled. "I'll get to that. But first, I have something for you to read." He handed me a folder from his desk. It contained many typed pages.

"Have you been following the Career Girls Murders?" he asked.

"Yes," I said, adding that I had assisted in the autopsies.

"Well, this is the signed confession."

"Wow," I said under my breath.

This had been the biggest unsolved case in the city—a brutal, high-profile double homicide of two young women that had captured the nation's attention. I first learned about their deaths a few hours after the women's bodies were found in their Upper East Side apartment on August 28, 1963. It was the lead news story that night. Reporters said the women's bodies had been taken to the medical examiner's office.

I knew Helpern might need help with the autopsies. So, the following morning, I headed straight there. When I arrived, newspaper and TV reporters were already in the lobby, waiting for any new information. I hurried to the autopsy room. A few police detectives were there, but they were quiet, respectful of the victims. Helpern was standing by the bodies of two women that had been placed on steel tables.

"I'm glad you're here," he said. "You can assist me."

Before we got started, he shared some details. Twenty-one-year-old Janice Wylie and her twenty-three-year-old roommate, Emily Hoffert, had been stabbed to death, Helpern said. Their bodies were discovered by another roommate when she returned home from work that afternoon.

"When she walked in, she knew something was wrong. Everything was out of place. So, she called Wylie's father, who came over and found them," Helpern said.

The autopsies would determine the cause of death and collect important information that could help police identify the killer. Helpern would perform an autopsy on one victim, while another medical examiner would examine the other. If they needed anything, I was there.

As we worked, I heard detectives quietly talking about the case. The women had been stabbed repeatedly. One cop said, "This was overkill. It had to be done by someone involved with one of the girls."

After the autopsies, Helpern told the waiting media that the women had suffered "vicious mutilation." They died of multiple stab wounds of the chest and abdomen, Helpern said, adding that Hoffert's carotid artery had been cut. Wylie's body was found nude; Hoffert's was fully clothed. It wasn't clear whether Wylie had been raped, he said. Their bodies were bound together with torn strips of sheets.

The tabloids called the gory slayings the "Career Girl Murders." The victims were representative of the thousands of young women who had come from all over America to New York and other larger cities to seek jobs and careers. Without a lot of money, some of the women would find roommates so they could make ends meet.

The daughter of a Minneapolis surgeon, Hoffert was about to begin her teaching career on Long Island. An aspiring actress, Wylie had just started working for *Newsweek* magazine. Her father was Max Wylie, a writer and producer who had created the television show *The Flying Nun*. His brother, Philip Wylie, was the more famous sibling, a prolific writer whose work spanned genres from men's adventure and detective stories to science fiction and social criticism.

The police were under intense public pressure to find the killer. Hundreds of detectives were pulled off their regular beats from every borough of the city to help with the investigation. Despite the manpower, months went by without an arrest.

But then, on April 25, 1964—eight months after the slayings—police officials announced they'd solved the case. They had arrested a Black man, George Whitmore Jr., nineteen, of Wildwood, New Jersey, who had confessed to the Wylie–Hoffert murders as well as other horrific crimes, including the slaying of Minnie Edmonds on April 14, 1964, and the assault and attempted rape of another woman, Elba Borrero, nearly a week later. Both women were from Brooklyn.

Brooklyn detective Edward Bulger and his colleagues were praised for their work. (Bulger even got a special police medal.) Prosecutors called the case airtight, saying they found an "incriminating" photo in Whitmore's wallet of a white woman who they said was Wylie.

The euphoria was short lived. Whitmore quickly recanted his confession, saying it was beaten out of him during a twenty-two-hour interrogation. At the time of the Wylie–Hoffert murders, Whitmore said he was in Wildwood, a resort town on the New Jersey shore about 150 miles south of Manhattan, in front of a television, watching the Reverend Dr. Martin Luther King Jr. deliver his "I Have a Dream" speech at the March on Washington.

Other than Whitmore's family and civil rights activists, few people believed him. Leaders with the National Association for the Advancement of Colored People (NAACP) said his arrest was racially motivated. They noted that Whitmore, an eighth-grade dropout with a low IQ, was Black; Wylie and Hoffert were white—and from affluent families. The NAACP said police treated Whitmore differently than they would have a white suspect. They echoed Whitmore's claim that the cops "beat him until he confessed."

Newspapers played up the race angle, too, with headlines like "19-Year-old Negro Has Admitted to Slaying Wylie and Hoffert." The cops tried to paint Whitmore as a monster. They ripped apart his character, calling him a drifter who was raised in a shack near his father's Wildwood junkyard.

The reality was that Whitmore had no criminal record. He was an unemployed laborer. The day of his arrest, he said he was in Brooklyn looking for work. The detectives said they questioned him because he fit the description of a suspect in the attack on Borrero, a twenty-year-old nurse.

The media followed the case closely, writing about every new development. In November 1964, Whitmore was found guilty in the Borrero case, largely as a result of media accounts of his arrest as the violent Career Girls killer. Now, prosecutors said they'd seek the death penalty against him for the Wylie–Hoffert murders.

Weinstein said the court had asked him to do a psychological evaluation of Whitmore to see if he was competent to stand trial for the Career Girl Murders. The evaluation would determine whether Whitmore had a mental disorder and a "rational and factual understanding of the criminal proceedings." As part of his assessment, Weinstein said he studied the confession.

"Michael, the man who ran into you was the Brooklyn detective who interrogated Whitmore," Weinstein said.

Weinstein said he had just told Bulger that he believed Whitmore's statement was a "false confession." Had Whitmore been coerced? Weinstein said he didn't know. What he did know was that, when false confessions occur, they almost always result from how an interrogation is performed.

Weinstein said Bulger was pissed off at his opinion and stormed out of his office.

"I want you to read this because this is a classic example of a planted confession. This way, you'll be able to recognize one in the future," he said.

I knew confessions were an important part of murder investigations. Most homicides were solved because someone confessed to the killing, or an eyewitness identified the person who committed the crime.

As I read Whitmore's statement, it was clear to me that Weinstein was right. Bulger and the detectives had manipulated Whitmore. They'd asked him to answer many questions "yes" or "no" after providing him with information in the question that allegedly only the killer would know.

> *Bulger: Did you enter the apartment at 3:30 PM?*
> *Whitmore: Yes.*

> *Bulger: Did you use three knives?*
> *Whitmore: Yes.*

> *Bulger: Did one of the girls have no clothes on, just a towel?*
> *Whitmore: Yes.*

After I read the confession, I handed the file back to Weinstein. "They fed him the answers," I said.

Weinstein nodded. "With a confession, you have to read the questions and look at the answers. That will tell you what you need to know." He added that if a suspect goes into great detail, that's usually a sign the confession is legit. But it's a red flag if they answer yes or no and provide very few details about the crime.

"What do you think will happen now?" I asked.

"I don't know," Weinstein said. But he said he'd share his opinion with Manhattan district attorney Frank Hogan. "He'll decide what to do."

I headed back to my office, but I couldn't stop thinking about the confession. I knew the New York City Police Department was under a lot of pressure to find the person responsible for the murders. But forcing a man to confess to crimes he didn't commit wasn't the answer. That would be something out of a Dostoevsky novel. Meanwhile, the real killer was still out there and could strike again. I hoped that Hogan would release Whitmore from jail and investigate the circumstances surrounding his statement.

When I got home that night, I told Judianne about my talk with Weinstein. She had been closely following the murders. New York was her home and she'd always planned to build her career here. But now, in the wake of the slayings, Judianne was having second thoughts.

The women's apartment was only a few blocks from ours. We loved our three-bedroom co-op on the Upper East Side. It was near Gracie Mansion, the mayor's residence. We had a uniformed doorman stationed in the lobby and a park outside our window.

But after the Wylie–Hoffert murders, we considered moving. Crime was soaring. Did we really want to raise our children in this kind of environment? We spent some time in Connecticut to see what commuting from there to New York would be like. But we agreed that we'd miss everything about living in the city—the hectic pace, the people, the food. Even more importantly, our work was intrinsically tied to New York, warts and all. So, when Whitmore had been arrested, Judianne, like so many others, felt relieved.

That night, however, Judianne listened quietly at the kitchen table as I recounted details of the confession. She understood its significance. Yes, it meant the murderer was still on the loose. But more importantly, it meant that an innocent Black man might be sentenced to death.

I told her that Weinstein would share his opinion with Hogan.

"Maybe he'll drop the charges," I said.

But Judianne wasn't so optimistic. She wasn't sure that Hogan or any-one else would do the right thing—especially since Whitmore was Black. She said there was too much racial bias in the criminal justice system. This was a high-profile case; if Whitmore was innocent, the public would ask what happened—why did he confess? That could open the Pandora's box of an investigation.

I wasn't naïve. I knew racism existed in every part of society. I saw it first-hand while I was growing up and in school. But I still believed that people in power would do the right thing. Judianne was much more skeptical. Maybe she was right when she questioned what the prosecutor would ultimately do with the information.

Judianne wasn't afraid to speak her mind about any subject, including controversial ones like race relations or drug abuse. If she were in my position, she'd probably have rushed to Hogan's office herself and confronted him. Me? At that point in my life, I was much more cautious. I focused on Bellevue Hospital and autopsies, and kept my opinions to myself.

Judianne and I came from very different worlds—and that helped shape our worldviews and how we handled things in our daily lives.

In the housing project where I grew up, my mother scraped for every penny. My teachers in New York's public schools never encouraged me. One time a teacher laughed at me in front of the class when I told her I wanted to be a doctor. I had to work while at City College of New York: shining shoes in Brooklyn, delivering alcohol to customers for a liquor store in Queens. I spent summers as a waiter and a tennis instructor in Catskill Mountain resorts and attended medical school on a scholarship. Otherwise, I wouldn't have been able to go.

Judianne's mother was a Republican attorney, an heiress of a paper-box company. Her father was also a lawyer and a leader in Eugene V. Debs's campaigns when he was the Socialist Party of America's candidate for president of the United States in the early twentieth century. He shared my mother's left-wing political sympathies. When Judianne told her parents she wanted to go to medical school, they said yes, with a caveat: she'd have to go to law school first.

I met Judianne in 1956 during my second year of medical school when I was living in a tenement across the street from Bellevue. I barely had enough money to get by. My roommate, who was attending Columbia Law School, said there was a girl in his class who planned to go to medical school after graduation.

The Memorial Day holiday was approaching, he reminded me. "Why don't you call her up for a date?"

I was intrigued—a woman who was going to be a lawyer *and* a doctor? I didn't have any classes that week, so the timing was right. I knew nothing about her background, so I wasn't intimidated. When I called, we talked a little, and then I asked her out. When she said yes, I had to figure out a place to take her that didn't cost much. Then it hit me. The morgue. We'd watch an autopsy. It was free. She thought it was fascinating.

We hit it off. Judianne was pretty and outgoing, with a good sense of humor and a social conscience. For our second date, I took her to another place that didn't cost money: Bellevue's delivery room.

In those days, medical students were allowed to "scrub in" on procedures. It was considered proper and ethical training—as long as they didn't interfere with anything.

Judianne was still a law student, but when we arrived at Bellevue we both got into surgical scrub suits and watched as a doctor tried to deliver a baby. It turned out to be a complicated delivery. At one point the doctor turned around and complained that there were too many people in the delivery room. He chased me out but let Judianne stay. So, for the next few hours, while the doctor worked to save the woman and her baby, I sat in the waiting room with the father. The delivery was a success.

When Judianne finally returned, we left the hospital, found a table at a nearby restaurant, had coffee, and talked for hours. I told her about my family, how I loved to play chess with my brother Robert, and that I found the morgue interesting. I said that I wanted to help people live better lives. She smiled, then said she wanted to do the same. I felt really comfortable with her.

Growing up, I'd had girlfriends, but I was shy, especially in high school. I mostly focused on school, as my mother encouraged. I knew if I wanted to escape the projects, I had to put my head down and work hard. I didn't have time for much else. Yet by the time I met Judianne, I was coming into my own. I was more outgoing. And I was in good shape from playing tennis with my brother and hustling between jobs. I was six feet, two inches tall, 180 pounds, with short brown hair parted on the left side and glasses.

Judianne knew my financial situation, but that didn't bother her. We had discussed getting married and, on October 26, 1957, I knew I was ready.

It was a Saturday, a day off from school but not from the medical examiner's office. I was at the old Bellevue morgue assisting with autopsies when Helpern called me over to the other side of the room. He was doing a "very important autopsy" on Albert Anastasia, a well-known Mafia boss, who had been shot the day before while seated in the Park Sheraton Hotel barber shop.

"Do the head," he said.

I had just been promoted.

In those days before electric saws, the most physically demanding part of the autopsy was examining the brain, because you had to use a handsaw to open the skull without injuring the brain. It was hard work—and this was the first time that Helpern had asked me to do it.

When I finished sawing, I was so excited I called Judianne to tell her about my promotion. "I'm standing here holding the brain of Albert Anastasia and I'm thinking of you. Will you marry me?"

It wasn't the most romantically phrased proposal, but she accepted. We decided to get married on June 14, 1958.

But things didn't go as we'd hoped. My mother was unhappy. She didn't like that, although Judianne's parents were secular Jews, Judianne didn't consider herself Jewish. She believed that Jewish women were treated as second-class citizens. For me, religion wasn't an issue. I didn't have a bar mitzvah or attend synagogue. I didn't believe in heaven or hell or that there was anything after death.

Her parents paid for a fancy catered wedding at a Manhattan hotel on Central Park South. Almost all of the hundred guests were her relatives or friends of her family. My brother was my best man, but my mother refused to go, and I had very few other relatives. All of my mother's and father's families had been killed in the Holocaust—one of the reasons I'd lost my faith in God.

We didn't go on a honeymoon right away. I didn't have the money. But then things changed. Shortly after we were married, I got a telephone call from the producer of a television game show called *Do You Trust Your Wife?* He said they were looking for interesting newlyweds to be contestants, and someone had recommended us. We didn't hesitate. We said yes.

The show was hosted by a largely unknown figure—Johnny Carson—who'd banter with couples before turning to the man and asking, "So, tell me, do you want to answer the questions, or do you trust your wife?" The more questions you answered correctly, the more money you won. It was that simple. Judianne and I had agreed beforehand that I would be the one who'd answer the questions. They asked me about songs from the hit Broadway musical South Pacific. We won $5,000—about $48,500 in 2022 dollars—and used the money to take a once-in-a-lifetime honeymoon trip around the world.

One of the things I most admired about Judianne was that she never rested. She went from law school to motherhood to medical school. And her main goal was to help people, especially those who fell through the cracks of society. She had a finely tuned sense of justice—which Whitmore's situation violated. That's why I told her about the confession.

By that point, we'd been talking about the confession for an hour. It was getting late and we both had to get up early. After we walked into our bedroom, she turned to me, clearly still troubled.

"We were so readily accepting of the police when they said he confessed. We didn't question it. And when he said he didn't do it, we believed the police, not him," she said.

The criminal justice system works for whites—not Blacks, she said. "I have no faith that Hogan or anyone in the system will do the right thing."

I tried to cheer her up. "The truth will come out," I said. But I'm not sure I believed it myself.

A few weeks later, the case took a stunning twist.

Selwyn Raab, a former newspaper colleague of mine back at CCNY, was now an investigative reporter for a New York newspaper. He found witnesses who placed Whitmore in Wildwood at the time of the Wylie–Hoffert murders, watching King's speech—just like Whitmore said. That purportedly incriminating photo of Wylie in Whitmore's wallet? It wasn't Wylie at all. It was actually a snapshot that Whitmore told police he found in his father's junkyard and decided to keep. Plus there was no physical evidence to corroborate his confession. No fingerprints. No witnesses. No nothing.

Then, in January 1965, a twenty-two-year-old drug addict named Richard Robles was charged with homicide in the Wylie–Hoffert murders. A drug dealer who had been arrested for a different murder had given police information that led to Robles.

Prosecutors dropped the murder indictment against Whitmore in the Career Girls case. But Whitmore's nightmare was far from over. Even though they knew police had coerced his confession, prosecutors continued legal proceedings in the other cases—despite the fact that the crimes Whitmore was accused of committing were based on the same flawed confession.

After Whitmore was convicted of the attempted rape of Elba Borrero, his lawyer filed a motion for a new trial. At the hearing in March 1965, Gerald Corbin, a juror in the Borrero case, testified that "practically everyone" on the jury knew that Whitmore had been charged with the Wylie–Hoffert crime. Corbin said that at least one juror "on more than one occasion" used racial slurs when referring to the sexual proclivities of Black people. He testified that the juror in question said Whitmore was guilty of attempted rape because "Negros are like jackrabbits" and "got to have their intercourse all the time."

The judge ordered a new trial, saying the jury had been racially biased. A month later, Whitmore's trial for Minnie Edmonds's murder ended in a mistrial.

While Brooklyn district attorney Aaron Koota said he wouldn't retry Whitmore for Edmonds's murder, he did for attempted rape in the Borrero case. Over the next few years, Whitmore would be tried twice for the attempted rape; both ended in convictions that would be overturned on appeal. Whitmore wouldn't be totally exonerated until 1973—nine years after he was falsely arrested—when it was disclosed that prosecutors had hidden from Whitmore's lawyer critical evidence supporting his innocence.

At Robles's trial in December 1965, his attorneys tried to use Whitmore's confession to create reasonable doubt that their client killed Wylie and Hoffert. But it backfired when prosecutor John F. Keenan summoned the detectives who had arrested Whitmore. His grueling questioning of the detectives under oath illuminated the sloppy analysis of physical evidence that had put Whitmore under suspicion. The detectives' threats and trickery had clearly helped elicit his confession.

But more worrisome, Keenan's questioning also exposed the detectives as bigots who were hell-bent on railroading Whitmore. They presumed his guilt on racist grounds, such as one detective's belief that "you can always tell when a Negro is lying by watching his stomach, because it moves in and out when he lies."

It took the jury only a few hours to convict Robles, who was later sentenced to life in prison.

Meanwhile, Whitmore's coerced confession was cited in the legislative debate in 1965 when New York outlawed the death penalty except for cases involving the murder of a police or corrections officer. His case was footnoted in the US Supreme Court's *Miranda* ruling, which required suspects to be told their rights, including the right to a lawyer.

For Judianne, the Wylie–Hoffert murders increased her interest in creating a drug treatment program that would truly help addicts—something she had wanted to do since Maldonado's death.

Robles was a bad guy. No question about it. But Judianne knew addiction was part of the equation. He had broken into the women's apartment because he was a hardcore drug addict looking for money to buy heroin. She said there would be similar homicides in the future unless something was done.

For me, Whitmore's saga made it clear how easy it was for rogue cops and prosecutors to manipulate the legal system to charge an innocent man, especially minority suspects. But I still didn't believe that police and prosecutor misconduct was systemic or that the law enforcement community as a whole was racially biased.

Years earlier, when Maldonado revealed how cops had framed him and others in his Hispanic neighborhood, I believed only a few bad police officers were involved. Most of the cops I knew were honest and would never do something like that. Even when I heard police officers talk about "dropsy," I didn't think the practice was widespread. Again, maybe a few bad cops—that's all. And when police and prosecutors made mistakes in cases involving Black or Hispanic individuals, I still didn't believe those mistakes were intentional.

But then, two cases emerged that made me begin to question everything, from police tactics to my office's relationship with police and prosecutors.

Chapter 4

. . .

PSYCHOSIS WITH EXHAUSTION

The hallway was full of cops and reporters. I slipped past them and through the autopsy room door. I had been there thousands of times before, but today I felt nervous. I wasn't there to perform an autopsy. No, I was there to see the body for myself, to make sure my boss hadn't made a mistake. If Helpern was right about the cause of death, it would put my doubts to rest. If he was wrong, I didn't know what I'd do.

It was the summer of 1967, and I was thirty-three years old. I had finished my pathology residency at Bellevue and was now working full time at the medical examiner's office. My wife had finished her psychiatric residency at Metropolitan Hospital and, true to her word, founded her own drug treatment program: Odyssey House.

The program was helping addicts get clean and deal with the underlying issues that led to heroin in the first place—without using legal substitute drugs like methadone. The patients lived together until they were able to live alone. Judianne had started with six heroin addicts. Now, she had dozens living in a treatment center in an East Harlem building, with plans to open more in New York and, hopefully, around the country.

If that wasn't enough, Judianne had just given birth to Lindsey, the third child in our growing family. We had just moved into a four-story nineteenth-century brownstone in Manhattan once owned by the Barrymore family.

But outside my family's orbit, it seemed like the entire world was spinning out of control. There was no escaping the bad news. The Vietnam War. Drug abuse. Racial unrest. I was conscious of the chaos. I opposed the war, but I didn't attend antiwar protests. I supported the civil rights movement, but I didn't march for social justice. Instead, I focused on my medical career and hoped I could make a difference with my studies on drug addiction. Driven by Maldonado's memory, I had since written or coauthored more than a dozen papers and discussed my findings at conferences in the United States and abroad.

Still, busy as I was, every now and then the racial injustice of a particular death would stop me in my tracks. And so it was in 1967 with Eric Johnson, who had been an inmate at Manhattan's Riker's Island jail awaiting trial on drug charges. He was Black, mentally ill, and poor. Now, he was dead.

When I arrived at work the morning after Johnson's death, Helpern was already dissecting the body. It was unusual for Helpern to be doing an autopsy at all—especially at 8:30 A.M. He only handled high-profile cases and he rarely visited the autopsy rooms in the morning; he was usually busy taking care of administrative matters in New York City's five boroughs. Normally he'd come downstairs to the autopsy rooms in the early afternoon to check on near-finished or completed postmortem examinations.

But there was something else that made this situation so unusual: Helpern was conducting the autopsy in the private room with a special table that was usually reserved for VIPs or decomposed bodies. Johnson wasn't famous or decomposed.

I was curious why Helpern was involved in the case. So, I began poking around. I examined Johnson's chart. A jail official had reported that the inmate was found lifeless in his bed and noted that Johnson had a history of seizures and that that disorder probably killed him.

But I discovered there was more to it. Helpern's long-time autopsy stenographer, Siegfried Oppenheim, shared some of the backstory with me. He said Mayor John Lindsay's office had received an anonymous tip that Johnson had been beaten by white guards. Then someone from the mayor's office had called Helpern, warning him that Lindsay didn't want any publicity about the case. New York City's jails and prisons were overcrowded, and Lindsay was concerned that inmates would riot if they knew what had happened to Johnson. Politically ambitious, Lindsay was worried that Johnson's death and a prison uprising would inflame racial tensions and that, in turn, would hurt his image as a dynamic crusader. So, Helpern found himself in a difficult situation.

PSYCHOSIS WITH EXHAUSTION ✦ 47

A burly, avuncular, articulate physician, Helpern joined the medical examiner's staff in 1931 and became chief in 1954. Over the years, he had acquired an international reputation as a forensic pathologist and medical detective. He had often bragged about the independence of his office, saying the position was protected from politics by Civil Service rules and regulations. Until age sixty-five, the chief medical examiner could only be fired for demonstrated cause.

But Helpern was now turning sixty-six and would no longer have Civil Service protection. If he wanted to remain in his position, he'd have to be reappointed each year by the mayor, who could fire him anytime, with or without cause.

I knew Helpern didn't want to retire. So, was he now beholden to mayoral requests? Was Helpern doing the autopsy because he wanted to please the mayor's political ambitions—or because he had come to appreciate New York City's growing race issues and wanted to make sure his findings were beyond reproach? And what would he do if he discovered that Johnson's death was caused by the guards?

New York wasn't immune to the country's racial tension, even though most city residents considered themselves liberal minded and progressive. Segregation, prejudice, and racially charged violence were Southern problems, they told themselves. They didn't happen here.

Many New Yorkers, like people all over the nation, had been following the civil rights movement in newspapers and on TV. They saw the shocking images of Southern police officers unleashing attack dogs or firing high-pressure hoses at men, women, and children marching for integration or voting rights.

They knew about Emmett Till, a fourteen-year-old Black boy who was murdered in August 1955 in an attack that shocked the nation and catalyzed the emerging civil rights movement. A Chicago native, Till was visiting relatives in Money, Mississippi, when he was accused of harassing a white woman. Several days later, relatives of the woman abducted Till, beat him to death, and threw his body into the Tallahatchie River. (Many years later, the white woman who complained about Till admitted that she made the harassment up.) Till's mother insisted on a public, open-casket funeral for her son to shed light on the violence inflicted on Black people in the South. Two white men were charged with Till's murder, but were quickly acquitted by an all-white jury.

Till's widely publicized death galvanized civil rights activists nationwide. But hundreds of similar deaths were known only to Black communities.

Many New Yorkers attended the March on Washington in 1963, where Dr. King gave his "I Have a Dream" speech from the steps of the Lincoln Memorial. They volunteered to go to the South to help organize voter registration drives and integrate restaurants and schools.

They also watched in horror as civil rights leaders were assassinated: Medgar Evers in Mississippi in 1963, and later King as he stood on a hotel balcony in Memphis, Tennessee.

Those terrible events took place in the South, but I knew Black and Hispanic people faced plenty of discrimination in New York as well. It wasn't usually as overt. Mortgage lenders kept minorities from buying homes in certain neighborhoods using redlining, an illegal discriminatory practice in which banks denied loans, or insurance providers restricted services, to certain areas of a community based on the racial makeup of an applicant's neighborhood.

Only a few could join the police force or fire department, or get good-paying city jobs. And a few years earlier, Judianne and I had seen just how deep New York City's racial divide was when we tried to help a Black medical school professor move into an apartment.

Mildred Phillips was a wonderful physician and pathology professor at NYU. She had taught both me and my wife and we had become good friends. One day, she called us and said she was planning to move to an apartment in our neighborhood.

"Great, we're going to be neighbors," Judianne said.

But a few weeks later, Mildred told us she didn't get the place. "They said they had already rented it," she said.

She was upset. And we thought it sounded a little suspicious, possibly discriminatory. She was trying to move into a predominantly white, upper-middle-class neighborhood. So Judianne and I decided to test the system. We would go to the landlord and ask if that very apartment was still available. If it was, we'd fill out an application and see what happened.

"If there was discrimination, we'll find out," I promised Mildred.

And sure enough, when we approached the leasing agent, she said the apartment was available. We visited the apartment with the agent and filled out forms. A few days later, the agent called us and said, "When can you move in?"

We immediately contacted the mayor's office. We talked to people in the housing department and filed a complaint. We kept following up. But in the end, the landlord denied the discrimination allegation, and the case died.

I learned that when it came to racial discrimination, it was all about political influence. We had the evidence, but the landlord had the power. It was discouraging. And for Phillips, it was devastating. She had the financial means. But in the end, it didn't matter because she was Black.

In New York, discrimination was hiding in plain sight. Most people didn't use racial slurs, instead speaking in "code." *Urban* meant *Black*. *Drug addict* referred to Blacks and Hispanics. Why did they think there was so much unemployment in communities of color? Residents there didn't want to work. Why were so many Black people in jail? They'd "earned the right to be there" by the way they behaved, not because of racial profiling or unfair sentencing.

I found it all appalling. As a Jew, I knew about prejudice and discrimination. My parents were Jewish immigrants who fled to the United States from Poland in the 1920s to escape poverty and persecution. My mother's brother was the first to arrive. After he found work, he encouraged his parents and twelve siblings to follow. The youngest, Fanny Linn—my mother—was the only one to take him up on the offer.

She worked long hours in the garment district, she saved her money, and years later returned to Poland to convince more family members to emigrate. They refused to go and would later perish in the Holocaust. But during her visit, a *Shadchan*—a Jewish matchmaker—set her up with a handsome electrician named Harry Baden. It was a whirlwind romance. They married in Poland and returned to the United States.

I was born in the Bronx in 1934, and my brother Robert followed me eighteen months later. During World War II, we moved to the Fort Greene housing project in Brooklyn because my father worked in the Brooklyn Navy Yard, and we still lived there when my parents divorced after the war. We were one of the few Jewish families in a neighborhood of Italian and Irish gangs. My brother was my best friend. We played tennis and chess together and did our homework on the kitchen table.

In this world, I was an outsider. As a history teacher once explained to me, the difference between Catholics and Jews was that Catholics would go to heaven in a boat, which represented the Church, "but in order for Jews to go to heaven, they have to swim. And they usually don't make it."

The first time I felt like an American was because of a very young Frank Sinatra, who made a ten-minute short film in 1945 called *The House I Live In*. It was intended to encourage people to oppose antisemitism and racism and was shown to the student body in our public-school auditorium.

In it, a group of kids surround a Jewish boy, ready to pounce, but Sinatra intercedes. He tells them that we are all Americans and that all religions and races are to be respected equally. Then, he sings a song. There was a stanza in it that has stayed with me to this day: "The house I live in / A plot of earth, a street. / The grocer and the butcher / And the people that I meet. / The children in the playground / The faces that I see. / All races and religions / That's America to me." It made a ten-year-old feel included—at least for a short time. (Years before, its composer, a New York City school teacher named Abel Meeropol, had written "Strange Fruit," a devastating song made famous by singer Billie Holiday that protested the lynching of Blacks in the South.)

My mother did more than encourage me. She was a role model, a liberal unionist in the garment industry. She brought coworkers home with her—Black, white, and Hispanic ladies, also with husband trouble—and they sat in the kitchen discussing politics and social issues. She was politically astute and outraged by this country's treatment of Black people.

She told me how Blacks were mistreated in America and helped me and my brother understand the importance of civil rights cases like the Scottsboro Boys—nine Black teenagers falsely accused of raping two white women aboard a train near Scottsboro, Alabama, in 1931. The case became a window into the South's unremittingly brutal system of justice. She said union leaders and activists from all over America had tried to help them. They were convicted but eventually pardoned, some posthumously.

She was a big fan of Paul Robeson, a Black Rutgers football star, actor, singer, and left-wing activist who spoke out against racism and lynching in the United States and was punished by the US government for it. She took a two-hour bus trip to Peekskill, New York, in August 1949, to see him in an open-air concert and described how the locals opposed his appearance. They threw rocks at her bus, breaking windows, and attacked the attendees.

I went to Boys High School in Brooklyn mainly because my mother thought it would be a good idea to go somewhere without girls. Yet there, too, I was a loner because I was Jewish and was more interested in my studies than in sports or parties, but I did become best friends with a Black teenager named Justice Taylor.

Justice was shorter than me, but muscular and very strong. We were both outsiders at school. In some classes, I was the sole Jew, he the only Black student. We did many things together, and he spent some nights at my apartment. My mother was pleased. We talked a lot about what we wanted to do with our lives and what we might face in the future. We had a lot in common; Jews and Blacks both lived with so much discrimination and hatred in America. But as Justice would often remind me, the prejudice he experienced was immediate and visceral.

"If we walk into a restaurant, no one knows you're Jewish," he said. "But me? You can see I'm Black. I can't hide that."

His father owned a shoeshine parlor in the Borough Hall section of Brooklyn, right next to a bar and grill. When we had time, his father would let us shine shoes to earn ten cents and usually a nickel tip. Sometimes his father would talk to us about the lack of justice for the Black community, which was why he'd named his son Justice. He told us about local problems that I had associated only with the South—police harassing Black New Yorkers, stopping them for no reason, or preventing them from going into white neighborhoods.

Most Boys High School students didn't go to college; they went to work. The school had no counselors to guide me in applying to college, and my parents knew nothing about scholarship applications. My mother didn't have the money to send me to college, but City College of New York and Brooklyn College were free. I chose CCNY, mostly because its basketball team had just won the NCAA and NIT national basketball tournaments. They had the best basketball team in the United States and some of the players would be headed for the Olympics. Justice went to Brooklyn College, where he shortened his name to Justus. After graduating with a business degree, he attended New York University law school. He later became a vice president at Chase Manhattan Bank, where he helped finance housing and community projects. We stayed close. I was the best man at his wedding. He was one of my only friends at mine.

Meanwhile, at CCNY, I discovered a more diverse community than in my housing project. There were many Jews and other minorities on campus. I was no longer an outsider. Suddenly, I had lots of friends. I was inducted into Phi Beta Kappa and elected senior class president. I joined the tennis team, and was elected editor-in-chief of *The Campus*, the student newspaper.

As a freshman, my first newspaper assignment was covering the trials of the CCNY college basketball players accused of shaving points. It was clear that Hogan, the Manhattan district attorney and a devout Roman Catholic, was being influenced by Francis Cardinal Spellman, as Hogan did not charge any of the basketball players in the Catholic colleges who had shaved points. He only arrested Jewish and Black students at CCNY, NYU, and Long Island University—an early and profound lesson for me in acceptable political, religious, and racial discrimination in the North.

When I got to medical school, I became interested in pathology. I was surprised to learn that the first public office to investigate deaths was established in 1194 by King Richard I of England as a way of collecting more taxes. Appointed by the king, the coroner was part tax collector and part detective. Part of his role was investigating sudden deaths because they represented potential windfalls for the king. Suicides were against the law because "self-murder" deprived the king of a subject and a potential soldier. But there was a religious reason, too: the monarchy believed that only God gave life and only God could take a life. Coroners had the power to seize the property of people who killed themselves. Families tried to hide suicides, while coroners tried to ferret them out.

Back then, the coroner's most important qualification was his loyalty to the king. The idea that doctors or medical knowledge could be useful in investigating deaths wouldn't come until centuries later. During the Renaissance, dissection of the human body became an integral component of medical education in Paris and other European cities. By the eighteenth century, doctors were using autopsies to study the effects of disease on internal organs.

In England, autopsies were how Sir Percival Pott became the first to associate occupational exposure with cancer. In the 1770s, he examined the bodies of men with cancer of the scrotum and discovered that the disease was confined to those who had been chimney sweeps in their boyhood. Sweeps had practiced their trade while naked, and rarely bathed; Pott therefore correlated the cancer with chemicals in the soot.

In medical circles, autopsies were becoming increasingly important for teaching medical students about treating disease. But there was a problem: there weren't enough bodies. The shortage spawned a thriving black market and schools were willing to pay for cadavers. At the University of Edinburgh's School of Anatomy, for instance, Professor Robert Knox paid ten guineas per body—no questions asked.

In 1828, two Scottish men—William Burke and William Hare—used this shortage to earn money. When they couldn't rob graves, they suffocated the living, using a technique that would become known as *burking*—putting a hand over a victim's nose and mouth, then sitting on the chest or back, which prevented the victim from breathing. It left no bruises or other signs of violence— much like today's police restraint deaths, except Burke and Hare's deadly scheme was about business, not race. Their moneymaking venture was discovered only when a medical student showed up for his autopsy class and found his girlfriend lying on the table. Authorities traced the body back to Burke and Hare.

Hare, the leader, turned on his partner and served a few years in prison. Meanwhile, Burke went to the gallows.

At the end of the nineteenth century, the state of murder investigations was dismal. Murders often went unreported, and the bodies were just buried. There were no death certificates. There was no sense of who was dying and whether the death was natural or unnatural. Then, in 1888—and following Jack the Ripper's unsolved murders—Scotland Yard began using hospital pathologists in murder cases. Police agencies in England and the United States slowly began applying forensic science—pathology, toxicology, and microscopes—to catch killers.

New York City established the Office of the Chief Medical Examiner in 1914 to replace the coroner system. For the first time, the medical examiner had to be a physician and pathologist trained in doing autopsies. But to this day, America has no uniform national system of death investigation. Every state has a different method—in some cases, they vary from county to county.

Worse, most US counties don't use trained forensic pathologists. In many places across America, coroners are elected, and neither have nor require any medical training. In some places, the only qualifications you need to become a coroner is being old enough to vote and a US citizen.

That doesn't mean police agencies aren't using science to solve crimes. Departments began establishing police labs in the 1920s. At first, officers compared bullet markings, fingerprints, tire marks, and shoe prints. They soon began comparing hairs, fibers, and handwriting. These police labs were renamed "crime labs" and then "forensic labs" to give an impression of scientific separation from actual police officers, despite their connection to law enforcement.

Forensic pathologists, by contrast, are specialist medical doctors. There are only a few hundred in the United States. In murder cases, their job is to perform autopsies to determine the cause and manner of death and to discover, collect, and document evidence.

While death marks the end of the body's functions, a victim's body is often a source of invaluable clues to what happened at a crime scene. The standard autopsy takes anywhere between one and four hours and begins with a careful examination of the outside of the body. Then, the front of the body is opened in the shape of the letter *Y*, using an incision from each shoulder to the top of the abdomen and a straight line down to the pubic bone to allow examination of the heart, lungs, and all of the abdominal organs. Another incision is made across the back of the head from ear to ear to expose the skull for access to the brain.

The internal organs are each removed separately and examined with the naked eye and then under a microscope, with the findings recorded in an official autopsy report. The skin is the most important organ to the forensic pathologist. It shows gunshot wounds, stabbings, blunt impacts, strangulation by injuries to the skin of the neck, and drug injection marks. The autopsy also includes toxicology tests to see if there's alcohol, cocaine, fentanyl, or other drugs in the person's system.

The basic autopsy technique hasn't changed much since the 1850s when it was developed by Rudolf Virchow, the father of pathology. And medical examiners still wrestle with the same questions: How long has the body been dead? Was the death natural or unnatural? If it was unnatural, was it a homicide—the killing of one human by another?

Such questions are what brought Eric Johnson's body to the medical examiner's office. Helpern was performing an autopsy to determine how he had died.

Rikers, a.k.a. "the Island of the Damned," was notorious for its violence and the brutality of the inmates and guards. Located in the East River near LaGuardia Airport, it is the city's largest jail, plagued by severe overcrowding that led to a spate of deadly uprisings.

The East River island was a military training ground during the Civil War. In 1884, descendants of the original owners sold it for $180,000 to New York City, which initially turned it into a garbage dump. In the late 1920s, the city picked Rikers as the site for a new jail.

When Rikers opened in 1932, the jail was designed for 4,200 inmates. But by 1954, it held 7,900. As time passed, the harsh conditions only got worse. There were constant scuffles between corrections officers and inmates. The place was a tinderbox—no one knew when one of those altercations might lead to a full-fledged riot. That's why Mayor Lindsay was so concerned. If the guards had caused Johnson's death—and that information was released to the media—it might trigger an uprising.

The circumstances surrounding Johnson's death were sketchy. Corrections officers said they went to his cell to give him medicine to control his seizures, but he refused to take the pills. He made "a cutthroat gesture" at them, they said, a sign that he'd resist. The officers put on masks and fired a tear gas canister into his cell. As a white plume of smoke provided cover, they entered his cell and dragged him out. Johnson was not responsive, they said. To their surprise, he was dead. Few of those details had made the news—not yet.

When Helpern finished the autopsy, he cleaned up and met with reporters who had come to the office. He told them that Johnson had died of natural causes, calling the death a case of "psychosis with exhaustion." That meant, he said, that Johnson died because of the way his brain and body reacted to the neurologic stimuli. In other words, Johnson got so excited that he collapsed and died. His own body's reactions were the cause of his death. Case closed.

Before I started working at the medical examiner's office, I had not heard of the term *psychosis with exhaustion*. It wasn't taught in medical school. It wasn't in medical textbooks. Yet, this wasn't the first time Helpern had used it. The other time also involved someone who died in police custody. That's when he explained the theory to me. He said psychosis with exhaustion occurs when a person's nervous system becomes overactive, as can happen during an altercation with a police officer.

I was concerned about Helpern's diagnosis. I didn't believe there was evidence that psychosis with exhaustion was a real condition. I also didn't want to argue with my boss about Johnson's cause of death. I respected Helpern, but I was afraid of how he'd react. So, I didn't say a word to him when I headed to the private autopsy room to examine and photograph Johnson's corpse. I wasn't sure why I was being so secretive. This wouldn't be the first time I had examined a body dissected by other assistant medical examiners in our office. I was always documenting cases as part of my research and for teaching purposes. With Johnson, maybe I could learn more. Maybe I could start documenting and researching psychosis with exhaustion and similar cases and collect enough information to write a journal article.

I found Johnson's body still on the table. I didn't waste any time. I began examining him and noticed bruise marks on his neck. When I inspected his eyes, I saw petechial hemorrhages—tiny red marks indicating ruptured capillaries, a condition that can be caused by neck compression. It looked like someone had squeezed Johnson's neck. I knew the incident had been obscured by tear gas so there probably weren't any witnesses who saw what happened. But here was something even more important than witness testimony: autopsy evidence that suggested Johnson died from neck compression, not natural causes. I took a deep breath, then hurried out of the room to find a camera. When I returned, Helpern was back in the room—and he looked annoyed.

"We don't need any more photos," he said, dismissively.

Usually, Helpern didn't mind if I took pictures. In fact, he encouraged me. He liked talking to me about cases. But not today, and I wasn't going to press him.

Later, when I put together all the pieces of the Johnson case, it seemed to me that Helpern's ruling had more to do with politics than science.

Medical examiners can rule a person's death natural, accidental, a suicide, or a homicide. If the manner isn't clear, they can rule the death "undetermined." But those determinations aren't made in a vacuum. Sometimes, medical examiners are pressured to make the wrong ruling. That pressure can come from an influential family who doesn't want anyone to know their loved one died of a drug overdose or suicide. Or it can come from a police chief who doesn't want the handcuffed, choked Black man in the police cruiser declared a homicide.

I don't know why Helpern said Johnson died of natural causes. But I knew he was friends with the police commissioner and district attorney. Our office had a good relationship with the cops and prosecutors. They looked at us as an extension of their own offices. They believed we were all fighting the same people, the ones who made our jobs miserable: drug addicts, poor people living in poor neighborhoods—what back then we called ghettos. We all had to look out for each other. We wouldn't be holding up our end of the bargain if Helpern ruled Johnson's death a homicide. Johnson was a mentally ill Black prisoner. A bad ruling could mean the end of the officers' careers. We wouldn't want to do that.

And maybe Helpern was just plain worried. If he ruled the death a homicide, it could mean the end of his career. He no longer had Civil Service protection. So, the mayor could fire him for making a "bad decision."

The tension between law enforcement and communities of color reminded me of the 1947 movie *Gentleman's Agreement*, in which Gregory Peck plays a reporter who pretends to be Jewish to investigate antisemitism. Along the way, he uncovers the titular agreement, a secret, unwritten, and usually unspoken rule designed to exclude Jewish people from neighborhoods, workplaces, and schools.

Did police, district attorneys, and medical examiners have their own gentleman's agreement—except instead of it being about protecting community homogeneity from Jews, it was about protecting cops when someone died suddenly after being restrained by police? Was there an understanding that medical examiners were expected to say someone died of psychosis with exhaustion instead of police violence to stop an investigation into the incident? Was it because district attorneys knew a probe—with witness statements—could lead to criminal charges and they didn't want to prosecute police?

Neither Helpern nor I were in the cell when Johnson died. Maybe we could have learned something from Johnson's death to prevent a similar incident, but Helpern's ruling eliminated any chance of that.

In the end, Helpern's cause of death ruling protected the corrections officers.

I was disappointed in Helpern and started wondering about Johnson. I didn't know much about him. Did he have a family? What did he do for a living? Would anyone miss him? Would anyone claim his body from the morgue? Or would he be buried on Hart Island, a grim, uninhabited place that was home to the City Cemetery of New York, better known as Potter's Field?

I knew if I said anything to Helpern it would upset our relationship. Unlike my wife, who didn't back down when she believed she was right, I didn't take risks. So, I stayed quiet. And nothing happened. Johnson became a statistic—just another Black man who died in police custody of natural causes.

Helpern was my mentor. He had taken me under his wing and helped me so much in my young career. I really wanted to give him the benefit of the doubt. But a few weeks later, Helpern disappointed me again in a case that raised more disturbing questions about how our office responded to possible police misconduct.

When I came to work one morning, the body of a young Hispanic man was waiting for me in the autopsy room. Police said they had arrested him the night before for buying heroin. They brought him to the precinct and put him in a cell, and he fell asleep. When officers tried to wake him up, he wouldn't budge. After checking his vital signs, they discovered he was dead.

They called the victim's family, and an aunt came down to the police station. She couldn't speak English, so they found someone who did. The stranger broke the sad news to her: her nephew had died of a drug overdose. And that's what the cops told us when he was transported to the morgue.

Of course, medical examiners are the ones who make that determination—not police officers. But I knew why they said it. They were trying to influence our findings before we started the autopsy.

When I began the postmortem examination, I discovered that the man had marks on his neck. It looked like he had been choked. Something was obviously wrong with the police narrative. So, I called the station. The officer there repeated the story, but I stopped him.

"Are you telling me nothing happened?"

"Yeah . . ."

"Well, I found marks on his neck," I said.

I could hear the officer sigh over the phone. "Let me ask around and I'll call you back."

A few minutes later, he got back to me—this time with a different version. He said police "struggled" with the man. They had to subdue him, but the rest of the story stayed the same. They put him in a cell; he fell asleep and didn't wake up.

By now, I didn't believe them. Was it a struggle on the street? In the police car? In the cell? I knew the autopsy could only answer some of my questions.

And it didn't take long before I discovered that the man's hyoid—a horseshoe-shaped neck bone between the jaw and Adam's apple—had been fractured. It was the kind of injury someone would have sustained from a chokehold. But before I could issue my finding on the cause of death, I'd have to wait for the results of toxicology tests, which could take weeks.

When they came in, they showed only trace amounts of heroin in his system. He didn't die of an overdose. He died of traumatic asphyxia. So, I ruled his death a homicide.

Armed with my findings, I asked Helpern if I should call the man's family. Wouldn't they want to know that he hadn't died of a drug overdose? Shouldn't there be an investigation? Shouldn't the police officers involved be held accountable?

No, Helpern said. It wasn't our policy to notify victims' families and share our findings with them. If they called us, we could disclose the cause of death. But we couldn't "volunteer" that information.

"We don't want to unnecessarily create a lawsuit," he said.

I was angry. Lawsuits? Was that what this was about? Shouldn't someone try to find out what really happened? It didn't make sense. But then again, it did.

The family was under the impression that their loved one had died of a drug overdose. They assumed what the police told them was true. And the man's body was already buried. So, why would they call us? Helpern and others knew that. They understood that many of the people we were dealing with were Black or Hispanic. They were poor. They weren't going to question the police version of events. Even if they suspected something was wrong, they didn't have money to hire an attorney. The system was rigged.

Not notifying the man's next of kin to explain our findings was wrong. But I knew there was nothing I could do or say to change Helpern's mind. Still, I couldn't stop thinking about the injustice. Two young men—one Black, the other Hispanic—had died in police encounters. But there would be no investigations. No one would be held accountable. No policies would be created or changed to prevent this from happening again. I was discouraged by Helpern's response. I was disillusioned with the whole damn system. And I feared that, if we didn't address the issue soon, the streets in New York would explode, like they already had in dozens of other US cities in 1967.

For instance, forty-three people died in Detroit in nearly a week of rioting. And in Newark, twenty-six people died in five days of protests that caused millions of dollars in damage. Most of the riots shared the same triggering event: a dispute between Blacks residents and white police officers that escalated to violence. But tensions didn't start in 1967. No, they had been simmering for years and years. Blacks and Hispanics faced high unemployment, poor housing, substandard schools. Add in daily harassment from white cops and it's a wonder the violence hadn't erupted sooner.

Both cases taught me a valuable lesson: forensic pathologists are scientists in a political position. We have to fight political pressure, not just bow to it. We have to tell the truth, no matter what the personal cost.

As the years passed, that became my North Star, my guiding principle. I would eventually study how other medical examiners handled fatal police encounters, particularly the ones involving restraints like handcuffs and chokeholds, back pressure, and spit masks—causes of death that are not as obvious as shootings. And when I did, it became clear to me just how far some medical examiners would go to cover up possible police misconduct.

Psychosis with exhaustion would eventually fade away, replaced by a new term: *excited delirium*. The rebranding didn't change the fact that both terms were nothing more than junk science, a way to protect bad cops from facing the consequences of their actions.

Chapter 5

• • •

ATTICA, NEW YORK

Rows of maple and oak trees flashed past as the recreational vehicle headed east on the rural two-lane road. Red, yellow, and orange leaves had just started to fall. Cows grazed on the rolling green hills. We drove past scenic rivers and streams that bisected the small towns east of Buffalo.

"Have you ever been up this way before?" the New York state trooper asked.

"No," I said. "But it reminds me a little of the Catskills. It's beautiful."

He smiled but kept his eyes on the road.

We had just met. Robert Horn was medium height and muscular with a baby face, crew cut, and a big, broad-brimmed felt hat with a high crown. In his early thirties, he exuded a quiet confidence and strength. Where we were going, I might need him as a bodyguard.

Horn had picked me up at the Buffalo Niagara International Airport. Our destination was thirty-five miles east of the city, a notorious maximum-security prison in the town of Attica, New York. By then, the whole country had heard of Attica. Prisoners had seized control of the Attica Correctional Facility on September 9, 1971, and a few days later, state police stormed the prison. Things didn't go as planned. By the time the September 13 raid was over, there were forty-three deaths—ten hostages and thirty-three prisoners. That's why I was here, just two days later. I was going to perform autopsies on the victims.

Monroe County's medical examiner, John Edland, had determined that the hostages were killed by friendly fire from police. But his ruling ran counter to what law enforcement authorities and journalists had reported. They said the inmates had slashed the hostages' throats. Russell Oswald, the state commissioner of corrections, and Vincent Mancusi, the prison's superintendent, didn't like Edland's findings. They accused him of being a "lefty"—a Communist who hated police.

They wanted a second opinion. They called New York City.

This kind of high-profile case would normally fall to Helpern. But he was away in South Africa at a forensic medical conference. James Bradley, the chief physician for the State Corrections Department, had heard me speak at a conference. He recommended me for the job.

I was on an Allegheny Airlines flight to Buffalo the next morning. Horn was at the airport to pick me up, dressed in his gray New York State Police uniform. He grabbed my bag and put it in the trunk. Then he headed to the driver's seat.

"They're waiting for us," he said. "We got a lot of work to do. The medical examiner says that we killed the hostages."

He said that he had been assigned by Captain Henry "Hank" Williams to stay with me and drive me wherever I had to go while I was here. On the drive, we made small talk. He told me he worked in the Ballistics Section of the State Police Crime Laboratory and loved his job. He said he'd be collecting any bullets or other evidence that I might find during my investigation.

When we were a couple of miles out of Attica, he glanced at me. "We're almost there," he said.

The great prison loomed in the distance like a medieval fortress. Guards kept watch from red-shingled turrets, thirty feet up. The prison's gray stone walls measured more than a mile around, and tear-gas stench still hung like a fog over the place. The only thing missing was a sign saying "Welcome to Hell."

The uprising was a huge national story. Every major radio and television station and newspaper had covered it. Some news organizations provided continuous coverage while negotiations were going on—unusual in the days before twenty-four-hour cable news channels. No one knew what would happen, so journalists didn't leave the scene. They'd break into scheduled programming to give updates.

Attica was not exceptional. Its grim conditions were typical of lockups all over America. Unrest had built in prisons in almost every state that summer. Inmates were crammed into hot, dilapidated facilities. They complained about poor medical care and cruel corrections officers. Some prisoners were forced to work long hours for little or no pay. There were few opportunities for education or rehabilitation. Many lacked even basic psychiatric care, or drug and alcohol treatment programs.

Yet, it was Attica that exploded.

Over the last twenty-four hours, I had tried to learn as much as I could about the prison. It was reminiscent of Rikers Island at first glance. Opened in 1931, it was supposed to house 1,600 of the toughest criminals in the state. By 1971, over 2,200 people were locked up there, in dehumanizing conditions. Sixty percent of the prison's population was Black and Hispanic, almost all from inner-city neighborhoods.

In addition to chronic overcrowding, inmates' letters home were censored. They were allowed one hour of exercise or recreation per day, one shower per week, and one roll of toilet paper each month. The prison had no air conditioning. Inmates said racist police brutality was so endemic they'd begun to see themselves as political prisoners rather than convicted criminals.

Most of the prison guards were local white men who'd received little training on how to deal with violent criminals. Each one was expected to oversee anywhere from 60 to 120 prisoners.

Early in the summer, Corrections Commissioner Oswald had received a list of demands from a prisoner group calling themselves the "Attica Liberation Faction." The letter said the administration and prison officials "no longer consider or respect us as human beings," and demanded a list of reforms.

Traditional racial and religious divisions among the prisoners were breaking down, prison officials realized; the men had forged a new solidarity. On August 22, the day after a prisoner was murdered at California's San Quentin prison, most of the prisoners at Attica wore a strip of black cloth as an armband and ate their breakfast in unnerving silence.

When Horn pulled up to the gate, a guard waved us inside. We parked next to a big camper van. The state trooper standing in front of the camper was Hank Williams, a muscular three-hundred-pound man with a crew cut and a campaign hat like Horn's. Replace the hat with a football helmet and Williams could've played defensive end for the Buffalo Bills.

Horn said Williams had been sleeping in the camper since the beginning of the uprising. He'd been in charge of the fatal raid and had been taking the brunt of the criticism for the disaster.

"You'll see, Williams is a good cop. He's a good guy," Horn said.

When we got out of the car, I scanned the scene. I still wasn't clear on what actually triggered the uprising, but Attica looked like a war zone. The inmates were housed in four long, separate buildings, or cellblocks, lettered A through D, that formed a square. Each had a fenced outdoor exercise yard. The cell blocks were connected by covered walkways that cut through the exercise yards and intersected in the middle at a control center called Times Square. That central spot was heavily guarded, as you had to cross through Times Square to get from one cell block to another.

Mattresses, papers, and other debris littered the exercise yards, where days before thousands of inmates had stood in solidarity, their right fists raised in protest. Now, there was an eerie quiet.

Horn escorted me to an office inside the prison, where Commissioner Oswald and Superintendent Mancusi were waiting. They stared at me in dismay. They were expecting a respectable old guy in a suit and tie. Instead, they got a thirty-seven-year-old dude with long hair, moustache, and jeans.

"Sit down," Oswald said.

For the next hour, Oswald and Mancusi recounted what happened.

They said they didn't know what prompted the inmates to start the uprising. They were still piecing it together. But on September 9, after breakfast, the uprising erupted "spontaneously" in Cell Block A. Then prisoners from all four cell blocks surged down the walkways toward Times Square, armed with clubs, makeshift knives, and whatever other weapons they could find.

William Quinn, a Times Square guard, saw them coming. He ran to slam the gates closed to stop them, but one of the gates had a faulty bolt and the prisoners broke through. They beat Quinn senseless and left him lying comatose, his skull fractured, as they moved through the facility.

The state police were summoned and wasted little time. Captain Williams and his men began retaking the cell blocks, successfully fighting their way through with tear gas and guns. But before they could retake the last one, Cell Block D, Oswald and Mancusi, against Williams's advice, ordered the police to stop.

The entire penitentiary was locked down. For four days, about 1,200 prisoners holed up in Cell Block D with forty-two hostages. The inmates were in control.

Oswald and Mancusi said they'd stopped the troopers because they were worried about the safety of the hostages. I didn't say a word, but it sounded to me like they'd just lost their nerve. Stopping had been a mistake. In prison standoffs, the longer you wait, the greater chance that someone will get killed. There are always grudges and enmities in prisons. When the inmates are no longer protected by guards, some will do what they can to settle old scores.

Oswald said he began negotiations to end the siege. To represent them, the prisoners had assembled a core inmate group, which included Black Panthers, Nation of Islam members, a white Weather Underground member, and a member of the Young Lords, a politicized Latino group. Hostages included guards who were well liked and sympathetic to the prisoners' cause. The prisoners designated typists, organized a security force, and drafted a list of outside people they wanted to appoint as observers—non-incarcerated notables who they felt might keep them safe by bearing witness. These included Louis Farrakhan, who later became the leader of the Nation of Islam, and Tom Wicker, the *New York Times* columnist and author.

The uprising became a made-for-TV event. Negotiators met with the prisoners in Cell Block D's exercise yard. Reporters and broadcast journalists were there with their lights and cameras. The prisoners' twenty-eight demands included better food, medical care, and access to books and newspapers. Oswald said he could agree to all but three: the removal of Superintendent Mancusi from Attica, amnesty for the inmates who were a part of the uprising, and passage to a Third World country for any prisoners who wanted to go.

Things went downhill from there. About fifteen prisoners emerged as leaders. They said everyone in the cellblock supported their action. However, in the prison yard during negotiations, as inmates Barry Schwartz and Kenneth Hess spoke with a reporter, Schwartz slipped the reporter a note that said not all prisoners supported the uprising. The reporter showed the note to one of the inmate leaders, who took Schwartz and Hess inside from the yard and cut their throats. Those wounds were not fatal; Schwartz was later seen leaning against the bars of a prison window, screaming for help with a bloody towel around his neck. But the leaders then took the pair to separate cells and fatally stabbed them. The leaders also killed another prisoner, Michael Privitiera, for starting fights among inmates. All three of the men were white. Schwartz and Hess were Jewish. Privitiera was Italian.

On September 11, Quinn, the guard attacked at Times Square, died at the hospital, converting the uprising to a much more serious murder investigation. As the negotiations dragged on, Oswald grew frustrated at the lack of progress. The prisoners knew Quinn had died and petitioned Governor Nelson Rockefeller for pardons. Rockefeller said no. He was worried the prisoners would kill the hostages. The prisoners began digging defensive trenches, making Cell Block D look like the Western Front during World War I.

The governor was feeling pressure from the White House. President Richard Nixon and the FBI saw the state authorities' patience with the prisoners as a sign of weakness—a concession to radicalism. So, Rockefeller gave the order for the state police to go in again. He barred the corrections officers from taking part because he knew they'd want revenge.

On the morning of September 13, a helicopter dropped tear gas canisters into the prison yard. The prisoners took eight blindfolded prison-guard hostages up to a catwalk overlooking Cell Block D, and stood behind them, holding knives to their throats. Several more blindfolded hostages were brought into the yard and made to stand in a circle. Chaos erupted. State police with rifles and shotguns and unauthorized corrections officers with handguns stormed in, firing their weapons. Endless rounds were shot into the chemical mist. When it was over, no one could say exactly what had happened. Cellblock D was secured, but with numerous casualties.

Witnesses said they saw dead hostages being brought out of the prison on stretchers, bloody blindfolds wrapped around their necks. Everyone there, including journalists, assumed the prisoners had carried out their earlier threat to cut the hostages' throats. Newspapers, including the *New York Times* in its front-page lead story, stated that the inmates had killed the hostages.

No single local mortuary was large enough to handle all the bodies.

Cadavers were sent to a number of mortuaries in the Buffalo and Rochester area. That's how John Edland, Monroe County's chief medical examiner, got involved; Rochester is in Monroe County. When Edland conducted the autopsies, he made a startling discovery. The inmates hadn't cut the hostages' throats. They had died from law enforcement shotgun wounds—almost all double-aught buckshot to the head. The blood around their necks was the hemorrhaging from the bullet holes to the head. They'd died from friendly fire.

Before Edland had a chance to say anything to state officials, one of his assistants told a reporter at the local newspaper, the Rochester *Times-Union*, about the autopsy results. When Edland confirmed the story, all hell broke loose. The media had to backtrack from earlier accounts.

The corrections officials at Attica were pissed off. They didn't believe Edland. This had to be a plot to blame the deaths on the troopers, they said.

"Look, we think Edland is a communist," Oswald said to me. "That's why he's lying about this."

Mancusi chimed in. "We saw the hostages being beaten and abused for days. I saw with my own eyes that the hostages' throats were cut . . . This has to be a communist plot of some kind. Why else would Edland lie?"

I told them that I said I wasn't there to prove Edland was a liar. I came to Attica to find out the truth. The men grumbled a little, but they couldn't contradict that.

Edland was a good forensic pathologist who I knew from medical examiner meetings. Politically he was very conservative. He was certainly no communist. But Attica had become a hot political issue. "Law and order" conservatives, led by President Nixon and Vice President Spiro Agnew, had pushed Rockefeller to stop negotiating with the prisoners and retake Attica by force.

"Attica proves once again that when the responsible voices of society remain mute, the forces of violence and crime grow arrogant," Agnew wrote in a *New York Times* opinion piece. "One need only recall the era of Hitler's Storm Troopers to realize what can happen to the most civilized societies when such a cloak of respectability is provided thugs and criminals."

Mancusi said he had a list of the funeral parlors with the hostages' bodies. They were the only ones he wanted examined. But I told him that to properly reconstruct what happened, I had to examine everybody, including the inmates.

"I want to look at all the bodies—prisoners and hostages. To understand one death, I have to understand them all," I said. "To do it properly, I have to make sure each gunshot perforation and track is identified—entrance and exit—so they can be matched to every weapon used."

Oswald and Mancusi shook their heads in disbelief. They shot me a look that said, *Who the fuck does this guy think he is?*

"We're not doing it that way," Mancusi said, irritated.

I let silence fall for a minute.

"If I can't examine all the bodies, I won't do any. I'll go back to New York," I said. "I don't have to be here." I got up and started to leave.

Then Oswald jumped in. He had only been the corrections commissioner for a year, and he believed that prisons should emphasize rehabilitation, not punishment. He had wanted to somehow resolve the uprising peacefully, but things kept going wrong. He overruled Mancusi. "What you say makes sense. Examine everybody," he said.

I asked Oswald for the list of where the prisoners' bodies were being stored. "We have no list. They're probably still at the different medical examiner offices that they were brought to. I don't think they've been identified yet."

At that point, I knew it was going to be a long week.

◆ ◆ ◆

I opened the door of the Holiday Inn by the Buffalo airport and plopped on the bed. I was exhausted.

My first day had been a media circus, for good reason. This was the deadliest US prison riot in a generation. Attica shone a spotlight on the biases and stereotypes firmly embedded in communities across the nation, and on how so much of the media fed into them: Black men are violent criminals. The white corrections officers were in the right—hardworking men just trying to do their jobs. Anyone in jail deserves to suffer.

From my work, I knew it was easier to arrest and convict Black people than white people. Stereotyping, particularly of Black males, played a big role in that. Generations of white Americans learned from parents, neighbors, teachers, cartoons, jokes, television, and movies that Black people were supposedly unintelligent and lazy, and more prone to commit crimes than white people—that's why so many were in jails and prisons, including Attica. White supremacists still adhered to and maintained these racist lies, which were upheld by politicians who wanted to keep their votes. Racial inequality was the reality, and Black people who wanted better treatment were asking too much.

Black people didn't want to overthrow society. They just wanted the same employment and educational opportunities as whites. They wanted to stop being targeted by police. They wanted to be heard. They wanted not to be "judged by the color of their skin, but by the content of their character." With the civil rights movement and its push for racial equality, I could see things starting to change. But it was moving too damn slow.

When the *New York Times* reported that the Black prisoners sliced their hostages' throats, no one blinked. But when Edland cast doubt on that presumption, saying that white state police officers were responsible for killing the white hostages, public opinion in the Rochester area turned on Edland. His loyalty to his country was questioned. He received death threats.

I'd seen something similar in a New York case during the summer of 1965. For years, racial tensions had been simmering in El Barrio, the East Harlem section of Manhattan. Police there were out of hand, Hispanic residents said. They were being stopped, harassed, beaten, and sometimes arrested for crimes they didn't commit. Few people in the white community believed them. Meanwhile, police officers patrolling that area used racial slurs and stereotypes to describe the neighborhood and the people who lived there.

Things came to a head when police officers chased a suspect into a sprawling El Barrio housing project. Many people watched from their windows, and then started screaming at the officers to leave. Shots rang out. When it was over, two of the residents by their windows were dead. The police said they had been attacked, and that the two tenants were killed by their neighbors, not by the cops. But residents said the police killed them. Many New Yorkers believed the officers.

Immediately after the shooting, thousands of people from the projects demanded that the mayor and police chief resign. There was no violence that night, but no one knew how long the peace would last.

I arrived to work the next day at 8 AM to crowds of people outside the medical examiner's building on the East Side of Manhattan. Reporters were waiting within.

"Who did it?" one of them shouted as I brushed past.

I shrugged. "I don't know," I said. "We'll have a look."

I headed to the autopsy room. Another medical examiner, Elliot Gross, was already there. He took one body; I examined the other. We both removed police-issued .38 caliber flat-nose bullets from the bodies. When Helpern arrived early, he looked at the bullets, then went upstairs to the lobby where the media were gathered. At an impromptu news conference, he stated that the two were killed by the police. He got an immediate call from then–Mayor Robert Wagner.

"Why did you say that the police shot them so quickly? Those people are going to riot," he said.

After the call, Helpern bounded back to the autopsy room and yelled at Gross and me, parroting the mayor. If we had waited longer before recovering the bullets, Helpern said, he could have told reporters that we didn't know yet who fired the bullets—and wouldn't know until ballistics finished their examination in a few weeks.

Despite Wagner's and Helpern's fears, the news conference had the opposite effect. Instead of inciting protests, our honesty calmed everyone down. No rioting. I learned a lesson that day: civil unrest takes place when people believe they're being lied to, when they feel that their voices and concerns aren't being heard. The quicker you come out with the truth, the better it is for everybody. It's when you delay—when you don't want to give the bad news—that people think there's a cover-up. That's when the people lose trust, and that leads to unrest.

No police officers were ever charged in those deaths. A police investigation said the officers' actions were justified. Now, after my meeting with Oswald and Mancusi, I wondered: If the results of my examination agreed with Edland's, would any white state troopers be charged in connection with the Attica deaths? If history was any guide, I already knew the answer.

The next morning, I met Horn in the lobby at 8 AM. We had a busy day ahead of us.

I decided to focus on the hostages first. Their bodies were in funeral parlors, identified, embalmed, and ready for burial. The death certificates had been filled out. No one who died had cut marks on their necks or stab wounds.

Edland was right. They had all died of bullet wounds, and the shots had come from a distance where the police were. Six of the hostages had died of double-aught buckshot pellet shots to the head. That happened when one of the troopers who entered the D yard fired his shotgun at a prisoner who the officer said was making a threatening gesture. The trooper missed and the pellets ended up 150 feet away from his position, spread out at head height, where the six blindfolded hostages were standing.

Then I examined the body of a guard who supposedly had been fatally beaten by inmates. That information had come from a funeral director who had prepared the man for burial. He told reporters at a news conference that there were no bullet wounds on the man's body.

The guard's eyes were indeed blackened, and he had bruises on his forehead. But when, with Horn's help, I turned the naked body over, there was a clear gunshot entrance wound in the middle of his upper back. The funeral director hadn't turned the body completely over when he was preparing it for burial. The injuries to the face and eyes were due to his falling face down onto the ground. My internal examination showed no skull fractures or brain injury. The guard had died from a shotgun pellet, not from a beating.

I called the funeral director at his home. "I hate to disturb you. But can you come back in?" I could tell he wasn't thrilled by my call, but he agreed.

Horn smiled. He had been driving me around all day, from funeral home to funeral home, helping me examine the victims and collecting bullets from the bodies. By the time the first autopsy was done, we were much more comfortable with each other. If someone had peeked into our car, they'd have thought we were filming a TV show. In his impeccably pressed uniform, Horn was the strait-laced, disciplined one, the meticulous crime lab guy. I was the free spirit: a young forensic pathologist whose long brown hair had a touch of gray. Together, we were searching for clues to solve a criminal mystery.

"When he gets here, what do you want me to do?" he asked.

I smiled. "Watch."

When he arrived, he was carrying a bowling-ball bag. He wore a white bowling shirt with his team's name emblazoned on the back.

"You bowl?" I asked.

"Yes," he said, annoyed. "I'm in a league."

"I want you to take a look at something," I said.

I had placed the guard's body on his stomach so the funeral director could see the back. He stared at the wound and his face turned red. He wheeled around and immediately picked up a phone on a nearby table. He called his wife in a panic.

"Honey, don't say anything more to the newspaper reporters. Not a word," he said.

"I guess I ruined his bowling night," I whispered to Horn.

When we left the funeral home, Horn dropped me off at the hotel. We were tired, but we felt good. We were contributing to the understanding of what had happened on that horrible day. We had worked hard but had made progress.

"See you tomorrow," he said. We had another long day ahead of us.

"Same time. Same place," I said.

In the hotel room. I yawned and glimpsed at the alarm clock on the night table. It was nearly midnight. Horn was going to pick me up early, and I wanted to be ready. I still had a lot of work to do.

◆ ◆ ◆

As Oswald had guessed at our initial meeting, the prisoners' bodies were still at various medical examiners' morgues in the area, mostly in Rochester and Buffalo. Each had been brought out of D yard with a coded tag tied around the left ankle—P-1 to P-33. No names; they were being slowly identified. I began at the Rochester Mortuary because most of the bodies—prisoners and hostages—had been brought there.

Edland fully cooperated with us. He said he was upset at the backlash for telling the truth. Meanwhile, Horn and I were working sixteen-hour days. The autopsies took longer than usual because they involved victims who had been shot multiple times. I had to check each bullet track to determine the entrance and exit perforations and the trajectory through the body, in order to see if it could contribute to the investigation.

Somehow we managed to examine everyone who died in the uprising—and recover many bullets still in the bodies. Some medical examiners only remove a sample of bullets when there are multiple gunshot wounds. I've learned that the bullet you leave behind is the one that may have come from a different weapon. By recovering all the bullets, we were able to confirm all of their trajectories.

During that week, I got a call from Arthur Eve, a Black state assemblyman from Buffalo who had been one of the hostage negotiators. He was concerned about Elliot Barkley, one of the uprising leaders. Barkley had been extremely outspoken and eloquent during the four-day standoff, criticizing Attica's conditions on television. Some of the prisoners told Eve that they saw Barkley alive after the state police retook Attica and speculated that he must have been shot after that. Edland had said that Barkley was killed by a single rifle bullet in the back. For some, that confirmed that he'd been executed.

When I examined Barkley's back wound, it was very large and wide, not the smaller wound indicative of a bullet scoring a direct, straight hit. The larger entrance perforation meant the bullet was "tumbling"—evidence that it had struck an intermediary target before hitting Barkley's body. In other words, Barkley was struck by a ricochet bullet. He was not deliberately targeted.

I finished my work on Monday, September 20. I had been with Horn almost a week, and we had actually become friends. I was asked to share my analysis with Oswald, Mancusi, and the state police, especially Captain Williams. I knew Williams wouldn't like my findings, but I wanted him to hear them from me.

We met in Mancusi's office at the prison. There, I recounted the work I'd done reexamining the hostages' and prisoners' bodies. In the process, I had confirmed Edland's findings that friendly fire had killed the hostages.

I walked them through the scene as I reconstructed it. The officers had stormed Attica under a cloud of tear gas. The initial barrage of gunfire was indiscriminate. All told, police fired three thousand rounds. They were lucky that more than two dozen hostages made it out alive.

I concluded that the hostages in the exercise yard were struck in their heads when a state trooper accidentally discharged his shotgun in their direction. Maybe he slipped and fell, and the gun went off. The hostages' blindfolds slipped around their necks and became soaked with blood. That's why witnesses believed the victims' throats had been slashed.

I told them there was another problem. Even though prison guards had been forbidden to take part in the raid, some had stepped in anyway and used their personal weapons. I'd found handgun bullets in some of the bodies, as well as rounds from rifles issued to the state police. It was a mess.

I learned that state troopers didn't have to sign their names to get a rifle. So while bullets could be tracked back to a specific rifle, we didn't have a way to find out who had actually used the weapon.

It would be hard to charge anyone in law enforcement.

Inmates claimed that some of the prisoners had been shot while trying to surrender. But it was difficult to tell by autopsy alone what a prisoner was doing when he was shot. We'd have to rely on statements by inmates and police—and they both had intrinsic biases. It wasn't like the prisoners were all lined up and shot. As the police swarmed Cell Block D, some of the inmates were shot in their backs and sides. It would be hard to determine the precise angle of fire without knowing if the inmates were standing or lying down when they were hit.

But one thing was clear: once the shooting stopped, the police vented their frustration on the inmates. Witnesses had reported officers yelling racial slurs at the prisoners, who were all stripped nude; many were beaten.

When I finished, the prison officials were angry, but there was little they could do. Williams listened and accepted my findings.

Meanwhile, Attica was still big news. The uprising was a watershed moment for prisoners' rights, sparking a national conversation about the treatment of incarcerated people and the need for reform. It was the most media attention any prisoner struggle had ever received, and it brought details about prison conditions into living rooms across the nation.

Upstate New York was suddenly flooded with civil rights attorneys and advocates. Attica guards were accused of retaliating against the prisoners. Potentially there could be countless investigations, possible criminal charges, and lawsuits.

But first, it was time to bury the dead. Politicians and law enforcement officials attended the prison guards' funerals. The slain inmates, many of whom had no family, were buried in a nearby cemetery.

Even with my confirmation, many residents and police refused to accept Edland's findings. The threatening phone calls to Edland continued. I could only imagine what would have happened if the internet was around then. How many conspiracy theories would have been floated and eventually worked their way into the mainstream? I understand that passions sometimes overtake truth and justice. But what Edland went through was unconscionable. He paid a heavy emotional price for telling the truth—for just doing his job.

My work at Attica was done. When I spoke with Williams, he said he wished his bosses had let him continue taking back Cell Block D that first day. If they had, there would have been no hostages. Instead, so many lives were lost.

"I appreciate your work, Doctor Baden. This riot, everything that happened, this is something that we're going to have to live with for a long time," he said. We shook hands and said goodbye.

Horn was waiting outside in the lot by his cruiser. "You ready?" he asked.

I nodded. "It's been a long week," I said.

"Yes, it has."

As we drove to the airport, he said he had enjoyed working with me. "Maybe we'll work together again."

"I'd like that," I said.

He pulled up to the departures curb. I shook his hand. "Let's keep in touch," he said.

I nodded, then grabbed my bag.

As I sat in the airport waiting for my flight, I still had some questions about the uprising. Could it have been prevented? But something worried me that day: Would prison officials call Helpern and others to complain about me because I pressed so hard for autopsies to be performed on all the victims? And if they did, how would Helpern react? Would he have my back, or would he be pissed off? Nothing I could do now, but I knew I needed to brace myself for the worst.

When I returned home, I was surprised but relieved to find there was no backlash for the way I had handled the case. Instead, something strange happened: a whole new world opened up for me.

Chapter 6

• • •

PATHOLOGY RULES

Back in New York, I settled into my routine of autopsies and research. But then, to my surprise, the telephone started to ring, and letters began to arrive from people asking for help.

At that time, I had a good working relationship with the media. Over the years, New York City journalists routinely called the medical examiner's office with questions about cases. My experience with my college newspaper had been positive—in fact, I had considered becoming a journalist. So I encouraged my reluctant colleagues to talk to reporters to make sure the reporters got the correct information. "They're just trying to make a living. Why don't you help them?" I'd say. After all, the *forensic* in *forensic pathology* derives from the Latin word meaning "of the forum," referring to speaking in public and in court to help educate others. So I saw speaking with reporters as part of our job.

But these calls were different. Criminal attorneys, inmates, and families of convicts or victims asked if I could reexamine evidence in their cases. When I asked how they knew my name, they said "Attica."

Attica was also why, in early 1972, I received a call from John Dunne, a Republican state legislative leader from Nassau County—one of the Attica negotiators who'd formed a rapport with the inmates. A man who'd urged Governor Rockefeller to go to Attica and meet the inmates face to face. A man who'd urged officials not to storm the prison.

"Do you think you can come to my office and talk?" asked Senator Dunne.

"Of course. It's about Attica, right?"

He said yes, and we set a date and a time.

Attica had changed my career. I was no longer just a deputy medical examiner. Now, my name was nationally known in law enforcement circles. Even Helpern praised my work. I didn't get any pushback from him or others, unlike what had happened to Edland. They knew I did the right thing, and public opinion in New York City was very much on my side. It also seemed that more and more politicians on both sides of the aisle were embracing prison reform.

Meanwhile, at home, I was seeing less of Judianne. Her Odyssey House program was a success. In just a few years, it had expanded from one drug treatment center in East Harlem to nearly a dozen in several states. She spent most of her time running the nonprofit and lobbying government officials for money so Odyssey House could treat more drug addicts. The only time she took a break was when she gave birth to our fourth child, Sarah. But within days, there she was, back in her office.

With both of us working so much, our marriage began to suffer. We still loved each other but we didn't laugh as much. We were serious about everything. We didn't go to movies. In fact, we didn't go out—not even to restaurants. Every time we talked it was about our jobs.

But it was more than that. When we got married, I was passive. Her parents helped us financially with our apartment and, later, our children. I was extremely grateful for their generosity. So, I went along with everything Judianne suggested for our family—from where to live to where to send our children to school. Later in our marriage, I began to speak up. If I didn't like something, I'd tell her. She didn't like that.

Each of us felt that our own work was more important than our marriage. She spent her waking hours at Odyssey House; I spent mine at the morgue. We argued more and more.

Not only were we not spending as much time alone with each other, we also weren't spending much time with our children. Yes, we'd see them when we came home. But our live-in housekeeper, Mrs. Bean, had become a surrogate parent. She was the one who made sure they got off to school and, later, prepared their dinner.

The three oldest—Trissa, Judson, and Lindsey—were very close. And they were doing extremely well in school. They were still young, just thirteen, nine, and seven. Trissa and Lindsey said they wanted to become doctors when they grew up. Judson said he was more interested in law than medicine. The brightest of my children, Judson was someone to whom everything came naturally. I knew his future was unlimited. And we had a special connection—it seemed like we could talk about anything. He was the one who always waited up for me. He was genuinely interested in my cases and I loved to tell him about them. As for Sarah, her siblings were protective of their baby sister. In a way, my children were a self-sustaining unit. At times, it seemed like they didn't need us at all. They had each other.

Still, I felt guilty about not spending more time with them. They were getting older, and we didn't do things together. We didn't sit down for family dinners. We no longer had time for family trips. Sometimes Judianne would take Trissa to work or events. And a few times, I took them to conferences with me.

I wasn't an absentee parent. I'd go to parent–teacher conferences at their schools, and to Lindsey's soccer games and Judson's chess matches. But just like many of my young doctor friends who were raising a family, I was always working. So was Judianne.

Maybe part of it was that Judianne and I hadn't come from homes that had family dinners or getaways. My mother worked as much as she could to help our family survive. Our biggest trip was taking the subway to Brooklyn's Brighton Beach. And I knew Judianne's lawyer parents were never home. The more I thought about it, the more I realized that we were raising our children the same way our parents raised us.

But what could I do? For me, being a forensic pathologist was not a job, but a calling. I knew Judianne felt the same way about Odyssey House. So, we didn't slow down. We stayed *too busy* to think about what all the hard work and long hours were doing to our marriage or our children. We didn't turn down time-consuming requests from government officials or the media.

So, any time a legislator or reporter asked me to talk about what happened at Attica, I did. Years earlier, when I'd begun presenting findings from my drug abuse studies at big conferences, I discovered that I enjoyed public speaking—but the key was being prepared. You couldn't do these presentations on the fly. That's why, to prepare for my meeting with Dunne, I began compiling notes about what I had learned at Attica, as well as my ideas for prison reform.

Dunne was an interesting legislator. He was a conservative Republican, but moderate on some issues. He also was a close friend of Governor Rockefeller.

An advocate of prison reform since his election to the New York Senate in 1965, Dunne had risen through the GOP. Now, he was chairman of the Senate's Committee on Crime and Correction. Over the last few years, he had visited nearly three dozen jails and prisons. His inspections included meetings with inmates to discuss conditions and problems.

In 1969 Dunne had issued a scathing report on the appalling conditions in New York City's nine jails, noting their alarming suicide rate. Eight months later, violence erupted in one of them, the Men's House of Detention in Manhattan, better known as the Tombs. The prisoners took several guards hostage but agreed to release them after officials promised to make changes.

Since then, inmates had inundated Dunne with letters complaining about harsh conditions in their jails. After prisoners took hostages at Attica, Dunne was one of the people their leaders asked to meet with.

When he arrived, the prisoners in Cell Block D cheered. He agreed to help them negotiate a settlement to the uprising.

The prisoners also asked to meet with Rockefeller, but the governor refused. And when Dunne discovered that Rockefeller planned to use force, he pleaded with him for more time to negotiate an end to the crisis. Dunne knew he had time on his side. The prisoners weren't going anywhere. But Rockefeller ignored Dunne and ordered state police to retake control of the prison.

If the governor thought Attica was going away after the raid, he was wrong. Attica was still in the public consciousness. A special grand jury handed up forty-two indictments against sixty-two prisoners. They faced over twelve hundred charges, most of them centered around taking the hostages. Civil rights groups protested that all the indictments were against prisoners. None were filed against guards involved in the post-uprising reprisals.

After they took back the prison, inmates said, the guards brutalized them. They forced them to remove their clothes, shouted racial slurs, and beat them as they crawled through the dirt on their elbows. (Their claims would later be corroborated by videos and witnesses.) Some said several prisoners were killed after they surrendered.

Rockefeller had set up a commission to investigate the uprising and its aftermath. Dunne led that effort. He was looking into both the causes of the Attica uprising and ways to ensure it never happened again. He needed input from a lot of people who were there. I was on his list.

I knew Attica's inmates had been imprisoned because they'd been convicted of serious crimes, including murder. But I also knew that something was clearly wrong with our criminal justice system. Why were the overwhelming number of inmates in our prisons people of color? Why were prisoners treated so inhumanely? Why was it so easy for us to simply throw them away? Could some of them be rehabilitated? Could some of them be innocent?

I knew some of the answers. Inmates were largely poor, uneducated, and considered the underbelly of society. But while I knew from my interactions with prisoners and addicts that many were decent, bright, hard-working, and worth saving, too many people believed they were "lowlifes"—vicious animals, whose criminality was genetic—and that tough treatment was the only way to control them.

Attica had opened a window into the penal system's racial injustice. In America, it was easier to arrest and convict poor people of color in particular because they didn't have money to hire good attorneys to defend them. The deck was stacked.

Maldonado. Whitmore. Johnson. Attica. Names and places that played a role in raising my own awareness of social injustice and racial bias in the criminal justice system. But I was still struggling with the idea that racial prejudice might be part of the culture in the law enforcement community. I wasn't ready to go that far. Not yet.

As I prepared for my meeting with Dunne, I began thinking about my own childhood. Where I grew up, crime was one of the few ways to climb out of the neighborhood. You didn't have many options. You didn't get much encouragement from your teachers. They all seemed pessimistic about your future. They thought that maybe you'd get a factory job or work on the docks—if you didn't end up in jail first.

You had to be tough to survive. A lot of us looked up to gangsters, like a skinny neighborhood kid I'd known named Joey Gallo. Sometimes Gallo and his brothers would visit their aunt, who lived in my project building. I was many years younger than Gallo, who was on his way to becoming a major Mafia figure. But he'd seen me hanging out in front of the building enough times to recognize me and say hello or tousle my hair. Guys like Gallo became your heroes because they escaped from the neighborhood. I felt that if my mother hadn't been so obsessed with my schooling, that could have been me. (Years later, he'd end up on my autopsy table after being shot while celebrating his birthday in Umberto's Clam House in the Little Italy section of lower Manhattan.)

When I was in elementary school, my parents fought often and loudly before their divorce. Sometimes my father stormed out of the apartment and disappeared for weeks. My mother was convinced that he had a girlfriend, and she railed at him for deserting us without any money. The tension at home affected my behavior at school. I was classified as a "deportment problem" and kicked out of the first grade for acting up. My mother and the local school psychologist decided to send me to a reform school for Jewish delinquents in Hawthorne, New York, when I was just six years old. I took to the disciplined environment and became very good at schoolwork, eventually skipping a few grades there. When I returned to Brooklyn three years later, I was three years younger than everyone else in the class.

I learned something else at Hawthorne that helped me even more when I returned to my old neighborhood: how to fight. I didn't back down. I can't tell you how many times I got into altercations as a teenager because I was Jewish or to protect my kid brother. When someone tried to bully either of us, I'd jump right in and punch them, and soon the bullies quit trying.

I was lucky to find a way out through education. Many of my classmates didn't have the same opportunities because of racial prejudice. For things to get better, that had to change, or else jails would continue to be filled with people of color.

I brought all these opinions to the senator's office. Dunne was tall and thin with round glasses. In his severe gray pinstriped suit, white button-down shirt, and tie, he looked like the Yale Law School alum that he was. Dunne understood the criminal justice system. He was tough, but compassionate.

He told me that his visits to lockups around the state had opened his eyes. He was appalled at the conditions, violence, racism, and lack of rehabilitation. Well before the riots he had tried to call attention to the out-of-control violence at the Attica prison, the racism, and the crowded, dirty conditions.

I nodded in agreement. "While I was there, one thing kept coming up," I said. "Inmates talked about the brutality. A main concern was the violent way prisoners were treated by the guards." Attica had become a symbol of racial hatred—white guards beating up Black prisoners.

When a convict was injured or killed at Attica or committed suicide, prison officials had devised a way to cover it up. Time and again, inmates told me, corrections officers restrained prisoners, then beat them. They would then be taken to the infirmary, where some died of their injuries. When a prisoner died, the guards took the body to the nearest hospital emergency room. There, they would tell the doctors the inmate had died of a heart attack. That's what was put on the death certificate. And that's what the family was told.

"No one would do an autopsy to see what really happened," I said. "Inmates believe the guards get away with murder. They believe their lives are expendable."

"What do you suggest?" he asked.

"Require that an autopsy and toxicology be done on every inmate who dies at Attica," or any other prison, jail, or lockup in New York state, I said.

The session lasted about an hour. When we finished, Dunne promised he would do something. And in 1973, he introduced legislation that created the New York State Corrections Commission Medical Review Board. This special board would provide oversight for the Department of Corrections, which ran the prisons. It would review every death that occurred in all of New York's sites of incarceration. It would have five members: a forensic pathologist, a forensic psychiatrist, a defense attorney recommended by the New York State Bar Association, a county sheriff, and a member of the community. Not only would the members review all deaths, they'd also have the power to report egregious activities by corrections officers, staff, or medical personnel to the appropriate authorities so they could take action. The new legislation required an autopsy and toxicology done on every inmate who died—the only legally ordered autopsies in New York state. And these findings would be immediately available to the families.

Back then, there were thirty thousand people in New York jails, prisons, and lockups and about two hundred deaths a year—mostly young, relatively healthy people. Dunne hoped the board would develop the trust of inmates and create a sense of fairness. In turn, that would reduce the chance of another prison uprising.

When the legislation passed, Dunne called me.

"How would you like to be a member of the new review board? There's no pay with that job."

I didn't hesitate. "Yes!" I said.

I could still work in the New York City Medical Examiner's Office. But in addition, I would be the state commission's forensic pathologist.

The board performed another important duty: it developed strategies to prevent deaths in the correctional system, whether from suicides, drug overdoses, inadequate medical care, or struggles with corrections officers.

After the board's first meeting, I jumped right into the prevention part. Suicides were a big problem in prisons. Hanging was the only way you could kill yourself when incarcerated because prisoners didn't usually have access to guns, knives, or pills.

After examining the problem, I determined that the most common way prisoners hanged themselves was by using the curtain rods in shower rooms where they were alone. So, I recommended putting in collapsible rods. "If someone attempts suicide, the shower rod will break," I said.

The board agreed it was a good idea and also recommended taking away prisoners' shoelaces and belts if they were suicidal. I also suggested another policy: if a guard heard a prisoner talk about suicide, he had to report it to his supervisors right away, and they would have to ensure the inmate got immediate mental health evaluation. Holding prison authorities accountable—letting them know someone is watching them—would help change harmful attitudes and behaviors.

We also developed a suicide-prevention screening form that had to be filled out for every new inmate. It was a way of evaluating a prisoner's suicidal potential so he could get early help. It was so successful that prisons and jails throughout the United States adopted it.

Further, we emphasized the need to more closely observe inmates who received bad news from their significant others or lawyers.

Another issue I brought to the board's attention was deaths that occurred during the use of tear gas to remove unruly prisoners from their cells—deaths like Eric Johnson's.

In some cases, corrections officers would use tear gas to punish prisoners they didn't like. They would don gas masks, fire canisters into the cell, and then go inside to grab the prisoner. Nobody could see what was going on because of the gas. If the prisoner ended up dead, the officers would say, "We couldn't see what happened." But the autopsy would show signs that the inmate had been beaten or physically choked.

We were able to establish rules that use of tear gas would have to be approved by supervisors. And the tear gas would have to be fired by an officer who wasn't involved in the initial attempt to remove the inmate. Since the rule was implemented, there have been no tear gas deaths in New York prisons and jails.

Dunne's good work won him national notice. He was later appointed by President George H. W. Bush as assistant attorney general for civil rights, the person in charge of enforcing all federal civil rights laws. He also founded Prisoners' Legal Services of New York, which has helped more than fifty thousand of the state's inmates. The nonprofit provides prisoners with nonviolent ways to resolve disputes, a move that helps reduce tensions and hostility in jails.

In the end, some good resulted from the Attica uprising. The Medical Review Board greatly reduced the number of jail suicides. By 2020, the annual average had been cut in half, from thirty to about fifteen, despite a 50 percent increase in the population of New York's jails, prisons, and detention centers. And inmates were receiving better medical care. It was exactly the kind of public service that I'd wanted to do when I'd first chosen forensic pathology.

Chapter 7

• • •

UNDER FIRE

This was it: August 3, 1978, my first "official" day as chief medical examiner for the city of New York.

I had worked in that office for eighteen years—first as a "tour doctor," then as a deputy chief medical examiner. I had studied and apprenticed for this for a long time. So, when I walked into City Council chambers with my family for my swearing-in ceremony, I knew I was more than ready.

Mayor Edward Koch had been waiting for me inside the big room, along with about a hundred guests—family members, friends, and colleagues. I was surprised that so many people showed up for the ceremony. After all, I had technically been the chief medical examiner for months. The mayor had appointed me in April after not reappointing my predecessor, Dr. Dominick Di-Maio, who had replaced Helpern when he retired in 1973.

Although I had been running the day-to-day operations of the office since then, I couldn't be called the chief medical examiner until DiMaio had exhausted his unused vacation and sick days. Until then, I'd been the city's "acting" chief medical examiner. But after today's ceremony, the word *acting* would disappear from my title.

Everyone in the room applauded as a smiling Koch escorted me to a make-shift stage in front of the room. I glanced at the crowd. My mother and brother were in the front row. So were mentors like Nobel laureates Dickerson Richards and André Cournand and many of the Bellevue Hospital doctors I had worked with over the years. I glimpsed the eyes of others who clapped or gave me the thumbs-up sign. They all knew how hard I had worked to reach this day.

Here I was, at forty-three, leading one of the city's most important agencies. In my new position, I'd earn $50,000 a year. If I had become an internist, I knew I'd be making at least twice as much. But I didn't care about that. No, I loved everything about forensic pathology. I really had followed my bliss.

With three of my children standing behind me (Sarah, my youngest, sat on the floor, trying to hide behind the podium) and Judianne by my side, Koch unleashed a flurry of praise and compliments, calling me one of the best forensic pathologists in the nation.

"Doctor Baden's influence extends beyond his office," said Koch, reminding everyone in the room that I served on the New York State Corrections Commission Medical Review Board, which investigated prison deaths, and was a special consultant to the US Department of Justice on federal murder cases. "For years, the law enforcement community has been reaching out to Doctor Baden for help on difficult cases."

Not only that, Koch continued, I had gained an international reputation as an expert on the effects of alcohol and drug abuse, adding that my articles had appeared in many professional journals and books. He noted that I was on the faculty of several medical schools, including those of Columbia, New York University, and the Albert Einstein College of Medicine.

As I stood there, I felt a sense of accomplishment. A kid from a tough housing project in Brooklyn, who had been sent to reform school, was now the chief medical examiner of the city of New York. At the same time, I wasn't satisfied with my achievements. I knew I had a lot of work ahead of me if I was going to carry out my ambitious agenda.

I planned to take a different approach than my predecessors. They had been happy with the status quo and content to deal with problems as they emerged. But I wanted to do more. I envisioned the office as independent, scientific, apolitical. I planned to make changes that would transform our office into a destination for the best and brightest young forensic pathologists—physicians who truly wanted to make a difference.

And so, I hit the ground running.

When I was appointed, my office had nine forensic pathologists who were responsible for 6,500 autopsies a year. (At the time, there were only 150 forensic pathologists in the United States.) I hired eight more full-time board-certified forensic pathologists and a serologist—a doctor who studies blood and body fluids.

We launched research projects, and I pushed for us to become involved in environmental medicine. We were public health doctors, and we had a unique opportunity to create research programs to study serious issues, such as the effects of dangerous chemicals in our drinking water. The possibilities were endless.

Our direction created quite a buzz in the medical community. Soon, medical students were calling, hoping for a chance to join our staff. When talking to the prospective job applicants, I was enthusiastic about our future.

"The job offers professional gratification. We're on the verge of something big . . . a renaissance of forensic pathology," I'd tell them.

We were moving fast, making changes. Everything was headed in the right direction. But then, problems began surfacing that threatened the independence—and integrity—of my office.

In the summer of 1978, police officers had strangled a respected Black man, Arthur Miller, while restraining him on a Brooklyn street, and they expected my office to cover for them. I refused. Some prosecutors had encouraged me to "bend and stretch" autopsy findings to help with their criminal cases. Again, I said no. Criticism began circulating that I wasn't a team player. Friends warned me that some city officials had been privately grousing about me to Koch.

So, they're angry at me because I'm doing my job with integrity?

Yes, it sounded crazy, but I wasn't going to back down. I promised myself that I'd keep moving forward with my plans. Thankfully, I had Civil Service protection. I suspected that without it, I'd already be gone, just like my predecessors—Helpern and DiMaio.

Helpern's time had run out a few years earlier, after a series of one-year contracts. His retirement on December 15, 1973, wasn't his idea. For most of his tenure, Helpern and his office had stayed free of scandal or controversy. But in his last year, things went awry.

The city's investigation commissioner heard that some employees in the medical examiner's office had taken bribes from funeral directors looking for business. Helpern was never accused of involvement in any such practice, but doubts lingered over his ability to police a staff of nearly 140 people.

In the end, it was rumored that his wife's behavior—and a bizarre lawsuit she filed against the city—was what brought his career as chief medical examiner to a close.

The medical examiner's office used to be in the old Pathology Building in the Bellevue Hospital complex. In the early 1960s, we moved across the street to a brand-new building. At about the same time Helpern, a widower, remarried. Beatrice, his bride, was installed at a desk outside his office and named his "voluntary secretary." She was not paid. She wasn't on the staff. She didn't work for the city. But Beatrice controlled access to Helpern.

At the time, the medical examiner's office had only one city-issued chauffeured vehicle, and it was assigned to Helpern. All the other doctors used their own cars or took the subway to death scenes. But Beatrice used the car to do personal errands.

One day, on her way to shop at Bergdorf Goodman, an upscale department store, the car hit a pothole near the medical examiner's office. Beatrice bumped her head. She wasn't seriously injured, but she sued the city for her pain and suffering.

At that point, then–Mayor John Lindsay declined to extend Helpern's tenure.

Lindsay was required to pick Helpern's replacement from the Civil Service's list of qualified candidates. He chose Dominick DiMaio, the longtime deputy chief medical examiner. I was pleased by the appointment. I had known DiMaio since I'd been a medical student volunteering in the autopsy room. He was welcoming and taught me much about performing autopsies.

When DiMaio took over, very little changed in the office. I remained the deputy chief of Manhattan and continued to speak at conferences to discuss medical studies. Many of my lectures were about drug addiction or prison reform in the wake of Attica. But I found that I was talking more to reporters and legislators about a wide range of issues related to medical examiner work. All of it caught the attention of a special congressional committee examining the assassinations of two American icons.

The chairman of the newly established House Select Committee on Assassinations called me in early 1976 and explained that they were reinvestigating the deaths of President John F. Kennedy and the Reverend Martin Luther King Jr. He said they hoped to finally answer the public's lingering questions about the cause of death in both murders.

The Warren Commission's conclusion that Lee Harvey Oswald had acted alone in killing Kennedy was being challenged. I was asked to lead a group of forensic pathologists reexamining Kennedy's death, and King's as well. I was honored to be part of the investigation. I assisted in appointing eight chief medical examiners from around the country to be part of the committee's autopsy unit, so that our conclusions would be accurate and acceptable to the public.

Conspiracy theories had surrounded the Kennedy and King murders for years. Kennedy was assassinated in Dallas, Texas, on November 22, 1963. Oswald was charged with the murder after being arrested that afternoon for killing a Dallas police officer, but was himself shot dead two days later under suspicious circumstances. More than a decade after Kennedy's death, his assassination was still cloaked with mystery.

Some facts weren't in dispute. Oswald worked at the Texas School Book Depository in Dallas. On the afternoon of November 22, Oswald was seen on the sixth floor of the building around the time Kennedy's motorcade was approaching. At 12:30 PM, as Kennedy's car drove through the plaza below the building, three rifle shots were fired. Two bullets struck Kennedy. The order in and timing with which they struck created doubt as to whether there was just one shooter. Also, Texas governor John B. Connally had been wounded. Had Oswald shot him—or a second assassin?

Kennedy died at Parkland Memorial Hospital shortly after the attack. He was forty-six years old. Police arrested Oswald later that day as a suspect in the police officer's killing, then charged him while in custody with the president's murder. But Oswald never stood trial. He was fatally shot on November 24 by Jack Ruby, a nightclub owner with Mob connections, while being taken from Dallas police headquarters to county jail. Ruby stated that he acted out of outrage over Kennedy's assassination.

I'd heard all the conspiracy theories: Ruby's actions might have been part of a larger web. The hit was ordered by Mob bosses angry at Kennedy and his brother, Attorney General Robert Kennedy, for cracking down on organized crime. Or the hit was ordered by Cuban dictator Fidel Castro, who was seething about covert US plans to kill him and overthrow his communist regime. Some people claimed there was a second shooter and that four shots were fired, not three.

King's death was similarly controversial. The civil rights leader was killed by a single rifle shot on April 4, 1968, while standing on the balcony of the Lorraine Motel in Memphis, Tennessee. He was in the city to show his support for striking sanitation workers. His assassin, James Earl Ray, was a suspect from the start. The FBI traced the shot to a rooming house across the street from the motel and found the gun that had fired the bullet. It bore Ray's fingerprints. Ray was arrested that June at London's Heathrow Airport with a ticket to Rhodesia, an African country ruled by a white minority. He was extradited to America and later convicted for King's murder.

A supporter of segregationist Alabama governor George Wallace, Ray was a career criminal. He had escaped from prison a year earlier and was still on the run when he shot King. At first, Ray confessed to the crime. A few days later, however, he declared his innocence, arguing that he had been set up by a man he knew only as "Raoul." The FBI never found Raoul. Still, some people believed Ray was innocent.

One conspiracy theory claimed there were two shooters, but the FBI said only one shot was fired in King's assassination—and it came from a bathroom window in the boarding house about a hundred yards away from the motel. The FBI found Ray's fingerprints on the windowsill.

From the beginning, I insisted we follow the science. We had to diligently examine all the evidence in both assassinations. We couldn't let elaborate theories influence our work. But the longer I was on the committee, the more difficult it became to separate fact from fiction. Outside sources pressed us to confirm their pet ideas.

With Kennedy, we analyzed every frame from a home movie shot by Abraham Zapruder on his 8 mm Bell & Howell camera. It was the only film that captured the exact moment of Kennedy's assassination. We pored over every detail of the 1964 report released by the Warren Commission, a group formed weeks after Kennedy's murder to investigate his death and led by Chief Justice of the United States Earl Warren. The Commission concluded that Oswald fired three bullets, two of which had struck Kennedy from behind. After an exhaustive investigation, we came to the same conclusion.

With King, we found there was no scientific evidence of another gunman. There was abundant evidence that Ray—and only Ray—pulled the trigger and fired the single fatal bullet that pierced King's jawbone and neck. We found nothing to dispute that. And as the spokesman for the panel of medical experts, that's the testimony I gave to the congressional committee in September 1978.

That should have ended things. All the wild theories should have been put to rest once and for all. The committee agreed with our conclusions on Dr. King. But with Kennedy, the committee ended the investigation with a hybrid theory. While it agreed with most of our forensic pathology findings, it insisted there was evidence of a second gunman in Dealey Plaza on the basis of controversial audio testimony. (A later FBI review found that the acoustical evidence that a second bullet was fired from the grassy knoll was incorrect.)

Meanwhile, DiMaio had come under fire for a scandal that rocked the Medical Examiner's Office. In 1976, police arrested three men—including DiMaio's chauffeur—for running a call-girl ring out of the city morgue. It included transporting prostitutes to clients in the medical examiner's official car. The enterprise would later be memorialized in a 1982 comedy film *Night Shift*, staring Henry Winkler, Michael Keaton, and Shelly Long.

In early 1978, DiMaio reached mandatory retirement age. And like Helpern, he said he wanted to stay. But Koch refused his request. And like Lindsay before him, under the city's Civil Service rules, the mayor had to pick DiMaio's replacement from the seniority list. I was one of several qualified candidates. Koch said he selected me because he had been following my career for years and I was "very capable and innovative."

When I told Judianne about the promotion, she was excited. But when I suggested we do something special to celebrate—maybe go away for a weekend—she hesitated. She said she wasn't sure she could find the time. Odyssey House had completely taken over her life. She was always on the road—or at least it felt that way. She now had therapeutic community group homes in a half dozen US cities, and had expanded overseas to Australia. Whenever she was home, she usually had one or two recovering drug addicts with her. It was her way of helping them integrate back into society.

I realized with pride that my wife had become famous and that, in a way, I was living in her shadow. I was comfortable with that. But we did have issues to deal with. We both knew we had to do something to turn our marriage around. We began marriage counseling but stopped after a few months. We didn't think it was helping. Maybe we gave up too quickly. I don't know. I only knew that I didn't want a divorce, for our children's sake. I knew what it was like to be the child of divorced parents. I didn't want that for them.

Rather than think about my marital problems, I threw myself into my new job. I worked long hours as I began implementing my ideas. Everyone was excited. We began research projects into child abuse and other causes of death. We were building momentum. Then I ran into a buzzsaw.

It was a humid early evening on June 14, 1978. The streets of Crown Heights in Brooklyn were alive with teens and children hanging out in front of stores, sitting on stoops of brownstone row houses, or shooting hoops in playgrounds. Some had boom boxes on their shoulders, and the deep, thumping bass turned the street corners into nightclubs. If people weren't outside, they were leaning out their windows to stay cool. Some called out greetings to neighbors or friends walking below.

At the turn of the twentieth century, Crown Heights had been an upscale neighborhood. Now, it was a tough section of the city. It was poor and predominantly Black, but Orthodox Jews also lived there. The men wore the uniform of their faith: long black coats and high black hats, full beards and long, curly sideburns—even in the scorching heat.

Crown Heights had been a racial tinderbox for years. Families in the poverty-stricken neighborhood struggled to buy the basic necessities amid high unemployment and crime. Violence had erupted there more than once. During the New York City blackout of 1977, more than seventy-five stores were broken into or robbed there.

But some in Crown Heights were trying to revive the community. Arthur Miller, a thirty-year-old Black businessman and entrepreneur, was well known in the community. He was a short, muscular, 180-pound man who liked to box. He played the congas, trumpet, and guitar, and was outgoing, a leader. Some in the neighborhood called him Samson. But Miller was a gentle man, a father of four who would lend a helping hand to anyone in trouble.

Miller was born in Nassau, Bahamas, to a family who immigrated to America when he was a teenager. After arriving in Crown Heights, Miller thrived as an entrepreneur, busy with several business and community projects. Construction became Miller's primary trade, but he also owned a grocery store on Nostrand Avenue.

He founded Brooklyn Renaissance for Jobs, which in 1977 helped obtain federal funds to employ one hundred neighborhood people. He had also helped to organize the Nostrand Avenue Community Commerce Association, which was awarded a $225,000 grant by the New York State Department of Commerce.

Miller regularly organized block parties for residents and led the Four Block Association, a group that was trying to revitalize Crown Heights. He had a good relationship with the cops. Many in the precinct would stop by and ask him how things were going.

In the spring of 1978, Miller was planning to open LoLisa's VIP, a club on Nostrand Avenue that would include a skating rink for children and a nightclub for adults. But that wasn't his only current project. His brother Sam had been helping him convert a vacant store into a wedding hall. For weeks, twenty-year-old Sam had been removing debris from the building. He'd leave it on the sidewalk outside until he had a chance to take it to a landfill.

That's how the trouble started.

Two white patrol officers, Anthony Curcio and Christopher Schiebel, said they'd noticed the debris piling up and for weeks had been unable to identify the owner of the construction project. That night, the officers drove by the building and spotted Sam shoveling the debris into the back of a pickup truck. They stopped him as he was pulling away and asked to see his license. The radio dispatcher said his license had been suspended. Sam protested. The suspensions had been lifted after he had paid his fines, he said. He had the receipts at his home, which he offered to show as proof.

But the cops didn't care. They started writing tickets. People from the neighborhood gathered around. They asked the policemen why they were harassing Sam. They believed it was another case of profiling, where cops stopped young Black men for no reason other than the color of their skin. The residents didn't trust the police. And the cops—mostly white officers—didn't like the residents.

"Why are you picking on the kid?" one of the neighbors yelled.

"Just leave him alone!" another shouted.

The two officers were scared, so they called for backup. More police cars arrived, and more residents poured into the street as word spread in the neighborhood.

Someone called Arthur Miller and told him his little brother was in trouble. Arthur was on a first-name basis with many officers in the Seventy-Seventh Precinct. When he got to the scene, witnesses said he raised his hands over his head and told the officers, "It's me. Cool it. You're wrong. Can't we talk this over?" He tried to calm the crowd.

The officers didn't recognize him. And when he raised his hands, it revealed a gun in his waistband—a weapon he was legally permitted to carry. Witnesses said that's when the officers pounced on him.

"This white detective runs up behind Arthur and shoves him down," a witness later said.

They handcuffed his hands behind his back. While he was prone on the sidewalk, witnesses said, officers kneeled on his back. One held a billy club across Miller's throat from behind. And just like George Floyd would more than forty years later, Arthur Miller whispered that he couldn't breathe. The only difference between Floyd and Miller was the absence of smartphone cameras set to capture the abuse.

The cops picked Miller up and threw him into the back of a patrol car. Foam was coming from his mouth. Witnesses said that as the car drove off, they could see his feet sticking out of the window.

Miller was still breathing when cops put him in the cruiser. But by the time it arrived at the precinct house, he was dead. When the cops brought his body to the hospital, they told doctors he died of a heart attack. They didn't say anything about restraining him, kneeling on his back, or choking him with a stick.

When Crown Heights learned that Arthur Miller was dead, the city braced for an explosion.

I knew that fatal police encounters had to be investigated immediately. Special care had to be taken because of the the authorities' power to cover things up. You needed an autopsy finding that was beyond reproach.

The examination fell to Milton Wald, a deputy chief medical examiner in Brooklyn. After Wald finished, he called me. He sounded worried, so I decided to go to his office in Brooklyn.

"Everything is normal. I can't find a cause," he said.

"Are there marks on his neck?"

"Yes, bruises."

"Any hemorrhages in the eyes?" I asked.

"Yes."

"Any damage to the windpipe?"

"Yes, there are hemorrhages in the neck muscles."

"Well, isn't that neck compression? With an arm or a nightstick?"

He nodded. "You're right."

I knew that police at the time would put a billy club or a forearm across the front of a person's neck to subdue them. The idea was to block the airway until the person passed out so he could be handcuffed. But if the neck or back pressure continued too long, it could be fatal.

When a person cannot breathe, they panic. They try to tell officers they can't breathe, but the cops often interpret that as resistance. So, even if the person is already prone, police sit on them to try to put on handcuffs. That cuts off even more air supply to the lungs. If this goes on long enough, the person dies from a lack of oxygen.

Wald reminded me of my predecessors' policies about deaths that occurred during a police encounter: "We're supposed to say 'pending further study' until the commotion dies down, or to say 'psychosis with exhaustion.'"

My experience with Eric Johnson's death had taught me that psychosis with exhaustion was a euphemism that exonerated police for using deadly force while pacifying the family and drawing a polite curtain of silence over the events. The death was really the victim's own fault. Nothing to see here. No need for the prosecutors to investigate or present evidence to a grand jury. Police and city leaders were betting that, with time, the public would forget about what happened. Everyone would move on.

That was the old way of doing business. Things were changing. On my watch, we would diagnose whatever the science and pathology showed. We would tell the truth—and do it quickly, so the community wouldn't assume a cover-up. Delaying would only inflame tensions.

I told Wald we didn't have to wait for further studies. We could make the diagnosis now on the basis of the circumstances and the autopsy findings. I told him to list the cause of death as "compression of the neck" and the manner of death as "homicide." I knew the cops would be angry, but it was time to be honest.

My experience with police up to that point had convinced me that the overwhelming number of officers are good people. It was a difficult job, and most of them did it well. They were professionals, just overworked and underpaid.

But as in any profession, there were some cops who shouldn't have had that job. They overreacted. They couldn't handle pressure. They were prejudiced. To them, people of color were not as American as their own white friends. Instead, they were the enemy—genetically bad and dangerously strong, requiring more force to be subdued. I thought if we started holding the bad cops accountable for their actions, they'd learn how to use de-escalation techniques instead of resorting to violence. They might stop using tactics that killed people.

After speaking to Ward, I began returning media calls. Arthur Miller was strangled, I said. We couldn't tell if a nightstick or a forearm had caused the neck compression. Police tactics like chokeholds had to stop, I added.

"This death raises issues that have been raised in the past about people who died in police custody," I told reporters.

I compared it to such crude tactics as prison guards firing tear gas into cells to subdue prisoners. I reminded them that, at my urging, the New York State Medical Review Board had recommended corrections officers only use tear gas with strict guidelines and proper supervision. And after they did, deaths from tear gas in prisons had stopped.

My office's ruling on Miller's death took the case as far as we could move it. The district attorney's office had to take the next step. They were the ones with the power to investigate, charge officers, and present evidence to a grand jury.

The Miller family didn't think they would be treated fairly. So, although we did an autopsy, they hired their own pathologist to do one, too. And to their surprise, their pathologist agreed with our findings.

Meanwhile, the Crown Heights community was angry. They held a march against the "cold-blooded murder of Arthur Miller." Six hundred people showed up and walked several miles to the Seventy-Seventh Precinct station.

"We went to the precinct to express some hurt, pain, and some outrage, too," said the Reverend Herbert Daughtry of the House of the Lord Pentecostal Church on Atlantic Avenue.

The protesters were met by dozens of helmeted police officers, but the scene remained orderly. The crowd gradually dispersed.

Mayor Koch called me the same day we released the cause of death. "You made a serious mistake here," he said. He believed our ruling would incite a riot.

I told him that was not my experience. As a medical examiner, I found that transparency prevents riots. "The community wants the truth, and they got the truth," I said.

I was proved right. The immediate release of autopsy findings helped calm the situation. Community leaders still wanted more answers, but at least they knew we weren't covering up what many of them had seen happen first hand. Days later, Koch sent me a letter praising our work on the Miller case.

Deputy Mayor Herman Badillo, chairman of Koch's new community-outreach committee, formed to reduce tensions in the city's neighborhoods, talked with Crown Heights civic leaders. The Brooklyn district attorney's office said it would investigate Miller's death.

But the police pushed back. Many of the officers who were at the scene refused to talk to police investigators or the DA. The police union criticized the medical examiner's office. We "went rogue," they said—we "weren't part of the team."

Their reaction made me think back to my earliest days as a full-time medical examiner. Helpern had called me to his office to introduce me to his "good friends"—the New York City police chief and Manhattan's chief homicide district attorney.

During the meeting, the district attorney explained how the offices were connected.

"We're a three-legged stool. We have three legs: the police, the district attorney, and the medical examiner. All three have to work together for justice," he said.

Clearly, they were initiating me into the club. We were all working together to convict the people *we thought* were guilty. Police only arrest and district attorneys only prosecute bad guys, and you, Mr. Medical Examiner, are part of the prosecution team.

But that's not how science works. Sometimes our findings don't support the prosecution's version of events. As chief medical examiner, my goal was to ensure my office's independence. We were going to do what was medically and ethically right, whether it aligned with the police and district attorney's theory of what happened or not.

The Miller case highlighted our office's independence, and that rubbed some police officials and one district attorney the wrong way. That's why, only a year after I was appointed, I got another call from the mayor—one that would change my life and the trajectory of my career.

Chapter 8

• • •

THE LAWSUIT

The Mob kingpin's body was on the autopsy table in the Brooklyn medical examiner's morgue. Outside, the media was gathered, awaiting new details. We were just about to start the autopsy when the telephone rang. The nasally voice on the other end was instantly recognizable.

"Michael, how are you?" Mayor Koch asked.

"I'm fine," I said, looking down at the body in front of me. "A little busy."

"Do you think you can meet me later at City Hall?"

I glanced at my watch. It was 10 AM. "Yes, I can be there at two."

"Fine. I'll see you then," he said, and hung up.

I was a little surprised at the call. What did he want? Koch and I didn't talk much. I put it out of my mind. We had a body on the table.

Carmine Galante, *capo di tutti capi* (boss of all "the bosses"), had just been shot dead with two other mafiosi at Joe & Mary's Italian-American Restaurant in Brooklyn. Galante had been a protégé of Vito Genovese and Joe Bonanno, heads of two of the most powerful Mafia crime families. In the 1950s, Bonanno had sent Galante to Canada to set up a heroin pipeline between Montreal and Newark. Galante exceeded expectations and made tens of millions of dollars for Bonanno.

In 1962, the law caught up to Galante. He was convicted of drug trafficking and sentenced to twenty years in federal prison. He kept his mouth shut and was paroled in 1974. Once freed, Galante went straight back to work, seizing control of the Bonanno crime family and importing a crew of young

Sicilian drug pushers for protection. Over the next five years, he built a network that flooded the streets of US cities with heroin. But like other mafiosi, Galante created many enemies on his way to becoming the "don."

On July 12, 1979, Galante and several friends were finishing a late lunch on the restaurant's outside back patio. The don had just lit a cigar when three armed men in ski masks walked through the eatery and caught the table by surprise.

Galante and two others were hit by handgun and shotgun blasts. Galante was blown backward by the force of a shotgun blast in his upper chest.

The morning papers featured photos of the blood-spattered patio with Galante's body in the center, a fat cigar still clenched in his mouth.

The Brooklyn medical examiner was performing Galante's autopsy. I was there to supervise. After the postmortem examination, I got cleaned up and headed to City Hall to meet with Koch.

I didn't know Koch personally before he took office in 1978, replacing the stiff, formal Abraham Beame. Unlike his predecessor, Koch was outgoing, a showman, a shrewd politician with plenty of chutzpah. He didn't look like a mayor. He was tall, squinty-eyed, and bald, with round shoulders and gangly arms. He wore baggy pants and spoke in a high-pitched voice. But he was a masterful storyteller and was candid about the city's problems. He also had a natural ability to connect with average city voters, especially Jews.

Our backgrounds were similar. His parents had immigrated to New York from Poland, and struggled to make a living in America. Shortly after Koch was born in the Bronx, his family moved to Newark, New Jersey, then back to Brooklyn. As a teenager, Koch took odd jobs like working in a delicatessen to help his family make ends meet.

He went to City College of New York and was drafted into the US Army. After his discharge, he went to New York University Law School. He was elected to Congress in 1968 and, after nearly a decade there, decided to run for mayor in 1977.

New York was in bad shape at the time. Running on a "law and order" campaign, Koch defeated Mayor Beame and Mario Cuomo—who would later become New York's governor—in a contentious Democratic primary. His message resonated with New Yorkers who had seen a surge in crime, and he won the general election.

Since taking office, Koch had been delivering on his promises. But not everyone was happy with him. Black leaders were upset with comments they considered insensitive. He said, for example, that busing and racial quotas had done more to divide the races than to achieve integration.

Still, he was popular. To Koch's trademark expression, "How'm I doin'?" most New Yorkers would answer, "Great."

When I walked into City Hall on Friday, July 13, 1979, Koch's greeting was warm and friendly. He led me to his office and closed the door behind us.

He said he wanted to talk to me about my job. I told him everything was going well. He nodded and paused for a moment. Then he blindsided me.

"Your first year of probation is almost over," he said.

First year?

I said my probation period was six months.

"No," he said.

An awkward silence fell over the room. Now, I was nervous. Did I just walk into an ambush?

Koch was direct. "I asked the city's five district attorneys and the health commissioner for letters to evaluate your performance. This is standard procedure."

But I knew it wasn't.

Then he got to the reason I was called into his office.

"Four of the letters were complimentary, but I got two negative ones," Koch explained. "I wanted you to respond so I'd have your replies on file. Nothing to worry about. This is routine."

Routine? Really? The negative letters, he said, were from Health Commissioner Reinaldo Ferrer and Robert Morgenthau, the Manhattan district attorney. I was confused about Ferrer. Two months earlier, he had praised me in a public speech. Morgenthau was a different story.

Morgenthau and I had had disagreements. He believed the medical examiner's office had become too independent, that we should be more cooperative in supporting his office's theories in court.

Each of New York's five boroughs had a district attorney. But I knew Koch believed that Morgenthau was the most important.

I told Koch that I didn't know of any complaints from Morgenthau or Ferrer.

"There must be a misunderstanding. I'd like to talk to them," I said.

"That's a terrible idea," the mayor said. The letters were supposed to be confidential. He said he didn't want Morgenthau to know he had shown it to me. My reply—in writing—was to be equally confidential. Just for his file, Koch said.

The mayor got up from behind his desk and handed me an envelope with copies of the letters. He shook my hand and smiled. "Don't worry about it. It's routine." I took him at his word.

When I got back to my office, I opened the envelope. The more I read, the angrier I became. Morgenthau's complaints were a direct assault on the integrity and independence of the medical examiner's office. Our job was to determine the cause and manner of death on the basis of medical science, not political wishes. The other four borough district attorneys praised me to the mayor for that.

Morgenthau particularly complained about one high-profile murder case: David Levine. His office had charged Levine with breaking into an apartment and raping and fatally stabbing the tenant on May 28, 1978. Levine was arrested when he tried to use the victim's credit cards.

The evidence against Levine for the murder was strong. But we had found no medical or scientific evidence to show that the woman had been raped. Also, Morgenthau's office had charged Levine with burglary once before, a few years earlier—but had lost a key piece of evidence. As a result, Levine went free. If Morgenthau's office hadn't lost the evidence, the victim would still be alive. I believed Morgenthau's office had added the rape charge to make the murder case even stronger.

As I continued reading over the complaints, one stood out for pure outrageousness. Ferrer said I had used "poor judgment" in the Arthur Miller case by disclosing that he had been choked to death by policemen who had been trying to arrest him.

"His conduct further exacerbated an understandably tense situation," he wrote.

Koch must have forgotten about the letter he sent me commending me for the way I had handled the situation and how it had calmed down a tense community. The next day, I sent the mayor a copy of that letter along with my responses to the criticisms.

On July 31, Koch called me back to his office.

I believed everything was going to be okay since I had answered all the issues raised in Morgenthau's and Ferrer's letters. I had documents to back everything up. But when I arrived, I noticed right away his tone was more formal than before.

When the office door closed, Koch stared at me. "Michael, we're demoting you," he said.

I was stunned. He continued talking, but I didn't hear the words. My heart was racing. My mind was numb. I had dreamed of being the chief medical examiner since the first day I stepped into the autopsy room in 1955. I loved my job, and now it was in serious jeopardy.

I took a deep breath as I waited for Koch to finish. "Mr. Mayor, why?"

Koch said it was nothing personal. He said his decision wasn't based on any individual complaint. It was based on my inability to get along with Morgenthau.

"Morgenthau says you're not a team player," the mayor said.

I was stunned. He was basing the demotion on the idea that the medical examiner's office *should not* be independent of police and the district attorney?

I wasn't sure how long I was in his office before Koch got up, shook my hand, and led me out. The sun shone bright outside City Hall. I was slightly disoriented. I wasn't fired, but I would no longer be the chief medical examiner. My new position would be the same as my old one: deputy chief medical examiner. Koch's decision was clearly well planned, but I'd no clue it was coming.

Somehow, I made it home.

But I'd just received a short course on how politics works and how it can trump medical science.

Koch announced my demotion at a press conference.

"I have decided on balance not to reappoint him," the mayor said. "It is very painful for me. But I have an obligation."

The *New York Times* ran a front-page story with medical examiners from around the country criticizing my demotion.

One of my pathology mentors at Bellevue, Marvin Kuschner, called me. He must have had some kind of radar because he always seemed to know when I needed a boost.

"Don't let them get you down, Michael. I know you're angry. But it may work out for the best. Only time will tell," he said.

In 1970, Kuschner had been recruited as the chairman of the Pathology Department at the new Stony Brook Medical School in Suffolk County, New York. He presided over the medical school's birth and was appointed dean in 1972 when the first classes commenced.

He said I could teach there. But he said he didn't think I'd be happy because it wasn't as exciting as being a medical examiner. He was right. I loved my job. "Just remember, if it doesn't work out, there are other places that would hire you in a minute. Keep the faith."

My wife, the psychiatrist/lawyer, thought I should fight back. "Koch has violated Civil Service laws, and he relied on misinformation," she said, "You should sue to get your job back."

She reminded me that there had been controversy about her approach at Odyssey House, too—how she shunned methadone to help drug addicts. Some people had personally attacked her, saying she was too rigid, too controlling. But she was committed to Odyssey House's approach. She knew it worked and vigorously criticized public officials, including the mayor, for not paying more attention to the heroin crisis. (Some even thought that was why the mayor demoted me.)

Judianne was right. I had to stop feeling sorry for myself. I had to fight to keep the medical examiner's office independent. The first step was to publicly answer the allegations against me.

A day after the demotion went into effect, I went on the offensive. I held a news conference.

"The allegations are untrue and unfounded. They're politically inspired," I said, adding that Ferrer and Morgenthau had objected to the independence of the medical examiner's office.

"If this office was more malleable to certain requests . . . if I change a cause of death from suicide to accident, some people are pleased. But we are not here to make better cases for the DA. We are not going to lie," I said.

In the days that followed, I discussed my next moves with family and close friends. It would have been one thing if I had done something wrong, or if my office had been corrupt. But I was being punished for doing my job.

They urged me to take legal action.

"So, I should sue the city?" I asked.

"Yes," said my wife. She had reviewed the case and her professional conclusion was that I had been removed illegally in violation of Civil Service law.

My brother Robert was a big supporter. He was someone I leaned on. After he got out of the Army, he'd stop by regularly. He was a bachelor and loved to hang out with the kids.

"Don't let them get away with this shit," he said.

Meanwhile, Koch had appointed Elliot Gross, Connecticut's chief medical examiner, to replace me. I knew Gross well. We'd attended NYU Medical School together and had both started as associate medical examiners in the New York City Medical Examiner's Office in 1965 before he left for Connecticut. He had also married Helpern's daughter.

I reached out to Gross. I said that I'd bring him up to date with everything that had happened in the office since he left in 1966. I promised that I'd do all I could to help him.

Quiet and awkward, Gross grunted, "Okay."

A number of attorneys that I had worked with called to echo Judianne's judgment that my demotion had been illegal. They advised me that it was important to fight to protect the independence of the medical examiner's office from politics.

I wanted to, but I didn't know where the money to fight the decision would come from. I didn't have much in savings. Then, people started coming forward, saying they'd donate to help with my legal fees. My mother insisted on giving me $5,000. Then, unexpectedly, a garment factory owner whom I had met while waiting tables in the Catskills twenty-five years earlier called to say he'd donate $50,000. That was it. I decided right then and there to sue the city for my demotion. I'd fight City Hall. If not me, who? This fight was bigger than saving my job. It was a fight for the independence of medical examiner's offices everywhere. If city officials could do this to me, they would do this to someone else. They would continue bending autopsy results to suit political needs.

I went public with the details of Morgenthau's and Ferrer's complaints. I gave copies of their letters to the media, along with my responses. The *New*

York Times published excerpts of the letters, including the complimentary one Koch had sent involving Arthur Miller.

"Regarding the death of Arthur Miller, Commissioner Ferrer states that Dr. Baden issued a report on the evening of June 14, 1979, prematurely," the *New York Times* wrote. My response: "The facts are quite to the contrary. Mr. Miller was pronounced dead at 6:29 PM on June 14, 1978. The Brooklyn Deputy Chief Medical Examiner, responding to the concerns about the death, performed an autopsy later that same evening and determined the cause of death to be 'Asphyxia associated with laryngeal trauma. Pending further study and police investigation.' At no time was that diagnosis changed by this office or by that deputy or by me.

"Mr. Morgenthau's letter magnifies the natural frictions that develop in this high-pressure system in which we work with mountainous problems. Our roles are different. My office ought not to co-opt the District Attorney any more than the district attorney should co-opt us," I wrote.

I was still contemplating what to do legally, but I knew it was time to get back to my job.

Wald had retired, and I was now deputy chief medical examiner assigned to Brooklyn. At work, my colleagues expressed their support. People on the street smiled and gave me a thumbs-up.

I received a call from Bob Tanenbaum, who had been chief of the Homicide Bureau under former Manhattan district attorney Frank Hogan and was now an attorney in Beverly Hills, California. I had known Bob since 1965 when I began testifying in murder cases. He had never lost a murder trial. And when Congress established the House Select Committee on Assassinations, Tanenbaum was put in charge of the investigation into President Kennedy's death. He'd been the one to recruit me as the committee's chief forensic pathologist.

Now, he said he had been reading about the demotion.

"Michael, it's wrong. They violated your due process and the ability for the medical examiner to disagree with the district attorney and the mayor without fear of repercussions and made-up complaints," he said.

He volunteered to represent me but warned that it could be a long legal battle.

"You could win, but they'd appeal. They could tie this thing up for years. And they'll drag you through the mud. Is this something you really want to do?" he asked.

"Yes," I snapped. "I've already been dragged through the mud. This is a matter of principle."

"Okay. I just wanted to make sure," he said, his smile evident through the line.

A few weeks after my demotion, Tanenbaum filed a lawsuit in US District Court in New York. The thirteen-page complaint said my ouster was illegal, that I was denied my due process in violation of the Fourteenth Amendment. It said I shouldn't have been fired without a public hearing and that my demotion was "arbitrary and capricious." Instead, he argued, Koch had demoted me at a whim on the basis of two secret letters.

The demotion, Tanennbaum said, cut my salary to $42,000 a year from $50,000. He also wrote that I'd suffered damage to my "good name, reputation, and standing in [my] community."

Tanenbaum noted that the chief medical examiner was the highest civil service position in the city, and according to the law could be removed only for cause, such as incompetence. At no time had Mayor Koch challenged my competence as a forensic pathologist. My transgression? I wasn't a team player.

"The mayor," Tanenbaum wrote, "should not be in the position to hire and fire a medical examiner at will. It interferes with the medical examiner's ability to act independently, and turns the job into a political appendage."

After we filed the lawsuit, I kept working, mostly in Brooklyn. I liked the work—going to death scenes, autopsies, testifying—and New York City was the best place for it.

Judianne encouraged my return to routine: "Do what you've been doing. Go to work. Don't give them any excuses to fire you."

And that's what I did. I wouldn't talk about the lawsuit or Gross, who had started alienating the other medical examiners. Gross had a different managerial approach to the job. I was open when running the office, but he was secretive about everything. If there was a problem or an error, I accepted responsibility, but Gross blamed others. Nothing reflected that more than an autopsy he performed shortly after he took office.

Boxer Willie Classen died on November 28, 1979, of injuries he suffered during a match five days earlier. But after the autopsy, several of Classen's organs got mixed up with those of a drug addict—and word leaked to the press.

How did it happen? Gross wouldn't say. He said that the office had been plagued by a series of mishaps since he took over, and he blamed it on medical examiners loyal to me. He said they wanted to make him look bad.

I knew that was ridiculous. Yes, I had a lot of supporters, but they were professionals. No one would deliberately undermine him.

Over the next half-dozen years, Gross's pattern of blaming others for his mistakes would continue, and Koch would eventually fire him in 1987.

But in 1979, I had to peacefully coexist with Gross. I promised myself I'd do my job and stay out of his way.

◆ ◆ ◆

My son Judson opened the door to my room, breaking the darkness. I was sitting on my bed, physically and emotionally drained. Judianne wasn't home. She had another late meeting.

I didn't travel much in those days, instead spending long hours at the Brooklyn Medical Examiner's Office. By the time I got home at night, the children had usually eaten dinner and done their homework and were in bed or ready to go to sleep. Our oldest child, Trissa, had just started college at Bryn Mawr, but my other children were still living with us. Judson was sixteen years old, his brother Lindsey was fourteen, and his sister Sarah, six. Judson and Lindsey were inseparable. Like all siblings, they fought at times. But they always looked out for each other.

Judson was a tough kid and very bright; he didn't have to study to get good grades. He was a leader—my other children looked up to him. And he always tried to make sure I was okay. We didn't have the typical television father–son relationship where we played ball or watched football games on TV. But we talked a lot. He always asked me about my cases, or how I was feeling—as if he were the parent. When I prepared lectures, I would project my 35 mm Kodachrome autopsy photos on a screen, and Jud and Lindsey would sometimes sneak into a corner of the dark room to watch.

Tonight, he'd come to my room to check on me. He had been reading the newspapers about my battle with the city. He had overheard my phone conversations. He was worried.

"Can I come in?" he asked.

"Jud, of course."

He sat on the edge of the bed. "Are you going to lose your job?"

"No. Who told you that?"

"No one. I was just wondering. I mean, you sued the city . . ."

"Right. But if they tried to fire me, they'd make everything worse. It would be seen as retaliation. They're not going to take that chance."

"Well, I just wanted to let you know that I'm on your side. You're going to win, Dad," he said.

I smiled. "I think I have a strong case."

I paused for a moment and stared at my son. He had grown up so fast. He was a handsome young man with long hair and a big smile. I was proud of him.

I told him so, and we reminisced about how he loved to listen to stories about my cases. "You'd hear about a murder on the radio on a Monday and ask me about the autopsy the next day," I said.

I knew Jud was worried. So, I reminded him of something I had preached for years: if you tell the truth, things usually have a way of working out. "I'm going to be okay," I said.

I got up and gave him a big hug. "Thank you, Jud," I whispered.

He smiled and jumped up from the bed. "Good night, Dad."

"Good night, Son."

When he left the room, I thought about how lucky I was to have such a sensitive son. He sensed that I was down, that I felt betrayed. And all he wanted to do was show me that he was concerned. That he loved me. And that lifted my spirits.

I didn't know what would happen with the lawsuit. I didn't know if they'd fire me. They could do anything. But as long as I had my family's support, everything would be fine.

◆ ◆ ◆

Judgment day arrived, and I was ready. On April 5, 1980, my attorneys and the lawyers for the city of New York waited in Judge Charles H. Haight's courtroom on the third floor of the federal courthouse in downtown Manhattan. It was packed with my family and friends and journalists. Cameras were forbidden in federal court, so one of the newspapers had hired a sketch artist to capture the trial.

It was a beautiful old courthouse with wine-colored carpeting and bright lights built into the ceiling. The blond-wood benches in the spectator section sparkled under the lights.

As Tanenbaum said in the lawsuit, there was no office more important in the city than the medical examiner's. It was the office that investigated suspicious deaths. Now, the question was: Why was the holder of an essential nonpolitical office removed and deprived of a hearing?

That was an issue Haight would have to answer. My attorneys decided to have the judge rule on the case instead of a jury. He had a reputation as a fair judge. That's what we wanted—someone guided by the law, not politics.

Tanenbaum and another attorney sat at one table in front of the room. The city's lawyers were at a separate table close to ours. Both tables were covered with binders filled with documents, including depositions that were taken during discovery.

I glanced at my wife behind me and smiled. I was a little nervous. We knew the proceedings could last a week or so.

When Haight entered in his flowing black robe, we all stood at the sound of the bailiff's "All rise."

And so, it began. Each side presented its witnesses. The city brought in people who had grievances against me from years ago, including lawyers who used to work for the Manhattan district attorney's office who claimed I was derelict in returning telephone calls. But under cross-examination, my attorneys picked apart their stories.

When Morgenthau testified, he looked stiff, uncomfortable being on the other side of a court proceeding. His body language and facial expressions said he didn't want to be there. He shifted in his seat and rolled his eyes.

He said things that contradicted his depositions. When my attorneys pointed out the discrepancies, he blamed the stenographers for the mistakes.

The stenographers didn't care for that. But more importantly, he was unable to answer questions about normal court procedure.

He also didn't seem to understand how the grand jury process worked. Morgenthau had complained that in one murder case, he couldn't show an autopsy report to a grand jury because my office took too much time preparing it—we'd held up everything, he said. But a DA is not allowed to show autopsy reports to a grand jury. That's illegal. His face turned red when my attorneys pointed that out during cross-examination.

When Koch testified, he was his usual jovial self. I almost expected him to turn to the judge and say, "How'm I doin'?" He told Haight that I was an excellent pathologist, "but excellence is really not the point. Doctor Baden's temperament was such that he couldn't work within the system. The main thing is the chief medical examiner has to get along with the most important district attorney in the city."

When Ferrer testified, he criticized the way I handled the Miller case. He cited newspaper clippings to prove I had made "inflammatory statements."

"Did this case involve public concern?" his attorney asked.

"Yes."

"Were the people in the community concerned?"

"Yes. There was some rioting. The administration believed everything should be done to minimize the unrest."

Then his attorney showed the judge clippings saying Baden ruled that the man was choked to death by a fatal force to the larynx. That it was "an object pressed to his throat, probably a police officer's nightstick." He said I had first stated a different cause of death.

But under cross-examination, my attorneys showed the judge that I never changed the cause of death.

Ferrer was annoyed. He sighed. He said the real problem was the medical examiner's office acted too quickly. "The report was issued too fast."

Of course I knew that, by issuing the report so quickly, we had prevented a potential uprising. The people believed that, because we told the truth about the autopsy, maybe the Brooklyn district attorney would do something, hold someone accountable for Miller's death. That didn't happen, but the possibility that it could had prevented the community's early grief and anger from turning to violence.

The Brooklyn DA had presented the Miller case to a grand jury. He had seventy-seven people testify. But in the end, the jury declined to recommend criminal charges against the officers.

In a press release following the grand jury's deliberation, the district attorney's office described the crushing of Miller's larynx as "a tragic unforeseeable accident which occurred during a lawful arrest." He concluded that "Arthur Miller was not savagely beaten by anyone"—even though dozens of people saw the brutality with their own eyes.

The DA concluded that officers used "uniformly recommended procedures" when restraining Miller. No officers involved were fired or criminally charged for Miller's death.

For me, the grand jury response wasn't surprising. I knew indictments often depend upon how a DA presents the evidence to the panel. The hearings are secret, so I didn't know what evidence was presented—or how it was presented. But it seemed to me that the district attorney probably made Arthur Miller seem like some wild man—someone who was out of control. What choice did the police have, but to take him down the way they did? In my opinion, the DA had presented the case to a grand jury only to placate communities of color—not to get indictments.

The Miller case had "protect the police" written all over it. And that was happening more and more in cases where someone died suddenly while being restrained by police. It was becoming clear to me that this wasn't limited to New York City—it was going on all over the nation. This was systemic. And the racial motives were in plain sight.

Police were saying they had to use tactics like chokeholds to subdue suspects—usually Black men who somehow had superhuman strength, especially when they were on drugs. The reality was that some police officers were afraid of Black men, believing they were predisposed to criminal activity and a danger to cops.

In my own way, I was fighting back. In police-encounter deaths, if the cops caused the death, I said so. But the next step was always in prosecutors' hands. Over the years, I had begun to realize that DAs were reluctant to hold bad cops accountable because they were afraid of alienating the law enforcement community.

After weeks of testimony, the judge was ready to rule. And on May 8, 1980, the New York *Daily News* headline said it all: "City Told to Reinstate Baden."

Judge Haight agreed that I had been removed from office in "a publicly stigmatizing manner" without receiving an opportunity to show that the charges against me were false.

"A number of Commissioner Ferrer's more serious charges were entirely false or almost so," the judge ruled.

"There is no truth to a charge that Dr. Baden had issued a report prematurely and without sufficient data in the Miller case," he added.

Not only did the judge order the city to reinstate me, he said the city should award me $100,000. Haight said Koch had illegally extended the probation period from six months to a year.

"No mayor can change the rules in the middle of the game," Haight wrote in his eighty-one-page ruling.

Outside the courthouse, Murray Gordon, one of my attorneys, told reporters that the city had altered critical documents in my files and records.

"'I won't use the word 'cover-up,' but we had to force them to admit they'd done it," he said.

I chimed in. "You can't take a person's reputation away without giving him a chance to defend himself. This is still a country of laws. The decision shows that the medical examiner's office has to be independent of political interference."

My family was ecstatic, but my attorneys tempered my expectations.

"The city is going to challenge his ruling. This isn't over," Tanenbaum said.

He was right. The next day, the city appealed. And seven months later, on December 17, 1980, a three-judge panel issued their opinion.

In a 2–1 decision, the Second Circuit Court of Appeals overturned Haight's ruling that I should be reinstated. They said the chief medical examiner was too important to be a Civil Service position. The mayor should have the power to hire and fire the chief medical examiner at will. But the appeals court also allowed Haight to proceed with a trial on my request for damages.

Tanenbaum was encouraged by the judge who dissented in the ruling, and who had said that I had completed my six-month probationary period and the city just couldn't change that rule.

"Dr. Baden was clearly denied his right to a due process hearing," he wrote. "The adverse effect of the Mayor's decision to remove him was exacerbated by the abruptness with which the Mayor acted with respect to the holder of an essentially non-political position. The Mayor's undue speed, which was wholly unnecessary, deprived Dr. Baden of a fair opportunity to face his accusers."

Tanenbaum said the fight wasn't over. We would appeal the court's ruling. And worst-case scenario, we could still move forward with damages.

"We'll continue to expose what the city did to you," he said.

While he was optimistic, by the end of 1980, I had been fighting for one and a half years. I was tired. The legal battle had put even more strain on my marriage. Yes, Judianne was supportive. But by this point, we had become more like roommates than husband and wife. Could our marriage be saved? Maybe the better question was: Did we want to save it? The answer must have been no. Otherwise, why hadn't we started counseling or taken steps to re-kindle our romance? In the end, we decided we'd stay together because of our children. We reasoned that it was better for them to have two parents at home than one. With all the turmoil in our lives, it was remarkable that our children seemed to be doing so well.

After the appeals court ruling, Sidney Weinberg, the chief medical examiner in nearby Suffolk County on Long Island, called me up.

"Why don't you come to work in my office?" he asked. "I'll make you the deputy chief medical examiner and you can get away from all that crap."

Weinberg was a good friend, and I appreciated his offer. I couldn't leave the city for good, not until the lawsuit was resolved. But I did need a break from the New York City Medical Examiner's Office. I had accumulated enough time on the job to take a two-year leave of absence. If they'd let me take the leave now, I'd work for Suffolk County during that period.

I talked to my wife and attorneys about my idea. They agreed a change of scenery might be a good thing. I told Weinberg and the city about my plans. They all agreed, and I began my leave of absence in January 1981.

Many medical examiners had been following my legal battle. Some told me about the pressure they were getting from cops and prosecutors to change autopsy rulings in police restraint deaths. If someone died from a chokehold, they said they were encouraged to blame the victim's underlying medical conditions, like heart trouble or obesity. Or it was suggested that they should wait to issue an opinion until the toxicology tests came back. After all, the person might have died of an illegal drug overdose. Whatever it took to avoid saying the victim was asphyxiated by cops.

I knew that cases like Miller's weren't isolated incidents. But it would take a young Black civil rights attorney from California to show me just how widespread they really were.

Chapter 9

• • •

JUSTICE FOR SETTLES

It was March 25, 1982, and there I was, standing next to a gray steel casket in the basement of the Suffolk County Medical Examiner's Office with three of the country's best-known forensic pathologists: Thomas Noguchi from Los Angeles, Werner Spitz from Detroit, and Sidney Weinberg from Long Island. Together, we stepped up to the casket and lifted the 210-pound body inside onto the autopsy table.

Journalists waited in a room outside, but we didn't know when we'd be done. I took a deep breath, tuned out the noise, and worked the scalpel in my right hand. A few weeks earlier I'd known nothing about Ron Settles, the young athlete whose body I was cutting into. Now, I knew just about everything, because of Johnnie Cochran, a bright Los Angeles lawyer who was hoping to bring him justice.

Twenty-one-year-old Settles, a running back at California State University, Long Beach, had been in the prime of his life. He'd grown up in nearby Carson, gone to Banning High School, where he shared the backfield with Freeman McNeil, who'd gone on to NFL stardom with the New York Jets.

Settles's athletic talent blossomed in college. Scouts from the Dallas Cowboys and Seattle Seahawks were in touch. "He was a tremendous athlete," Cochran told me. "More importantly, he was a great kid." He'd helped coach a youth baseball team in his off hours and held a summer job.

Settles was on break from school on the morning of June 2, 1981, and running late for work. He decided to take a shortcut, the road through Signal Hill—a town notorious for its violently racist police force.

Officer Jerry Lee Brown said he pulled over Settles's red Triumph convertible (a gift from his parents, both teachers, during his senior year of college) when he clocked it going 50 miles per hour in a 25-mile-per-hour zone. Hours later, after Brown took Settles into custody, police said Settles hanged himself in a cell in the Signal Hill lockup.

Cops—and the medical examiner—called it suicide. Settles's family and friends called it murder.

They hired Cochran, who filed a wrongful death lawsuit against the city. "This is as bad as it gets," Cochran said.

A second opinion was needed on the cause and manner of death, and that's why Cochran called me. "I want you to do another autopsy," he said, adding that the medical examiner had badly botched the first. He'd seen my name in the papers, he said, referring to the legal battle with Mayor Koch and the Arthur Miller case. He'd been impressed by my fight to keep medical examiners' offices free from political pressure.

"I need someone who's going to be fair, someone who's not afraid of doing the right thing," he said. He clearly knew which of my buttons to push.

I wanted to help, but I couldn't say yes without running it by Weinberg, who as Suffolk County chief medical examiner was then my boss. I asked Cochran for more information.

"I'll drop the autopsy report and other material in the mail today," Cochran said.

I had been working at Suffolk County during my two-year leave from the New York City Medical Examiner's Office. Dr. Weinberg and I had known each other for twenty-five years. He'd worked for Helpern when I was a medical student. In 1960, Weinberg left Helpern's office to create a similar agency in Suffolk County, the easternmost part of Long Island.

Weinberg was affable, friendly, slightly overweight with a ready smile, a great medical examiner, and a good friend. Weinberg's visits to the Suffolk County government building were punctuated with "Hi, Doc!" greetings from public officials and ordinary citizens alike. He was skilled in negotiating Suffolk County's difficult political terrain. His department was a national model of efficiency and overall excellence, and no politician wanted to cross him.

I was happy there. It was good to escape New York City politics. But I didn't plan to stay there long term. I knew Weinberg was planning to retire soon. He asked if I wanted to succeed him, but I told him no. The pace was too slow. Too few autopsies. I missed the more challenging New York City cases. I wasn't sure what to do next.

The nature of the job had changed radically since its inception—even since I'd started as a part-time medical examiner in 1960. Medical examiners had become prominent but controversial public figures. At the turn of the twentieth century, the job of determining cause of death had been an obscure political appointment for people with wildly varied medical backgrounds and abilities. Since then, it had evolved into a highly technical function carried out by board-certified forensic pathologists with years of study behind them. Now, in the 1980s, the scope of the medical examiner's office had stretched beyond performing autopsies into the fields of criminal investigation, public health, and environmental analysis. Technology enabled pathologists to determine the causes of disease, crimes, and deaths with unprecedented accuracy. This sometimes brought them into conflict with other agencies, including the police and district attorney's office—people they're expected to work alongside cooperatively.

Government-employed forensic pathologists earned much less money than those in private practice or working for hospitals. At the time, I was one of approximately 150 physicians in the United States who were certified by the American Board of Pathology and working as full-time forensic pathologists. We had to be dedicated to the profession. We regarded ourselves as scientists whose sole aim was to determine the truth no matter whom it helped or hurt. But most of us were also public servants, answerable to taxpayers and the media and vulnerable to political attacks. Even Noguchi, one of the nation's most prominent medical examiners and the ME on whose career the popular television show *Quincy* was based, had drawn plenty of hostile fire—including, as the chief coroner for Los Angeles County, for the results of Settles's first autopsy.

When I leafed through the package from Cochran, I understood why he was so upset at Settles's death. The details were worse than I had imagined. No one could explain why a professional football prospect and local hero who'd only ever been issued parking tickets would kill himself after being arrested on minor charges.

Officer Brown claimed that Settles refused to turn over his license and keys when asked. When he searched Settles's car, he said he found a knife and a baggie with a small amount of residue he believed was cocaine. He also said Settles was acting strangely, like he was on phencyclidine—PCP—a hallucinatory drug known as angel dust.

The officer said he handcuffed Settles and drove him to the city jail. Even though Settles's hands were bound behind his back, Brown said Settles managed to grab his groin in a failed attempt to escape. "The suspect . . . was extremely difficult to control because of his brute strength," Brown wrote in his report. The officer said it took five minutes for him and others to "control" Settles.

The district attorney's office investigated. They found holes in Brown's story.

A man in the cell next to Settles's said he had talked to him after the police beating. "He didn't seem depressed," the man said. Settles was asking questions about how he could get released from jail.

The DA found that Settles had asked to make a telephone call, but the cops refused—a violation of California law. About forty-five minutes later, Brown's report said Settles was discovered hanging in his cell with a mattress cover around his neck. Police said they cut Settles down, but it was too late.

Signal Hill's history also figured into the case. Incorporated in 1924, the city of about 5,700 people sat on a hilltop near Long Beach overlooking the Pacific. It was a tough, majority-white, working-class city. Many of the residents worked in the nearby oil fields.

The city had a reputation for racism, with federal investigations of police brutality reaching back to the 1960s. Between 1968 and 1981, twenty-nine complaints and sixteen lawsuits had been filed against the police department for unjustified beatings and false arrests. The city had paid out more than $80,000 in settlements.

Brown, the officer who arrested Settles, had been fired from the Los Angeles Police Department in 1970 for using excessive force. His situation wasn't unique. Five other Signal Hill officers had been fired from other departments before landing there.

As I continued reading, I found that the police and the medical examiner had made critical mistakes in handling Settles's death. There was no evidence that CPR was ever performed. Police lost his clothes and stored evidence improperly, including the mattress cover.

Although Noguchi's office was responsible for Settles's postmortem examination, Noguchi himself did not perform the autopsy. It was handled by a doctor who was not a board-certified forensic pathologist. She didn't do everything she could have, including taking autopsy photographs. She said Settles died of asphyxia by hanging and declared his death a suicide.

Settles's parents and the community raised questions, but the suicide ruling would have stood—if not for a funeral director. Johnny Leggert's funeral home prepared Settles's body for burial. Leggert had worked for the San Diego Coroner's Office for three years before opening a mortuary. During that time, he said, he'd observed the remains of more than one hundred suicides by hanging.

When the body arrived at his mortuary, Leggert said he observed various bruises that appeared to him to have come from a beating.

"I felt that there had been excessive brutality and that was uncalled for," he told Cochran and reporters. "And I felt that all of the swelling and the distention was on one side of the face, so it couldn't have been attributed to a hanging. I felt that he had been severely beaten, and that somebody somewhere hadn't told the truth."

The resulting public outcry prompted a coroner's grand jury, a rare type of investigation where a panel reviews evidence in a mysterious or suspicious death. If the panel concludes the person was a victim of foul play, it can name suspects, refer the case to a grand jury for criminal prosecution, and change the cause of death. Noguchi was the coroner in charge of the Settles hearing—the first such inquest in Los Angeles County in forty years.

And that's when a different story began to emerge.

Officers claimed Settles had a knife and drug paraphernalia with him in the car. They said he was arrested and charged with assault with a deadly weapon on a police officer, possession of cocaine, and refusing to identify himself.

A witness testified that she saw two officers holding guns to Settles's head after he was pulled over. The drug paraphernalia was a plastic bag with some kind of residue inside, but no one could say for sure what it was. Brown admitted to beating Settles on the head and legs for being "belligerent" while he was being booked. At the end of the hearing, the coroner's grand jury ruled 5–4 that Settles's death was a homicide—he had died at "the hands of another." Noguchi had accepted that conclusion. He didn't have to if he had disagreed.

A special criminal grand jury was then empaneled by Gil Garcetti, the Los Angeles County assistant district attorney, to determine whether Settles's death was a homicide and, if so, who to indict. He was the chief of the special investigation division, the department that handles all official corruption and police brutality cases.

The criminal grand jury met for two weeks, hearing witnesses and reviewing hundreds of pages of documents. Garcetti named Officer Brown as the target of the investigation. Brown's fellow officers initially refused to testify, invoking their Fifth Amendment rights.

Garcetti demanded the officers be suspended without pay until they talked. They ultimately testified, but they corroborated Brown's story. The grand jury concluded that there was not enough evidence to indict anyone. It would later come out that Noguchi testified to that jury that he thought Settles committed suicide, even though he had accepted the coroner's inquest ruling that the death was a homicide.

In January 1982, Los Angeles County district attorney John Van de Kamp announced that the special grand jury "found no direct evidence or criminal homicide" in the death of Ron Settles.

But the case wasn't over.

Cochran sued Signal Hill on behalf of Settles's family, saying his client's civil rights were violated when the police beat him. The lawsuit sought millions in damages.

Settles's family and a broad coalition of community supporters created the Ron Settles Justice Committee. They raised money for the lawsuit and held rallies demanding answers.

Cochran planned to have Settles's body exhumed from where it was buried in Memphis, Tennessee, and to have a nationally known forensic pathologist reexamine the body. The second autopsy would determine whether Settles's death was suicide or homicide.

"That's where you come in, Doctor Baden," he said during our first call.

After reading the case, I talked to Weinberg. I wouldn't have to travel, I said. I could do the autopsy on Long Island, in our offices. Weinberg agreed that we should help—with only one caveat: we'd do it for free. Pro bono. "We will do it as a professional courtesy," he said.

Weinberg said he'd be there, but he wanted us to invite Noguchi, too. He was the coroner in charge, and if any change to the death certificate was warranted, he'd be the one who'd have to make it. He extended an invitation to the district attorney in charge of the case. Also, Weinberg said Signal Hill police could also have a forensic pathologist attend. When it came to our findings, there had to be total transparency.

Cochran told the media he agreed with the plan. Settles's body was exhumed.

"We feel very strongly that the autopsy should be open to public scrutiny to answer whatever questions we can once and for all," Cochran said at a news conference.

Noguchi accepted Cochran's invitation. So did Garcetti. And Werner Spitz, the chief medical examiner for the city of Detroit, was hired to represent Signal Hill.

In the following weeks, I got to know Cochran. We talked at length, not only about Settles but also racial issues dividing America.

I had seen how racial bias played a role in New York cases like Eric Johnson's and Arthur Miller's, as well as in Settles's treatment. But Cochran opened my eyes to something else: it wasn't just random cases here and there. America's racism was systemic and ingrained. It was everywhere, hiding in plain sight. Most white Americans didn't believe that police were targeting communities of color. They didn't believe that law enforcement used racial profiling. They didn't believe that police were killing innocent Black and Hispanic people. What they did believe was that if police killed a person of color, they were probably justified—to have attracted police attention, the suspect must have been doing something bad.

Black and brown people knew otherwise. They lived with the consequences of racist policies. They were pulled over by cops without probable cause, or stopped and questioned for walking down a quiet street at night, and then didn't make it out of the encounter alive.

Maybe that's why racial tensions were so high in cities across America—and why so many minority neighborhoods saw law enforcement as an occupying force. Cops weren't there to help and protect them. They were there to stop Black and Hispanic people from committing crimes—because that's what Blacks and Hispanics did. The police were there to keep people of color out of white neighborhoods. A group of Black teenagers spelled trouble, so police stopped and frisked them. That didn't happen to white teenagers.

Cochran described how a Black man driving a nice car would draw the ire of police officers, who would stop him for no reason other than "driving while Black."

I had never heard that expression before. "What does that mean?" I asked.

He laughed. "Racial profiling," he said. Black drivers were routinely pulled over not because they had violated any law, but because they were Black. Black parents had to explain to their children what to do if they were stopped by police. Keep your hands on the steering wheel. Be polite and respectful. Keep your mouth closed. Stay calm. One wrong move and you could end up dead. It was a conversation white people didn't need to have with their children.

"You know why Ron was killed?" Cochran asked me.

"No."

"Because a white cop didn't like to see a Black man with a fancy car."

That would have been hard for me to believe when I began as a medical examiner. But not now, not after what I'd seen on the job, examining the results of so many fatal encounters with police.

Cochran was fascinating: a charismatic man who was able to synthesize complicated issues and put them into language that everyone could understand. Born in Shreveport, Louisiana, his family moved to California in 1943 when he was six years old, part of the massive twentieth-century migration of Black Americans out of the Jim Crow South. In 1959, he received his bachelor's degree from the University of California, Los Angeles, and later attended Loyola Marymount University Law School.

After graduating in 1962, Cochran worked as a deputy criminal prosecutor in Los Angeles. By mid-decade, he'd entered private practice and launched a firm of his own. He built a reputation for taking on cases involving questionable police actions against Black people.

Settles was his biggest case to date. He felt that if this could happen to Settles—a well-known star college football player—it could happen to any Black person, any place at any time.

"This case is important," he said. "His family is hurting. They're good people. They did everything right. But right now, they're numb."

Listening to him, it was hard for me, as the father of four, to imagine the grief the Settles family was feeling. As Settles's mother told a newspaper, "When a person goes into a jail facility the epitome of health, and a couple of hours later comes out beaten, mutilated, and dead, there has to be a reason."

His uncle had expressed the same raw emotion. "My nephew was innocent of everything they charged him with except maybe speeding," Strong Matthews said. "That was the infraction that cost him his life. He made the gross mistake of driving through Signal Hill as a shortcut to get to work."

He also noted that Signal Hill cops were using Settles's strength as an excuse to beat him. It was a stereotype the police used time and again to justify using excessive force in cases involving Black men.

"They claimed he had aggressive behavior, that he had a substance in the car they claimed looked like cocaine, and they said he acted out, like he would resist arrest. In some accounts, it said he had superhuman strength. It was all a lie," Matthews said.

On the morning of March 25, 1982, the forensic pathologists and others began arriving at the Suffolk County Medical Examiner's Office in Hauppauge, Long Island. I had set up the room with chairs, notepads, tools—everything we'd need for the autopsy—and I was dressed in my usual green morgue shirt and pants with thin surgical gloves. I had my favorite knife—the one Kuschner had given me when he stopped doing autopsies after becoming dean of Stony Brook's medical school. The two Suffolk County Medical Examiner autopsy photographers were also present to take photos and videos of the proceedings.

I made it clear that if any of the other pathologists wanted to closely examine an organ or bruise or do a dissection, that would be fine. If someone had a question or an observation, we'd stop and discuss it. We were scientists, a team, all looking to find answers.

By 11 AM, everyone else was there and ready: Weinberg, Noguchi, Spitz, Cochran, and Garcetti. It felt like my days in medical school when groups of students observed a professor around the autopsy table.

We placed Settles's body on his back on the autopsy table. Even after being in the ground for nine months, he was in very good shape. Settles had been well embalmed and his dark skin hadn't deteriorated much. I took a deep breath, then began by opening the stitches from the Y-shaped incision made during the first autopsy.

I was slow and methodical and dictated what I was finding, including whether there was any hemorrhaging in the eyes or other parts of the body. I was creating an audiovisual record for evidence.

I noticed bruises on Settles's body that hadn't been described in the original autopsy report, especially around his neck and face. And I had been on my feet for a few hours when I turned Settles's body on his stomach. Noguchi stopped me.

"Let me do it, Michael," he said politely.

He knew my next step was to do a subcutaneous dissection, a technique that would reveal any hidden bruises on Settles's back in the fatty tissues just beneath the skin caused by blunt-force trauma. Noguchi had more experience than I did with cutting below the top layer of skin to look at the yellow fat just beneath.

"Tom, go ahead," I said.

I stepped back. Noguchi put on a pair of gloves and reached for a scalpel.

When a person is struck, blood vessels under their skin rupture. On a white person, this creates a highly visible bruise—usually a black-and-blue mark. On a Black person, the same bruise might not be as apparent, because dark pigmentation can hide the hemorrhage. So, you have to flay back the top layer of skin and look underneath to find evidence of injury. If Settles had been struck on the back by fists or a nightstick, it would show up there. The medical examiner who performed the initial autopsy hadn't cut under the skin to look for hemorrhage, because it wasn't the standard procedure.

Noguchi peeled back the skin. We saw no subcutaneous bruising on Settles's back. But when we repeated this method of dissection elsewhere, we found hemorrhages on and under the skin of his arms, legs, and chest, suggesting that he had been struck many times. When I dissected deeper into his neck, there were hemorrhages in the soft tissues behind the esophagus. Hanging doesn't do that. Deep hemorrhages in the neck are more typically caused by a severe chokehold-type compression. Hanging only leaves furrow marks on the outside of the skin. All evidence pointed to the same verdict the coroner's grand jury had offered: death at the hands of another.

The autopsy lasted ten hours. By the time we finished, the media had already left. The next morning, we held a press conference at the Suffolk County Medical Examiner's Office. Weinberg and I stated that the hemorrhages in Settles's neck behind the esophagus and the many bruises on his body showed that he was beaten and choked to death, and that his hanging was staged to cover up the crime. We believed the manner of death was a homicide.

Spitz, the Detroit forensic pathologist, said he didn't feel the findings were conclusive enough to support our opinions. He still believed it was a suicide. Noguchi said he was on the fence; it could be either. But maybe that had to do with the news he had gotten after he arrived in Suffolk County: his bosses in Los Angeles had just demoted him from his position as chief coroner.

I commiserated, telling him I knew how he felt. He just shrugged. "Maybe I'll grow bonsai trees," Noguchi said.

We also issued a brief statement saying the autopsy revealed no evidence of fractures, but we had discovered additional injuries to Settles's extremities. The police had admitted to striking Settles "one or two times." But we found that he had sustained at least twenty blows.

"The pathologists will attempt to determine the cause and manner of death after additional toxicology and microscopic studies are completed, including additional findings with respect to the neck," the statement said.

Two months later, when the tests came back, Weinberg and I reviewed everything. The studies confirmed our initial opinion: Settles's death was a homicide.

"The hemorrhage found on Settles's esophagus is not associated with a simple suicidal hanging," I told reporters, adding that I had performed autopsies on hundreds of such suicides. Settles had no drugs in his system. No cocaine. No PCP. So much for the theory that he was high on angel dust.

But Weinberg and I acknowledged that we could not say who had strangled him or staged the suicide. That would be a job for the police and district
attorney.

Cochran and Settles's family and supporters were appreciative of our work.
Based on our analysis, they pushed the Los Angeles Sheriff's Department to
reopen the criminal case. But despite the pressure and new evidence, the department refused.

In January 1983, the city of Signal Hill told Cochran they didn't want
to go to trial. They agreed to pay Settles's family $1 million to settle the civil
lawsuit.

"A substantial measure of justice has been achieved," Cochran told the
media.

But it wasn't over for me. Not yet.

Officer Brown filed a $20 million lawsuit against me and Weinberg, alleg-
ing that our analysis defamed him.

"In effect, what Baden and Weinberg are saying" is that Brown "killed
Settles," the officer's attorney, Steven Yagman, told reporters.

Weinberg and I had to testify in Los Angeles before a federal judge that
we had not mentioned Brown's name. In April 1984, the judge dismissed the
lawsuit, holding that our statements were constitutionally protected opinion,
and imposed sanctions totaling $250,000.00 against Yagman for "unreason-
able and vexatious conduct" during the trial. On appeal, the court upheld the
verdict but reversed the fine.

Settles's was one of several controversial deaths of Black men in the 1970s
and 1980s that changed the way police departments dealt with prisoners. Many
law enforcement agencies now video-record jail areas, a measure intended to
decrease the chances of excessive use of force by police or corrections officers.

For me, the Settles case represented another step in my gradual evolution.
I knew bad things happened to people of color in New York City. With Attica,
I saw that it happened across the state. From the news, I knew it happened in
Southern states. Now, with Settles, I realized it was systemic. It just wasn't
New York or the South. It was everywhere. And sooner or later, if we didn't
change the way our justice system treated Black and Hispanic people, there
would be a reckoning.

I had tried to address this injustice by serving on the New York State Corrections Medical Review Board and handling cases as fairly as I could. But now, with the Settles case, Cochran had pushed me in a new direction. He showed me not only that racial bias was widespread in our criminal justice system, but also that a forensic pathologist could make a difference.

After my two-year sabbatical ended, I returned to the New York City medical examiner's office. My new boss wouldn't let me speak out on or investigate civil rights cases. But an unexpected offer would soon change that.

Chapter 10

• • •

A NEW BEGINNING

I sat at my kitchen table with the phone receiver pressed against my ear. The man on the other end had just identified himself: Hank Williams, New York State Police. I didn't recognize the name at first, but then it hit me—big guy with a crew cut, upstate, lived in an RV. I hadn't heard from him in years.

I had met Williams in 1971 while I was at Attica. Back then he was a captain, but now he was the deputy superintendent. He said the state police was establishing a forensic sciences unit in Albany and expanding their crime laboratory. They needed a forensic pathologist.

"Doctor Baden, would you be interested in the job?" he asked.

I leaned back in my chair. I had turned down similar offers in other cities and states. But given recent changes to the New York City medical examiner's office, his offer was something to consider seriously.

"Let me think about it," I told him. "I'll get back to you in a couple of days."

It was July 1985. My legal battle with the city was over. Plus, as a result of the federal appeals court overturning my reinstatement, they had also ruled that the chief medical examiner position was too important to be included in the Civil Service. The mayor, they determined, should be able to hire and fire the chief medical examiner as he could other high-level employees. So they ended the position's Civil Service protection and made it just another political job. If the mayor didn't like the ME's ruling in a high-profile death, they could be fired. This meant the current New York City chief ME, Elliot Gross, now had no job security.

Gross was short, quiet, and introverted. He had attended elite schools, including Horace Mann and Columbia College. We'd both joined the New York City Medical Examiner's Office full time in July 1965. Then he left a year later to become Connecticut's first chief medical examiner.

Back in medical school, we'd been friends as well as classmates. Yet when he returned in 1980 to replace me as chief medical examiner, the first thing he did was to have security guards sweep my former office for hidden telephone-bugging devices that could listen to his conversations.

With the federal appeals court ruling, Gross knew his job depended on staying in Mayor Koch's good graces. For years, Koch had received strong support from police and the police unions. A "law and order" mayor, his philosophy was simple: if someone died during a police encounter, it wasn't the cops' fault. Minority community groups were upset by many of Gross's autopsy findings, which supported police officers' versions of events in a number of fatal encounters.

In the mid-1980s, police encounters with New York City's minority residents were increasing. The city was a mess. Crime was soaring in many neighborhoods, mainly because of the arrival of crack, a concentrated, highly addictive form of cocaine. Instead of powder, crack was sold as small rocks, white or pink in color, that addicts smoked in a pipe. When it burned, the rock made a popping or cracking sound—thus the street name.

The tactics police were using to fight drug trafficking and related crime were under fire, especially from leaders in minority communities. At times, it seemed that police were indiscriminately arresting these communities' residents. Some of those arrests turned deadly. When they did, the chief medical examiner was at the center, often accused of producing misleading or inaccurate autopsy reports.

One of Gross's earliest changes was to have the bodies of police-encounter victims brought from the other borough offices to Manhattan so that he could perform or supervise the autopsies. Previously, they were performed in the borough where the person died. Some medical examiners complained that he intervened to alter the findings of other forensic pathologists in our office.

In 1985, the *New York Times* published an investigative series criticizing Gross and the medical examiner's office for producing inaccurate or misleading autopsy reports, especially when someone died in police custody. Mayor Koch said he supported Gross. But an investigation by the State Health Department Board for Professional Medical Conduct concluded that allegations against Gross were warranted. (Later, in 1989, the board reversed itself, concluding that Gross's conduct should not have been disciplined. And, after a five-year investigation, the New York State Board of Regents dismissed all charges of misconduct against Gross raised in the *New York Times* investigation. The lack of widely accepted standards for conducting autopsies played a significant role in the reversals.)

Of all the problems the investigation highlighted, the ones involving police killings of Black men and women were the most disturbing. The reporters examined several racially charged deaths that continue to reverberate to this day.

Eleanor Bumpurs was a sixty-seven-year-old Black woman with a history of mental illness. She lived alone in her Bronx public-housing apartment and was four months behind on her monthly rent of $98.65. So, the New York City Housing Authority decided to evict her on October 29, 1984.

That morning, they sent Housing Authority marshals to her fourth-floor apartment to serve an eviction notice. She refused to let them inside and screamed what marshals described as "hostile threats" at them through the door. The marshals then called the New York Police Department Emergency Services Unit.

Six officers stormed through the door. They said they found Bumpurs, who weighed 260 pounds, brandishing a ten-inch kitchen knife. Police ordered her to drop the weapon, but instead, they said, she lunged at them. An officer fired two shots from his 12-gauge pump-action shotgun. Police officials later claimed only one hit her.

The shooting raised many questions. Did the police really have to force their way into her apartment? They knew she was mentally ill. Wasn't there a better way to handle the situation?

The autopsy raised more troubling questions.

The report, issued a month after Bumpurs's death, showed that she was hit by both shots. The first shot hit the hand that was holding the knife—"nearly amputating three fingers" and stripping away the weapon.

Jon Pearl, the associate medical examiner who performed the autopsy, said the second shot was the lethal one. The cause of death was "shotgun wounds (two) of chest, hand and lung." He said he included the number of shots as part of the cause of death. He would testify later that, after receiving the wounds to her hands, Bumpers would have been unable to hold a weapon.

The autopsy report angered the community, especially since Bumpurs's death came less than a year after another outrage.

In the early hours of September 15, 1983, Michael Stewart, an aspiring artist and model, left a nightclub in Manhattan's Lower East Side and headed to the Fourteenth Street subway station to catch a train back home to Brooklyn.

As he waited, the slender twenty-five-year-old Black man pulled out a marker and began scrawling graffiti on the wall. He didn't know that several Transit Police officers were watching him.

According to witnesses, the officers grabbed Stewart, handcuffed him, threw him to the ground, and began punching him. When Stewart screamed in pain, the cops choked him with a nightstick until he went silent.

The officers then hogtied him and carried his limp, 140-pound body to a waiting police van. The driver transported him to Bellevue Hospital, where hospital staff managed to get him breathing again, but he remained in a coma. Thirteen days later, he died.

From witness accounts, it was clear that police officers had beaten Stewart while restraining him. But Gross's autopsy whitewashed the use of excessive force.

Although Stewart's body was severely bruised, Gross said he had found no evidence that physical injury had caused his death, declaring that the police encounter hadn't caused or contributed to it. After the autopsy, Gross determined that Stewart had died from complications of drinking too much alcohol. Stewart's family charged that it was a "classic cover-up."

The public was appalled. Stewart was a healthy young man—before the police grabbed him. Black leaders and members of Stewart's family organized protests against police brutality and racism. They began a petition to remove Gross from office. Stewart's family filed a wrongful-death lawsuit against the city. (Years later, the family would be awarded $1.7 million.)

If Gross and Koch thought the issue would go away, they were wrong. Stewart's death continued to dominate the news. Part of the *New York Times* investigative piece focused on it.

Times reporters interviewed dozens of people involved in the Stewart case, including Siegfried Oppenheim, the chief medical examiner's office stenographer, who took the official notes during the autopsy. Oppenheim had worked on hundreds of cases with Gross and thousands total in his twenty-five years in the office, mostly with Helpern. He told the newspaper that he was convinced Gross was trying to hide the true cause of death.

"I was horrified," he said.

Doctors in the medical examiner's office supported Oppenheim's contentions.

Gross later amended his original autopsy. He reported the death was due to "injury to the spinal cord in the upper neck." But things only went downhill from there. Gross would make a third assessment in which he said Stewart died from blunt-force trauma, but he did not specify what caused the injury.

Stewart's family hired a forensic pathologist to conduct a second autopsy. He concluded that strangulation was the cause of death.

Six white officers were eventually charged in connection with Stewart's death. But in 1985, they were acquitted of all charges related to the case by an all-white jury. After the last defendant had heard his verdict, the entire right side of the courtroom, where the officers' families and colleagues sat, erupted with cheers and applause. Minutes later, as the officers drove away from the courthouse, dozens of protesters, shouting angrily and banging on their car hoods, heckled and jeered them.

"Murderers!" some of the protesters screamed. "Blood is on all your hands!" others shouted.

In response, American artist Jean-Michel Basquiat created *Defacement*, an acrylic-and-marker piece on wood, to memorialize Stewart and protest anti-Black racism and police brutality. With a ghostly black figure standing in between two cartoonish characters resembling cops with batons, the work has never been sold, having been painted on the studio wall of fellow artist Keith Haring, and is rarely displayed.

Sitting in silence at the kitchen table after Williams's call, I mulled all these things over. Blood on cops' hands. Then, Williams's offer, out of the blue. This was a sign. It was time for me to go.

I called Williams back. We talked for about thirty minutes. Williams said the state police was handling more and more murder investigations. But he was worried that many of the doctors who did the coroners' autopsies weren't qualified, which interfered with the state police's ability to investigate homicides.

I understood. Even then, the shortage of forensic pathologists was a national problem. The United States was almost equally divided between counties that had a medical examiner, who is an appointed physician, and those that had a coroner, who is elected and not required to be a doctor. Despite usually having no medical training at all, coroners were nonetheless responsible for issuing death certificates and investigating unnatural deaths.

Williams knew the statistics. Ninety-two percent of deaths in the United States were natural—cancer, heart attacks, strokes, and other diseases. The rest were unnatural: accidents, suicides, drug overdoses, or homicides.

If there was an unnatural death, county coroners would decide whether an autopsy should be done. And if they did, they'd usually get a local hospital pathologist to do it. The problem is that hospital pathologists are trained in diseases that cause natural deaths. Unnatural deaths are the focus of forensic pathologists. They're trained to analyze traumatic injuries—gunshot and stab wounds, blunt force and poison.

Coroners and hospital pathologists might misinterpret injuries that could lead to murder charges or exonerate a suspect. That's why forensic pathologists are so important. And that's why Williams said he needed me for his agency's new forensic sciences unit.

Lacking resources, most of New York's small towns and rural areas depended on the state police for help in murder investigations and other cases. As the agency's forensic pathologist, I knew I'd be in a unique position. People in communities all over New York State would be able to consult with us about cases. And the organization could offer its services to local police departments for free.

It was a great opportunity. But I wanted to run an idea by Williams.

"Can I work half-time?" I asked. "I would always be available on call, but that way I'd have more time for private consultations."

To ensure the state police would always have a forensic scientist available, I suggested they contact Lowell Levine, a good friend, a prominent forensic dentist, and a captain in the US Naval Reserve. He and I could serve as codirectors of this new body, formally called the New York State Police Forensic Sciences Unit. One of us would always be available.

Williams didn't hesitate. He said that he was fine with the arrangement as long as my private work didn't interfere with New York State investigations.

Williams was a straight shooter. He said he knew about my problems in New York. He assured me that my unit would be independent—free from politics. State troopers would be held accountable if they did something wrong, just like anyone else.

I was excited. This was an incredible opportunity to handle a wide range of cases.

But I had one last question: "Whatever happened to Robert Horn?" I reminded Williams that I had spent a week with Horn back during the Attica investigation, driving around the western part of the state, collecting bullets and other evidence.

"Bob's still here. Now, he runs the crime lab and you'd be working together," Williams said. "Doctor Baden, there are good folks here."

"Hank, I'm going to talk to my wife tonight and I'll let you know my answer in the morning."

So that night, when Judianne got home, I broached the subject. By now, only two of our four children lived with us. Our oldest, Trissa, was finishing medical school, while Lindsey was attending Bowdoin College in Maine. Judson was starting at Columbia College in New York, so he was in and out of the house. Sarah was in the sixth grade.

We had been married more than twenty-five years. Both of us knew our marriage was in serious trouble, but we had known that for years. We'd come together briefly when Koch demoted me. She'd been my biggest advocate. But after that, our marriage slipped back to the way it was. If I took this job, we'd see even less of each other. But the stark reality was, we were already living separate lives. We only stayed together for our children.

"If I take the job, I'd have to live in Albany for part of the week," I said.

Judianne was blunt. "Take it."

She said I'd be much happier with the state police than in the medical examiner's office with all the turmoil. She was right. She didn't mention anything about our marriage, and neither did I. I said I'd share more information with her about my living arrangements when everything was finalized.

I knew the position had the potential to open a new chapter in my life. I had thought about writing a book about forensic pathology. And I wanted to spend time helping communities solve crimes and reexamining cases where someone was convicted of a crime they hadn't committed.

What I didn't need was more time to deliberate. I picked up the phone and dialed Williams's number. "Hank, it's me. It's a yes."

"Doctor Baden, welcome aboard."

The next day, I submitted a letter stating that I was transferring to the New York State Police.

During my last two weeks in New York, I didn't hear a word from Gross or Koch. Many years later, when Koch and I were in the Fox News green room, waiting to appear on different programs, he approached me with an outstretched hand.

"I hope you didn't take that medical examiner demotion personal," Koch said, smiling. "It was just politics. I have always said that you are a great forensic pathologist, just not a team player—that's necessary in politics."

I could have walked away or ignored him. I could have berated him or dropped a few choice expletives. But I had closed that chapter of my life a long time ago. Instead, I responded drolly: "They don't teach us politics in medical school."

I won't say Koch did me a favor. The experience of losing the chief medical examiner position was harrowing. But in retrospect, many of the good and interesting things that followed my demotion would not have happened if I had spent my whole life working in the New York City Medical Examiner's Office.

After I left, Gross's troubles continued. And in October 1987, Koch fired Gross, saying he lacked the "'level of leadership and level of management'" needed to head the medical examiner's office.

The move came after a special mayoral advisory committee had recommended Gross's replacement.

Gross protested. But it didn't matter. Public pressure had reached a tipping point. And two years later, Koch himself would fall to the same pressure, losing the Democratic primary in a failed bid for a fourth term to Manhattan borough president David Dinkins. A few months later, Dinkins became New York's first Black mayor.

I didn't have time to think about all of that. New York City was in my rearview mirror. The highway in front of me was clear. What I didn't know was that I'd soon be taking a detour along a road that harkened back to a dark chapter in America's past.

Chapter 11

• • •

THE GHOSTS OF MISSISSIPPI

In the basement of the Albany Hospital Medical Center, I waited anxiously for the casket to arrive from Arlington National Cemetery in Washington, DC. I didn't know what I'd find when I opened Medgar Evers's casket. It was June 3, 1991 and Evers's body had been in the ground for almost twenty-eight years.

Evers's son, who'd been three years old when his father was murdered, had asked to be there. He had no memory of ever being with his father and wanted to see him. I said yes, but that I needed to look first to see if the body had deteriorated too much for viewing. Now, I had just gotten word that the hearse was on its way around the back of the hospital. In a few minutes, Evers's exhumed body would be in the autopsy room.

This was a deeply disturbing case, one steeped in racially motivated hatred. Throughout his life, Evers had heroically spoken out against racism in the Deep South. In the 1950s and early 1960s, he spearheaded demonstrations and boycotts of businesses that practiced racial discrimination and organized voter registration drives to make sure Black people had access to the polls. His success made Evers a big target for white supremacists. Maybe a re-autopsy would finally give his family the closure they had pushed for so hard and so long, by convicting the man responsible for the civil rights leader's death.

The phone rang. The casket was on the way to the basement. I switched on the overhead lights and took a deep breath. In a way, this autopsy summed up everything I had hoped to accomplish when I joined the State Police Forensic Sciences Unit.

Lowell Levine, the codirector, and I had been traveling to police agencies across New York, letting them know about the new forensic science resources the state police had on hand to help them solve criminal and other cases. Our reputation grew not only in New York, but with law enforcement agencies nationwide. And that's why I was here, on a Saturday, ready to reexamine the body of a civil rights icon. When Mississippi officials were considering reopening the Evers case, they turned to us. And my bosses at the New York State Police did everything possible to make it happen.

My transition to the state police had been an easy one, thanks to Hank Williams, Robert Horn, and others, like my new boss, Major Timothy McAuliffe. Williams had arranged for Levine and me to have an office at the state police headquarters building in Albany and one at the agency's office in one of the World Trade Center's twin towers in lower Manhattan. (That office was moved a few years before the September 11, 2001, terrorist attacks; otherwise I might have been in the building that horrible day.) I lived in Albany most of the week, and my colleagues became my friends. We'd eat lunch together in the state police cafeteria and go out to dinner sometimes.

About a year after I started, Williams died of bladder cancer. It was a blow, but others stepped in and helped fill the void. When there was a murder or other difficult case, we'd pull together. Nothing emphasized that more than when part of a bridge on the Governor Thomas E. Dewey Thruway collapsed on the morning of April 5, 1987, a Sunday. A 60-foot section of the 540-foot-long Schoharie Creek Bridge in upstate New York had fallen 110 feet into the swollen creek, together with a tractor trailer and four cars.

An hour after we heard of the disaster, McAuliffe picked me up at my house. We raced to the scene, about forty miles west of Albany. Levine was already on his way.

McAuliffe filled me in. After a few days of heavy rain, the center of the bridge had broken apart without warning. At least ten people had died but there were probably more casualties.

The plan was to go to the scene first and see if anyone needed our help. Then, we'd head to a hospital where they had set up a place for the victims and their families. McAuliffe was the right person to talk to the families. He was a devout Roman Catholic and a deacon in his church, an empathetic, kindly man who knew how to comfort people in pain.

In his late thirties, McAuliffe was stocky with grayish brown hair that made him look a little older than his years. He was a by-the-book trooper, the kind of guy who'd stop at a yellow traffic light before it turned red when others, like me, would have blown through it. I once asked him why he stopped. "I have to be a model for everyone who's watching," he said without missing a beat. "The police should behave better than everyone else."

As we approached the bridge, traffic was backed up for miles, so we drove on the shoulder until we reached the spot. We parked, and I walked to the edge of the roadway. The steel-plate girder bridge had collapsed in the middle. Cars could be seen in the water below.

"If they fell in, there's no way they could have survived," I said to McAuliffe.

A trooper approached us. He said several bodies had already been recovered. Salvage experts were pulling slabs of concrete off cars in the creek to see if anyone was inside. He said they were continuing to search the stream for more bodies. "We're doing everything we can. But it's really moving too fast," he said of the water.

McAuliffe nodded. He glanced at the scene. The troopers had everything under control. So we headed to Saint Mary's Hospital in Amsterdam, New York, where the bodies had been brought, so I could perform the autopsies.

Levine met me when we arrived, then led me to the morgue. On the way, I saw several families anxiously awaiting word about loved ones whose cars had plunged into the creek. Two nuns greeted us and led me into a side room while McAuliffe stopped to talk to the families.

For each retrieved body that arrived, I'd perform the autopsy and Levine would handle the identification. McAuliffe stayed with us. So did the two nuns, Sister Mary and Sister Ann. They were wonderful and extremely helpful. In their flowing black habits, they'd run back and forth between the autopsy room and the radiology department, ferrying the X-rays that would help us make identifications and document injuries.

Over a few days, we conducted ten autopsies. We helped as much as we could. Before I left, Sister Mary and Sister Ann handed me a small green cloth medallion—a scapular. Out of the corner of my eye, I spotted McAuliffe—who knew I was Jewish—smiling as the nuns gave the Catholic object of devotion. The nuns said I should keep it with me and hold it in my hand when I pray. They said it would give me hope in time of need.

"Thank you, Sisters," I said, before gently placing it in my wallet. It's been with me ever since.

The friendship and spirit of collaboration I had with my state police colleagues was inspiring to me. We all tried to come up with ideas to improve the Forensic Sciences Unit. In honor of Williams, Levine and I began an annual week-long seminar for New York State homicide investigators to showcase new techniques, science, and technology that could help detectives solve murder cases. The New York State Police Henry F. Williams homicide seminar rapidly grew so popular that it attracted homicide investigators from police agencies across the United States and in countries worldwide.

We also began receiving lecture invitations to law enforcement conferences across America. That's what brought Levine and me to Biloxi, Mississippi, in early 1991. We had been asked to present to the state's association of police and district attorneys.

Just before the conference began, Bobby DeLaughter, an assistant district attorney in Hinds County, and his boss, DA Ed Peters, approached us with a lunch invitation, adding they wanted to run something by us.

Over lunch, they told us they were considering reopening the Medgar Evers case.

"Medgar Evers?" I asked. "It's been a long time since I had heard that name."

DeLaughter gave us a quick history lesson. In the early 1960s, civil rights leaders throughout the South organized protests and voter registration drives and pushed for school integration. They were met at every step with violent resistance. Thirty-seven-year-old Evers, a national figure who worked closely with the Reverend Martin Luther King Jr., was one of their leaders in Mississippi.

Born near Decatur, Evers had enlisted in the still-segregated US Army in 1943 and served in Europe during World War II. When he returned home, he tried to vote in the 1946 election, but left the courthouse in Decatur without casting a ballot. Twenty armed white men had learned of his plan to vote and turned up to threaten his life.

Evers went to Alcorn College and, after graduating in 1952, began organizing chapters of the NAACP—an incredibly dangerous venture. He was targeted by the Ku Klux Klan, a white supremacist group that terrorized Black families across the South. He applied to the University of Mississippi Law School but was rejected because of his race. That only increased his resolve.

Named the NAACP's first field secretary in Mississippi in 1954, Evers moved his family to Jackson, where he worked to dismantle segregation. He led peaceful rallies, economic boycotts, and voter registration drives around the state. In 1962, he helped James Meredith become the first Black man to attend the University of Mississippi, a watershed event in the civil rights movement. Evers received numerous death threats, and several attempts were made on his life.

On June 12, 1963, Evers arrived home from a NAACP meeting just before midnight. He always tried to be careful. So when he pulled into his driveway, he turned off the engine and sat there for a moment. He scanned the yard and the block, then hurried out of his car. As he began the short walk up to his one-story home, the sound of a gunshot cracked down the silent street. A bullet struck Evers in the back. He staggered up to the front steps and collapsed.

Across the street on a lightly wooded hill, the shooter jumped up in pain. The recoil from the Enfield rifle had driven the scope into his eye, bruising his face. He dropped the weapon and fled.

Meanwhile, Evers's wife, Myrlie, and their three children—still awake after watching an important civil rights speech by President John F. Kennedy on television—heard the shot outside. Reena and Darrell, the two oldest children, followed the drill their parents had taught them: they grabbed their little brother Van, dropped to the floor, and crawled to the bathroom. They put Van in the tub—cast iron and bulletproof—and ran outside when they heard their mother's cries. They knelt by their father while he bled in the driveway.

They were soon joined by neighbors and police. Evers was barely alive when he arrived at the University of Mississippi Medical Center three-and-a-half miles away. Although there were separate entrances at the hospital for "whites" and "colored," he was allowed to enter through a third entrance: "Emergency." But he died an hour later of massive internal bleeding from his punctured right lung.

Word spread quickly in Jackson and beyond. Many people across the country were horrified. President Kennedy said he was "appalled by the barbarity" of the sniper-slaying of one of the NAACP's top integration leaders. The local newspaper, the *Clarion-Ledger*, offered a $1,000 reward to find Evers's killer.

"The death of Medgar Evers is most regrettable. We join practically our entire community in this feeling," the newspaper said in a front-page editorial.

But not everyone felt that way. White supremacists celebrated and promised even more violence if civil rights activists continued to push for desegregation.

The local police immediately found the rifle where the assassin had dropped it. A fingerprint was recovered from the scope and submitted to the FBI, which matched it to the military service prints of a local man named Byron De La Beckwith.

He was arrested several days later. Beckwith, a fertilizer salesman and known white supremacist, had been asking about the location of Evers's home for some time prior to the shooting. He had an obvious motive; further, he had owned the weapon, his fingerprint was on it, and he had a scope-related injury around his eye. Beckwith clearly appeared to be the killer.

But in Mississippi in 1963, none of that mattered. Beckwith sat through two separate trials. The all-white juries in both failed to reach verdicts. So Beckwith went free.

DeLaughter said that, afterward, Myrlie Evers moved her family to California and started a new life there. She stayed involved in civil rights, remarried, and became a commissioner on the California Board of Public Works. Any time she visited Mississippi, she dropped into the prosecutor's office to press them to reopen the murder case. But she was always told, "Don't dredge up the past."

The killer walked free. Nothing changed.

In 1989, a reporter at a local newspaper, Jerry Mitchell, uncovered records of the Mississippi Sovereignty Commission, a secret state agency set up in the 1960s to investigate and intimidate civil rights leaders—including Medgar Evers.

The commission included the governor, lieutenant governor, and a slew of high-powered state officials. It spied on civil rights leaders and accumulated more than 132,000 pages of records. The papers were supposed to be sealed for fifty years, but somehow Mitchell got hold of the archive. The newspaper stories he wrote raised troubling questions about the Evers case.

"The commission was working to get Beckwith acquitted," DeLaughter said. "When Myrlie found out, she pushed even harder for our office to reopen the case."

His boss told him to reexamine the prosecutor's records. When DeLaughter pulled the case file, he found it was only three pages long. All the original witness statements, police reports—even the murder weapon—had vanished.

"Everything was missing," DeLaughter said.

The DA said he had to start over from scratch. He went to the library and studied old newspaper stories on microfiche to find the witnesses who testified in the trials. And when he went looking for the murder weapon, he discovered Beckwith's gun in an unlikely place: the home of his own ex–father-in-law.

Judge Russell Moore III, who died in 1989, had presided over the Beckwith trials. And after the second mistrial—when the case was closed in 1969—Moore took the rifle for his collection.

"We keep looking for evidence and talking to witnesses," DeLaughter said. "We're hoping that with time, some of them will finally tell the truth." He paused for a moment, then looked at me. "We don't even have an autopsy report. If we don't find that, we can't move forward with a trial." The bullet that had gone through Evers and landed in his kitchen also was missing.

"Well, do you know where the body is buried?"

"I believe in Arlington National Cemetery."

"Then I don't think that will be a problem," I said.

"What do you mean?"

"For a medical examiner, burial is just long-term storage," I explained. "We can exhume the body and reconstruct the path of the bullet—even at this late stage." Yes, there might be some problems. If the body was too badly decomposed, it might be difficult to track the bullet's path. But if the bullet had struck bone—like a rib—a fragment would still be there, as well as the chip out of the bone. "We'll be able to get an accurate picture of what happened."

DeLaughter was fascinated. "Really?"

I nodded. I explained that we would have to get permission from the family to exhume the body. DeLaughter could get a court order to do it, but it's always better to get the family on board, I said.

Levine would be there with me to help confirm identification. If the body was too badly decomposed, he could use dental records to identify it. "*You* may know it's his body, but when you go before a jury, you don't want anyone to doubt that it's him," I said.

DeLaughter was quiet for a moment. "I think Myrlie would say yes. This is really important to her. Hell, it's really important to us."

"While you're reaching out to her, we'll talk to our boss just to make sure it's okay. I don't think it will be a problem. We would do the autopsy as a courtesy so there would be no charge. But you'd have to bring the body to Albany."

DeLaughter smiled. "It sounds good. Let me call Myrlie."

◆ ◆ ◆

The mortuary, the widow, and the bosses all agreed: we could exhume Evers's body in Arlington National Cemetery, bring it to Albany, and perform a second autopsy. "Let me know what we can do to help," McAuliffe said.

With a green light from McAuliffe and the superintendent of the state police, now we had to keep things quiet. We didn't want to tip off Beckwith.

Ever since Jerry Mitchell had written about the secret Mississippi spy agency and Evers's death, Beckwith had been talking a lot. He maintained publicly that he didn't kill Evers, but he showed no remorse about his death, either. Beckwith was a dyed-in-the-wool racist and proud member of the KKK. He made no apologies about it. If he kept talking, maybe he'd say something that prosecutors could use. But if he knew we were doing another autopsy, he'd know DeLaughter was serious. And if he had a shred of common sense, he would clam up.

I had read everything I could find about Medgar Evers. He had enlisted in the Army at a time when the US military was a reflection of much of the nation. It was segregated, and Black units were relegated to support roles. White officers regarded Black men as inferior combat soldiers. Evers served in an all-Black port battalion in the quartermaster corps. His unit unloaded supplies from Allied ships onto convoy trucks, which then transported them to the front lines.

While serving in England and France, Evers grew frustrated with the demeaning treatment that he and other Black service members received while serving their country. So, when Evers returned home, he decided to do something about it. That's why he got involved with the NAACP.

As I was reading, I got a call from his youngest son, James Van Dyke

Evers. Van had been three years old when his father was killed, and now was in his early thirties, a photographer living in California.

"I don't have any memories of my father. I'd like to be there, to see him, when you open the casket," he said. "Is that possible?"

I was caught off guard. I was confident there would be significant skeletal remains, so I'd be able to reconstruct the path of the gunshot wound. And I was hopeful that the skeleton would reveal the bullet's trajectory. But I was concerned about how difficult the sight of the exhumed body might be for the man's son to witness.

Still, I understood why Van wanted to be there. It was a chance for him to finally say goodbye to his father. It might be a gruesome sight, but it also might be fine. I just didn't want to sugarcoat anything. I wanted him to know every possible scenario.

"I have no problem with you being here. But with decomposition, it may not be possible to see your dad. So, let us look at your father's body first. Then, we'll show you what we can. Is that okay?"

"That's all I'm asking," he said.

Then, I called Myrlie for more information about whether the body had been embalmed and what might have been placed in the casket alongside Evers before burial. She told me her husband's body had been prepared by Collins Funeral Home in Jackson. Mourners had placed some personal items in the casket, like his NAACP pin. She said she wouldn't be at the autopsy, but that Van would represent the family.

"Thank you for taking an interest," she said.

Myrlie was a courageous woman, as much an activist as her husband was. Born in Vicksburg, Mississippi, and raised by her paternal grandmother, a retired teacher, she grew up in a family of educators. She was at Alcorn College, majoring in education, when she met Medgar her very first day. After they married, she actively helped Medgar organize NAACP branches and fight for integration. In June 1963, she was the young mother of three children.

It was heartbreaking to think about what they'd gone through. I couldn't stop thinking about my own children. What if they had seen me shot, bleeding to death, in front of our house? How would that have affected their lives? I was happy that we were playing a role in trying to bring the killer to justice. If Van wanted to be there with us in the autopsy room, I'd do everything possible to make it happen.

◆ ◆ ◆

On Monday morning, June 3, 1991, a backhoe carefully lifted earth from a grave in Arlington Cemetery, then set it to the side. Anyone walking by would think the groundskeepers were preparing for a burial. No one would have suspected it was an exhumation.

Van Evers was there watching with a man from the Collins Funeral Home, who confirmed that the unearthed casket was the one that his father had been buried in so many years earlier. They put the casket inside the hearse and then began the 370-mile-journey north to Albany.

Meanwhile, we prepared the autopsy room. A new one was still being completed at our forensic science building, so we decided to use the old one in the Albany Medical Center.

Our tools—scalpels, scissors, forceps with toothed tips, an electric bone saw, and a ruler—were laid out. We had an X-ray machine and a camera ready, and Levine had Evers's dental records. The autopsy would take several hours. DeLaughter would later release the results.

DeLaughter had arrived a little earlier, along with another member of Levine's and my team, William Maples, a forensic anthropologist from Florida.

The call came. Several state troopers helped place the long box on a gurney and wheel it inside. We all felt a little anxious. It had been thirty years since the casket was buried. What would we see when we opened it?

As the stretcher and casket were wheeled in, I glimpsed Van Evers right behind the troopers, looking a little nervous.

I reached out my hand. "I'm glad you're here," I said.

He smiled. "Thank you again for letting me come."

I explained again that I wanted to open the casket first. "If you could just wait outside the room. I promise I'll—"

Van stopped me. "I understand, Doctor Baden. Just let me know when you're ready." He turned around and disappeared into the hallway.

I turned my attention to the dark brown metallic casket in front of me.

We photographed it. It was intact and still watertight. I began to work on the fasteners to open the lid. After I loosened the last fastener, I turned to everyone in the room. "This is it!" I said.

We swung the lid open. And there he was, in excellent condition: Medgar Evers in his suit and tie, his hands crossed over his chest. It was uncanny. It looked as if he had just died the day before. Pine needles that had been placed alongside him thirty years ago were still green. The white linen lining was still clean and dry. The fabric was in perfect shape.

Van Evers, the man waiting in the hallway, was the image of this dead man. He was a little younger than his father was when he was assassinated, but they were clearly father and son.

I glanced around at everyone in the room. Apparently we all felt the same awe. Time stood still. I didn't say a word.

I walked outside the autopsy room and found Van. He was holding pictures of his father.

"You can go inside," I said.

He nodded. We walked in together. I had asked an assistant to pull a hospital partition around Evers so Van could have privacy. Van moved slowly to the open casket, as if afraid of what he'd find. Then he saw his father's face, his head resting on a white pillow. Van's body began to shake. He tried to hold back the tears but was too overwhelmed. DeLaughter walked over and the two men embraced.

"I'd like to be alone for a moment," Van whispered.

"That's fine. Take as long as you want," I said.

Before we left the room, Van turned to me. "Thank you," he said. Then I saw him lean down and kiss his father's cheek.

A few minutes later, Van walked into the hallway. "I'm ready," he said.

"Are you going to wait?" I asked.

"Yes. I'll be here."

I turned around and entered the room, followed by Levine. Before I began, I took photographs of Medgar Evers so DeLaughter could show them to a jury if the investigation went that far.

Then, I stood there for a moment in silence. I'm not sure why but I thought about all the autopsies I had done over the years. I had seen the human body in so many different states of being and it was still beautiful to me. Each body is a miracle of nerves, blood vessels, millions of capillaries. Trillions of cells, all in their proper place. Feelings, insights, pain, and pleasure—those things were, in a way, secondary. When the earth was created, there were two important elements: hydrogen and carbon. Billions of years later, those elements gave rise to the human body. When we die, we decompose back down to hydrogen and carbon, and all of that helps create more life.

An autopsy is a holy thing for me. The person on the table in front of me, on any given day, has lived maybe fifty or sixty years, and I'm going to learn more about them than anybody in the world. I'm going to look at their kidneys and hold their heart in my hands and examine their brain. Life is a gift. When we perform an autopsy, we have a responsibility to take care, to try to learn things to help the family, and to teach others about life and death. You can't make fun of dead bodies. You have to treat each one with the respect you would give a living person. You have to be appreciative of the miracle of life, even after death.

I took a deep breath, thought about that green medallion in my wallet, and picked up the scalpel.

A few hours later, I walked into the hallway. Van Evers was there, sitting in a chair.

"Everything went well," I told him.

Before I could say another word, a phone rang. A trooper picked it up and turned to me, "It's for you," he said.

"Take it, Doctor Baden. I'll fill Van in," DeLaughter said.

I picked up the phone. To my surprise, it was a reporter. Word had gotten out that we were performing an autopsy on a man from Mississippi. We hadn't written Evers's name on any list, so no one knew it was him. But the hospital's diener—the person responsible for handling, cleaning, and moving dead bodies before an autopsy—had spotted a Mississippi label on the casket. He knew about the hush-hush autopsy, put two and two together . . . and concluded the body on the table must belong to Elvis Presley.

Elvis had died in Memphis, Tennessee, in 1977, but he was born in a shotgun house in Tupelo, Mississippi, and that's also where many people believe he was buried. For years, people had puzzled over Elvis's early death: Had drugs caused it, or a heart attack? The reporter had already published the story that we had Elvis on our autopsy table. Now, he wanted to know our findings. I discovered that his story had since gone viral around the world. And no matter how many times I told him and the other reporters who called that they were wrong, the story wouldn't die.

I continued getting phone calls about Elvis for days after we finished the Evers autopsy. I even received a telegram from China asking for a photograph of the dead Elvis. But at least we didn't tip off Beckwith before any new charges could be filed.

◆ ◆ ◆

It was January 1994 and I had just finished packing. I was headed to Jackson, Mississippi, to testify at Beckwith's third murder trial, but I had something else to do before I left. I called Judson. I wanted to let him know that I'd be gone for a few days.

My other children were doing well. Trissa had finished medical school and started her residency. Lindsey was at the Albert Einstein College of Medicine, and planned to become an internist. Sarah would be starting Brown University in the fall.

But I was worried about Judson. So was everyone else. He had graduated from Columbia, but we knew he was struggling with addiction. And one afternoon, in 1988, Sarah and I found him passed out in the bathroom.

It looked like he was sleeping. I could hear him snoring. We called 911 and by the time the ambulance arrived, Judson was groggy but awake. The paramedics checked him and didn't think he needed to go to the hospital.

After they left, I talked with Judianne. We both agreed Judson needed treatment. We didn't want him to go to Odyssey House because he might have prior relationships with the therapists there. And we didn't want him on a methadone program. So, we sent him to a program we knew well: Daytop, in California. When he finished the year-long program, he was clean.

In retrospect, the first sign of Judson's addiction came a few years earlier, back in 1988. I'd gotten a call at the medical examiner's office from a police officer who wanted to inform me that he had just taken my son home. He said Judson had been riding his bicycle in Harlem and that he had watched Judson buy drugs from a man on a street corner. When the officer checked the boy's identification, he knew it was my son. He said he just wanted me to know what had happened. I thanked the officer and rushed home from work.

On the way, I kept thinking: *Why was he there? Was he using drugs?* When I talked to him, Judson denied he was buying drugs—or getting high. He said he was riding his bicycle and got lost. Somehow, he ended up in Harlem and was just asking for directions. I wanted to believe him. I didn't do anything. And I didn't say anything to Judianne. I believed Judson when he said he had never used drugs. And as far as the cop bringing him home, I figured I had been in a lot worse trouble as a kid—I was sent to reform school—and I turned out okay. So would Judson. But that hadn't turned out to be the case.

I was also having mixed feelings toward Judianne. When the kids were growing up, she'd often bring home heroin addicts in treatment who were trying to get clean, some of whom were very bright and nice to the kids. I went along with it even though I wasn't sure exposing our children to drug culture at such a young age was a good thing. Judianne was the psychiatrist, I told myself; she'd know best. Now I wondered: Had Judson's early exposure to drug addicts contributed to his own addiction? My wondering certainly didn't help my marriage.

I asked Judson one time: Why did he start using? He told me he liked the way it made him feel. But at that point, why he'd started shooting up wasn't important. The only thing that was important was making sure he had the emotional and peer support to help him stop. And part of that was calling him frequently to tell him that I loved him and that I'd always be there whenever he wanted to talk. He was never far from my thoughts. It was difficult to know if he was really recovering, and I couldn't help but fear the worst. I dreaded getting a phone call in the middle of the night that Judson had overdosed.

Whenever I called, Judson would answer on the first ring. He was living and working in California. He also was a docent at a local museum. He sounded good. I told him I was headed to Mississippi to testify in the Medgar Evers murder trial. He knew all about the case, and like so many in his generation, he believed the criminal justice system was biased against Black people.

"You're doing a good thing, Dad," he said.

"It'll be on the news. You should follow it."

"I will. Maybe one day we'll work together on a case," he said. Judson had been hinting that he might want to go to law school—something he had been talking about since he was a kid. If he did, I knew what kind of law he'd probably practice. He was always for the underdog.

"I don't know what's going to happen. But I'll let you know. And please let me know if you need anything," I said to him, before hanging up.

◆ ◆ ◆

In the cab on my way to the Albany airport, I tried to put aside my worries about Judson as I thought about how long it had taken the Evers case to even get to this point. He was killed in 1963. I had conducted the autopsy in 1991. Three years later, after my autopsy and other evidence had come to light, Byron De La Beckwith was finally going to trial.

It was big national news. The trial would certainly open old wounds, and maybe Mississippi could finally exorcise its guilt for the racism that led to Evers's murder and De La Beckwith's mistrials. But it was more than that. Evers's death represented the worst of the old South. So many Black men and women had been killed during the civil rights era in the fight for integration, social justice, and voting rights. And so many of the white people who committed those crimes had gotten away with it. This was a chance to right a wrong that had cast a pall over the entire community.

Yet, there was some debate over whether to prosecute Beckwith. Some people said that he was too old, and that that his crimes were long ago, in the old days. No need to dredge that up again. I felt the opposite. We should be trying to prosecute every open civil rights case. What would we say if we found a Nazi hiding in Argentina? Just let him go? Let bygones be bygones?

When I arrived in Jackson, DeLaughter greeted me at the airport. "Are you ready?" he asked.

"Yes. I think everyone is ready," I said.

As we drove to the hotel, I glanced out the window. This was the capital of Mississippi, the heart of the old South, where it seemed every other home had a Confederate flag flying in the front yard.

It was really a small town. Not much of a downtown, just a few office buildings and the courthouse. I could only imagine what it was like here that summer, thirty years earlier, when Evers was killed—with "white only" bathrooms and water fountains and segregated schools.

Or one hundred and fifty years earlier, when just about every Black man or woman on the street would have been someone else's legal property. Or during Jim Crow, when legislators wrote laws targeting newly freed slaves that police would enforce. Racial hatred and injustice weren't things you ended with the stroke of a pen. No, they are generations-long legacies of pain that manifest in so many different ways. DeLaughter was doing the right thing in prosecuting Beckwith. But by itself a guilty verdict wouldn't change anything. How do you address the prejudice that has been passed down from generation to generation? The racial bias that continues to live on in our schools, courthouses, and police departments? Not an easy question to answer.

I checked into the hotel and got some sleep. The next morning, I got up early. I put on a gray suit with a white shirt and navy blue tie.

Having testified at dozens of trials, I'd found the key was presenting scientific evidence in a clear, concise, and understandable way, so the jury wouldn't lose interest. I'd watched too many scientists drone on and on, putting jurors to sleep.

But there was something else I always tried to keep in mind, something Helpern once told me about testifying: Listen to the questions. Answer the questions. Don't volunteer information that isn't asked for. If you do, you run the risk of veering off course and getting into trouble. So, just answer yes or no.

"An expert who testifies should have white hair and hemorrhoids," Helpern had also told me.

"Huh?" I responded.

"White hair to look wise and hemorrhoids to look concerned. You have to impress the jurors," he said.

One of DeLaughter's assistants drove me to the courthouse. Outside, dozens of reporters were waiting to get in. Cameras weren't allowed in the courtroom, but one of the newspapers had hired an artist to sketch scenes from the trial.

When I walked in, there he was. Beckwith. He was seventy, but the deep lines etched in his face made him look older. He wore a three-piece gray suit with a Confederate flag pin on his lapel. He was smirking. He'd seen all this before. He looked confident that the outcome of this trial would be the same: another hung jury.

But unlike the all-white juries of the first two trials, this one had eight Black jurors and four white ones. And one thing was certain: the current governor of Mississippi wouldn't be walking over to shake Beckwith's hand the way then–Governor Ross Barnett did during his first trial, in full view of the jury.

Beckwith was a child of the South. He was born in California, but after his father died, his mother moved back to her hometown of Greenwood, Mississippi. After she died, Beckwith was raised by relatives. He served in the US Marines during World War II, and joined the KKK in the early 1950s.

A Black man like Medgar Evers embodied the worst fears of white Southern men like Beckwith. Evers was a local "boy" who didn't know "his place," and as his eloquent drive for racial equality brought him national prominence, Beckwith's hatred grew—and he wasn't quiet about it. This time, DeLaughter had witnesses who had heard Beckwith talk openly about killing Evers at a KKK rally.

After the jurors were seated, DeLaughter told them all about Beckwith's past as "an unrepentant racist." He called him a violent coward who waged a one-man campaign against integration—"a war to purge society of anyone and anything that was for integration."

DeLaughter said the evidence would show that Beckwith killed Evers with "a bullet that was aimed out of hatred, propelled by prejudice and fired by cowardice, a back-shooting coward at night."

His opening statement was gripping.

When it was Beckwith's attorneys' turn, they didn't dispute that their client's weapon was used to kill Evers. But they said Beckwith had nothing to do with the civil rights leader's death. They told jurors that Beckwith's gun had been stolen before the murder and that someone else had fired the fatal shot.

Then Myrlie was called to the stand. I was curious to see the way prosecutors would address Myrlie when she testified. Three decades earlier, even the prosecutors refused to call her "Mrs. Evers" because of a common practice among white Mississippians to ignore courtesy titles for Black men and women.

This time, it was different. "Mrs. Evers, can you describe that night?" he asked her.

"We were waiting for him to get home," she said. "We heard the car pull into the driveway and the horrible blast, and the children fell to the floor as he taught them to do. I ran to the front door, opened the door, and there was Medgar at the steps leading to the front door with the keys in his hand."

Her voice cracked and her eyes filled with tears when DeLaughter showed her a photo I had taken of her husband after his 1991 exhumation—a picture she had never seen.

"That's Medgar in his casket," she testified.

It was a powerful, emotional testimony.

When I took the stand, I looked at the jurors. I wanted them to feel comfortable with me. I wanted to make the evidence accessible. I described the condition of the body. "It's in a remarkably good state of preservation. It looks as if it was just embalmed the day before."

I said the autopsy and police investigation showed that the bullet ripped through Evers's body, then a window and kitchen wall, before landing on a countertop. From the trajectory and damage, I testified the bullet came from a high-powered rifle.

To make my point, I placed a view box with an X-ray of Evers's chest by the jury. Turning on the machine, I pointed to fractured ribs caused by the bullet. I showed the jury the bullet's trajectory by tracing small lead fragments in Evers's body. The bullet had entered his right back, punctured his right lung, and exited through the right side of his chest.

"This pattern is the trademark of a high-powered rifle," I said. The gun recovered from a thicket of honeysuckle vines in a vacant lot near the Evers home was a 1917 Enfield .30-06 with a scope.

"That rifle can produce that kind of destruction and had Beckwith's fingerprints on it."

Then I showed them a glass test tube with the lead fragments I removed at the autopsy. The jurors passed the tube around, shaking it. The fragments made a tinkling noise against the tube's sides.

I wanted to show that Medgar Evers was a human being—that he was a real man who lived a real life in this very town. The autopsy photos and bullet fragments did that for me. The jurors were engrossed by the evidence. But one person clearly was not. While I testified, I heard what sounded like a snoring noise coming from the right of me. When I turned, I saw Beckwith slumped over the table, fast asleep.

The trial lasted about a week. It didn't take the jury long to come back with a verdict: guilty. Beckwith was convicted and given a life sentence. He lost all his appeals and died in prison in 2001. He was eighty years old.

After testifying, I walked a few blocks to the Collins Funeral Home. I had to find out what they'd done to preserve Evers's body so well for so long.

It was an old, one-story, red-brick building with a wrought-iron awning. When I went inside, I asked for anyone who had worked there in 1963. A sixty-something Black gentleman with gray hair sitting on a three-legged stool said he had worked there for decades. Now, he was one of the owners.

"Are you here from the trial?" he asked.

"Yes."

He broke into a wide grin. "I'll be . . ." Then he recalled the Medgar Evers funeral. It was a high point in their history.

"I was a younger fella then. But everyone was coming in for the funeral from all over the country. Doctor King was coming. Every civil rights leader you could imagine," he said.

"I was very impressed by the good job you guys did in embalming Medgar Evers," I said.

"Well, I started out as an embalmer here. I learned from the best," he said.

Back then, they didn't have refrigeration in the funeral home. They had to bury people quickly, in a day or two, especially in the hot Mississippi summers, or the bodies would begin to smell, he said.

"But we couldn't do that with Medgar. We had too many people coming in," he said.

"So, what did you do?" I asked.

"Well, we gave him three times as much embalming fluid as we usually do."

"That's it?"

"Yup."

People had been looking for "secret ways" to preserve the dead for centuries. And the Collins Funeral Home's secret? More embalming fluid. It made sense. It would prevent the growth of any bacteria that could eat away at the body. As long as you kept water out of the casket, who knows how long the body would stay preserved?

I thanked him and shook his hand, then hurried back to the courthouse. DeLaughter was there, waiting. "You okay?" he asked.

I nodded yes. "I went to the funeral home. The one that handled Medgar Evers body. And a man there shared with me how they preserved his body," I said.

I paused for a moment. I didn't want to get philosophical. But it was striking how well all the pieces had come together for the trial. "His body was in excellent condition. That was important because it meant we could show the jury his picture. That helped them see he wasn't just a name in a history book. And it reminded me of something else."

"What?" he asked.

"What was it that Doctor King said? 'The arc of the moral universe is long, but it bends toward justice'?"

"That's it," he said.

"You know what? After all this, the way Evers's body was preserved, the way the trial turned out, maybe it's true."

I felt good that justice was finally served. And the case had reminded me how vitally important it was for law enforcement agencies to communicate with each other. It was law enforcement cooperation that finally led to Beckwith's conviction.

Maybe there was hope for righting wrongs that occurred decades ago. Maybe things were changing, I thought. But my optimism was short lived. I was about to get involved in a murder case that would show me just how deep the racial divide was in America—and how deep the mistrust between communities of color and the police.

Chapter 12

• • •

O.J.

Over the phone against my ear, an interviewer was peppering me with questions. On the television screen before me, a white SUV was rolling down the freeways of Los Angeles with a suicidal celebrity inside and more than a dozen police vehicles trailing behind.

It was late afternoon on June 17, 1994. O.J. Simpson was in the back seat of that Ford Bronco with a handgun in his lap. His former football teammate, Al Cowling, was driving while trying to talk sense to his friend. Police said that Simpson was periodically pointing the gun at his own head, threating to kill himself.

Around the world, people watched it all on live TV.

This wasn't a high-speed chase. The Bronco didn't exceed the speed limit. No one knew where O.J. was headed, but everyone knew he was on the lam. He had vanished that morning, after police told Simpson's attorney they were coming to arrest the former football star for the murder of his wife, Nicole, and her friend, Ron Goldman.

"Doctor Baden, you were with O.J. today. Can you tell us his state of mind?" Larry King asked through the phone.

"Not good, Larry," I responded. "He was very depressed. I'm worried that he might kill himself."

"He never admitted to the killing, right?" King asked.

"Not to me. He seemed to be bewildered, Larry, why people were so sure that he had killed his wife when he was so bereaved, when he was so upset. He didn't understand why suspicion was pointed at him."

Twelve hours earlier, I had gotten a call from Robert Shapiro at my home in Manhattan. It was 11 PM. He apologized for calling so late, but he wanted me to fly to Los Angeles early the next morning so I could examine Simpson, who was about to be arrested for the murder of his ex-wife. That call was the start of my involvement in one of the nation's most controversial murder trials. At first it seemed like just another celebrity murder case. But I'd soon discover that it was much more. The case would reveal deep divisions in our nation related to race, class, policing, and the criminal justice system. And it brought me back into the orbit of Johnnie Cochran, the lawyer I'd worked with on the Ron Settles case.

In 1994, I was busier than ever. The Medgar Evers trial had just wound up, and everything was going well with the New York State Police. We had helped solve a number of homicides. I had written a book, *Unnatural Death: Confessions of a Medical Examiner*, which looked at some of the most challenging cases of my career. And I had just been approached by HBO to host a new documentary series called *Autopsy*, where I'd reveal the stories behind the cases of unnatural or suspicious deaths that I'd helped to solve.

My work with the state police allowed me to take private cases as long as they didn't conflict with their own possible cases. I was selective, but the cases I did work on outside of New York seemed to raise my public profile a little more. That, in turn, led me to Los Angeles, and the "trial of the century."

My road to the Simpson case began a few years earlier. I had been working at my kitchen table when my phone rang. The man on the other end of the line said, "This is Marlon Brando."

I would have recognized his voice even without him saying his name. He asked if I knew anything about his son Christian's legal troubles. I said I had read a few things in newspapers, but I hadn't been following the case too closely. So, he recounted the basics.

His daughter Cheyenne had been staying at his house in the Hollywood Hills with her boyfriend, Dag Drollet, while she was pregnant. Brando said Drollet had physically abused her. On May 16, 1990, Christian arrived at the house with a gun to confront Drollet and warn him to stop beating his sister.

Brando said his son told him the weapon went off accidentally when Drollet tried to grab it. He said Christian only wanted to scare Drollet—not kill him.

But police were telling a different story. They said Christian didn't shoot Drollet during an argument. They said he murdered Drollet in cold blood, while he was sleeping on a sofa in Brando's house with the television remote control still in his hand.

Only one shot was fired, Brando said. It went in and out. "The medical examiner and the police can't find the bullet."

"What?"

"Investigators haven't been able to find the bullet," Brando said. He explained that the medical examiners didn't find it during the autopsy, nor anywhere in the room. They confirmed it had left Drollet's body, but the police didn't find it in the room, either.

Brando said he didn't know what to do. So, he said called his close friend William Kunstler, a prominent civil rights attorney. The actor said Kunstler recommended hiring me to try to find the bullet.

"Can you do another autopsy?" he asked. "Maybe they missed it."

I agreed to do it.

When I investigate a death, I don't look for motive. I'm not out to prove anyone's guilt or innocence. I look for the cause of death, the time of death, and how the person died. My findings are based on science, not a hidden agenda. I share my conclusions with clients and advise them as to whether those conclusions support or contradict their theory of what happened.

In this case, if I found the bullet and determined that its trajectory matched the "shot-while-asleep" prosecution story, Brando would know that the district attorney had a strong case and that perhaps Christian should consider a plea bargain. If I found what Christian claimed, then the prosecutor might want to reduce the charge.

Brando asked me to fly out quickly, so the next morning, I was on a flight to Los Angeles. He'd made arrangements for me to do the second autopsy at the Los Angeles County Coroner's Office. When Brando's son, Miko, met me at the airport, he drove me directly to the coroner's office, where I conducted my postmortem examination. During the autopsy, I confirmed that the bullet had entered Drollet's jaw and exited the back of his neck—and was not in the body. Miko then drove me to his father's house on Mulholland Drive.

I had been a Marlon Brando fan for decades, but the man I saw inside the big home was not the young, cool Method actor of the 1950s. This Brando weighed about three hundred pounds and was draped in a gray muumuu. His face looked the same, but his body was huge, like Colonel Kurtz, the character he'd played in *Apocalypse Now*.

Brando smiled, then reached out his hand to shake mine. "I'm glad you're here," he said.

He led me into the kitchen, and that's when I first met Robert Shapiro, who was representing Christian. He stood up and greeted me. A moment later, a woman who appeared to be Brando's housekeeper opened the freezer and handed him a carton of vanilla ice cream.

Brando turned to us. "Do you want any?" he asked.

Shapiro and I shook our heads. Brando got up from the table, pulled out a cabinet drawer, and removed a spoon. Sitting back down, he opened the carton and dug in.

I tried to make small talk as he ate. I said I was a big fan and I loved him in the movie *The Rose Tattoo*—the Tennessee Williams story about an Italian American widow in Mississippi who has withdrawn from the world after her husband's death and expects her daughter to do the same.

Brando stopped for a moment and looked at me. "I wasn't in that movie. That was Burt Lancaster."

I felt about two feet tall. I'm not sure why I mixed that up. Maybe I was a little nervous. But Brando was gracious. When I took my notepad from my carry-on bag, he noticed that I had a New York State Police magazine with my photograph on the back cover, holding a smiling baby. He asked me about the infant. I said it was a baby I had examined for the state police in an abuse case. For some reason, he asked me if he could keep the magazine.

"Of course," I said.

I wanted to ask him for a photograph of himself. But I felt that it wasn't professionally appropriate.

As we sat there, we talked about Drollet's death.

"Here's what I think," I said to him. "The medical examiner and I didn't find the bullet in Drollet. That means it still has to be in the room."

"But they already tore apart the place," Shapiro said.

"I understand. But sometimes the cops can miss things. Can I see the room?"

Brando nodded and led me to the large living room where Drollet had been killed.

"Has anything been touched in the room?" I asked.

"They moved some of the furniture, including the couch," Brando said.

I stared at the rug—pink shag carpet. "You can't see bullet holes in shag rugs," I said. "You have to lift the rug or get on your knees to palpate it. Police don't like to do that." So, I dropped to my knees and started patting the carpet surface. A few minutes later, I felt something hard under the carpet. I made an incision in the rug and there it was—the bullet, which had partially flattened when it struck the hard surface underneath.

I showed the bullet to Brando. He had a very curious look on his face. I could tell he was thinking, *Was the bullet good or bad for my son?* But before he had a chance to say anything, I wanted to make sure he understood what we had to do next.

"We've got to call the police. This is evidence. We have to give this to the police," I said.

He sighed. "Yeah. Yeah. Yeah."

Shapiro called the police and they said someone would be there right away. A sergeant arrived pretty quickly and I gave him the bullet.

"This was such a high-profile case. How could they have missed it?" I said to the sergeant.

He looked at the bullet for a moment, then shook his head sadly. "Doc, if you don't do a good job on the ordinary, routine cases, you can't do a better job on the high-profile ones," he said.

It was a lesson I'd learned a long time ago. You have to do things the right way on every case. You can't cut corners on some and do a good job on others. Whether the deceased is a homeless person or a celebrity, you do the best job possible for everyone. That's how you're able to find the little things, the clues that lead you to the truth. And when you discover the facts, you can't cover it up—no matter who it helps or hurts.

I'd later testify that the bullet's trajectory through Drollet's neck and into the shag carpet showed that he had been sitting up on the couch. Gunshot residue tests performed by police showed that Drollet's hand was near the muzzle when it discharged—consistent with Christian's statement that the weapon went off accidentally when Drollet tried to grab it. Christian would plead guilty to involuntary manslaughter and illegal possession of a gun. He was sentenced to a total of ten years and served five before being released.

As for Brando's lawyer, several years later, when Simpson found himself in possible legal trouble, he hired Shapiro. Shapiro then called me to do a second autopsy on the football star's ex-wife.

On June 13, 1994, the bodies of Nicole Brown Simpson and Ronald Goldman, a waiter at a nearby restaurant, were found outside Nicole's Los Angeles home. Nicole had been stabbed seven times in the neck and scalp, and her throat had been slashed. Goldman had been stabbed at least twenty-two times. The steps in front of the house were coated in blood.

Simpson was the prime suspect from the start. He and Nicole married in 1985 and divorced in 1992. During their marriage, Nicole had accused O.J. of domestic violence.

The double homicide generated worldwide attention. A Heisman Trophy winner and a former star National Football League running back, Simpson was retired from football, but he was still a celebrity. He acted in movies and commercials and worked NFL games as a broadcaster. And there was something else: Simpson was Black; Nicole was white.

Three days after the murders, Shapiro called me at home. It was about midnight, but I was often up late, working. He said he had just been retained as Simpson's attorney and wanted me to fly out to Los Angeles as soon as possible.

"He hasn't been charged yet, but I think it's just a matter of time," Shapiro said.

He didn't only want me to do a second autopsy on Nicole. He also asked me to go over all the forensic evidence. He was trying to be proactive, to get a head start on the prosecutors. He told me that Simpson was innocent, but police didn't want to look at other suspects.

"They want O.J. Their total focus is on O.J.," he said.

In retrospect, I didn't know much about O.J. Simpson. I wasn't a football fan. I recognized his name and image from the ubiquitous Hertz commercials, where the handsome athlete ran through airports, jumping over obstacles, on his way to his rental car.

I told Shapiro I would come.

"One more thing," he added. "Do you know a good criminalist?"

A criminalist is someone who examines physical evidence and creates links between scenes, victims, and offenders. They work in crime labs at local, state, and federal law enforcement agencies throughout the United States. I knew just the person. Henry Lee was a high-profile criminalist known for finding the tiniest clues—he once even solved a murder without a body. In the "Wood Chipper" case, Lee discovered that the remains of a flight attendant had been fed through a rented machine that cuts wood into chips. After a tip led authorities to the wood chipper, Lee found enough evidence nearby to lead to the conviction of her husband, an Eastern Air Lines pilot.

Lee was the chief criminalist and director of the Connecticut State Police Forensic Laboratory. He had consulted on thousands of criminal cases, authored countless studies, and written two dozen books. Now, he was focusing on DNA matching, a technique that was just starting to be applied in criminal cases.

"Henry Lee is the best. Let me call him. I'll get right back to you," I said.

I wasn't sure if he'd take this case. He usually testified only for prosecutors in criminal cases. This was different. We were being asked to find trace evidence in the case before charges were filed—information that might point to Simpson or lead police in another direction. Armed with that information, the defense team would come up with a strategy to defend Simpson. They'd also know whether prosecutors were being truthful about the forensic information they were presenting at trial.

When I called Lee a little after midnight, he picked up on the first ring.

"Henry, I know it's late," I said, "but this is important."

I explained that Shapiro had called and wanted us to help with the Simpson case, even though no charges had yet been filed.

"A lot of people are following it," he said.

"I know," I said. "But it seems pretty straightforward."

Lee didn't hesitate. "I'll do it."

"Okay. I'll let Bob know. He wants us out there tomorrow."

"Well, then I'd better get some sleep."

I laughed, then called Shapiro. "Doctor Lee is on board."

"Great." I could hear the excitement in Shapiro's voice.

After I hung up, I sat at my desk. It was 1:30 A.M. I was wired. I knew that, unlike Lee, I wouldn't be able to sleep. So, I packed my bag and gathered my papers. I'd have to let the state police know I would be gone, but with a little luck, I'd have everything wrapped up in a few days.

◆ ◆ ◆

Shapiro booked Henry Lee and me on an early-morning flight from JFK to Los Angeles International Airport.

On the long flight, I was a little worried that some people—including my colleagues—might think my involvement meant I believed Simpson was innocent. If they did, they were wrong.

Forensic pathologists don't testify whether a defendant is guilty or innocent. What we do is discover, collect, and document evidence. Then we testify as to the significance of that evidence relative to the issues in question. Our testimony about the facts should be the same whether we're called by a prosecutor or defense attorney. Whether a defendant is guilty or innocent is decided by the judge or jury and often depends on the attorneys' presentation.

When I'm hired, I don't have an opinion about someone's guilt or innocence, because I don't want that to influence my analysis of the forensic facts. And when I testify as an expert forensic pathologist, my job is to answer the attorneys' questions. As Joe Friday, the detective from the TV show *Dragnet*, would say, "All we want are the facts, ma'am."

Was Simpson guilty or innocent of the two murders? Did he cover up for someone? I couldn't testify about that. I could only testify about the cause of

Nicole Simpson's and Ronald Goldman's deaths, how they died, and when they died. I wasn't there to exonerate Simpson or convict him. I hoped my colleagues at the New York State Police would understand.

When we arrived, Shapiro greeted us at the gate, then led us to his car. He said he was taking us to a house where Simpson had been hiding from the media.

Lee and I had no idea where that was or what to expect. We just sat back and enjoyed the scenery. But as we approached a spectacular pink Beverly Hills mansion, Shapiro slowed down. The front gate slid open and he drove up the long driveway through a small forest of manicured plants and trees.

Shapiro said it was Robert Kardashian's place. Kardashian and Simpson had been friends since 1969, and Simpson had holed up here in what had become his second home. Kardashian was also one of Simpson's attorneys. When the door opened, Shapiro introduced us to Kardashian and his wife, Kris, and their three small daughters, all dressed in white.

"Where is he?" Shapiro asked.

"Second floor," Kardashian said.

"How is he doing?"

"Not well."

Lee and I followed Shapiro through a lobby with marble floors and high ceilings, and up a wrap-around staircase to the second floor. There was an Old World elegance to the five-bedroom, 7,100-square-foot house. The California sun flooded through the tall windows and reflected off the polished stone.

I took a deep breath. I was a little tired after the long flight. Now that we were here, I was hoping my adrenaline would kick in.

Kardashian opened a door, and there was Simpson, sitting on a chair. He lifted his head to acknowledge our presence. His eyes were blank. He looked depressed.

"O.J., this is Doctor Baden and Doctor Lee. They're here to help," Shapiro said.

He nodded. Simpson understood why we'd come, but his mind clearly was a million miles away. I knew that look. I had seen it many times on inmates who'd run out of hope. I sensed this man was on the verge of a breakdown.

We told Simpson that we needed him to undress to his underwear so we could collect hair samples and look for bruises. He nodded and began to disrobe.

As he was removing his clothes, I turned to Shapiro and quietly said, "Bob, there's a problem. I'm worried about O.J."

"I know. He's taking it hard."

"No. He has to be watched. He can't be left alone. He's obviously very depressed. I think he could be suicidal," I said.

The last few days had probably been a blur for Simpson. He was in a daze. And, now, he had to face reality. He might be charged with murder. His world was collapsing. I told Shapiro that if Simpson were arrested, he should be placed on suicide watch.

According to media reports, if Simpson did commit the murders, he had done so in a very short window of time.

Nicole had gone out to dinner with her family at a local restaurant but had left her eyeglasses there. Goldman, one of the waiters, volunteered to bring them to her house. He left the restaurant at 9:50 PM.

At the same time, Simpson was getting ready to leave on a business trip to Chicago. His house was a few miles down the road from his former wife's.

At 10:15 PM, one of Nicole's neighbors heard a dog incessantly barking. Meanwhile, at Simpson's house, a limo driver arrived at 10:25 PM to take him to the airport for a business trip. Simpson kept him waiting. He didn't go outside to the car until sometime after 11 PM. The limo arrived at the airport at 11:35 PM, and his flight left around fifteen minutes later.

The bodies of Nicole Simpson and Goldman were found at about 12:10 AM.

The timeline was tight. If Simpson had killed them, he had moved very fast and disposed of the evidence with incredible efficiency.

Of course, we didn't know anything yet. The forensics might help fill in the gaps, or open new possibilities.

Simpson was ready, so Lee and I put on surgical gloves and began working. Lee pulled hair samples from Simpson's head and groin area. I took pictures of Simpson's body as we looked for bruises, scratches, and blunt-force injuries. We didn't find anything except a healing cut on one finger. Simpson said he hurt himself when he broke a glass in a hotel bathroom in Chicago, after he was told about his wife's death.

"I was upset," he told us.

Kardashian occasionally poked his head into the room to see how things were going. Then Shapiro's cell phone rang. It was the prosecutor's office. The district attorney was writing up an arrest warrant for Simpson.

"Where are you?" the person on the other line asked Shapiro.

"I'm with O.J.," he said.

"Where are you?"

"I won't tell you now. You get the arrest warrant, then I'll tell you," he said. He hung up and said we had to hurry. About fifteen minutes later his phone rang again. He took a deep breath, then clicked on the call.

"We got the warrant," the voice said.

Shapiro sighed. "We're at Kardashian's house." He hung up and turned to Lee and me. "You guys better hurry up and finish. The police are on the way over."

"We're done," I said.

Simpson dressed and went into an adjacent bedroom. He didn't come back. We asked where he was, and Shapiro said he was probably saying good-bye to his girlfriend, who was also in the house. Shapiro left the room.

Lee and I went to the window, which overlooked the front entrance to the house, to see if the police had arrived yet. Moments later, Kardashian opened the door and took us to another room on the second floor. This one faced the backyard. Time dragged on. After about fifteen minutes, Lee and I began wondering if we'd been forgotten.

"It's taking a long time for them to get here," I said to Lee.

Suddenly Shapiro barged into the room, frantic. "Is O.J. with you?" he asked us.

"No," Lee said.

"The police are here, and they can't find O.J. I can't believe this is happening," he said.

Moments later, police officers walked into the room. "What the hell is going on here?" one officer said.

We shrugged. We had no idea.

"Don't go anywhere," an officer told the two of us.

It looked like O.J. had slipped away, and the cops thought we'd helped him along. Then, recognition dawned on another policeman, who had met Lee at a seminar. "Doctor Lee, what are you doing here?" he asked, incredulous that he might be working for the defense.

They let Lee go but held Shapiro and me a little longer. While I was waiting on the second floor, I looked down to the lobby below and saw Kardashian surrounded by a group of reporters. As he stared into the TV cameras' bright lights, Kardashian began reading aloud a note he said Simpson had written and left behind.

Simpson professed his innocence, adding that he loved Nicole. Toward the end, Simpson's letter began sounding more and more like a suicide note, especially when he said goodbye to his friends: "I can't go on. No matter what the outcome, people will look and point. I can't take that. I can't subject my children to that. This way, they can move on and go on with their lives."

Eventually, they released me, and I headed to my hotel. When I checked into my room, I immediately turned on the television. And there he was, Simpson, in that white Bronco on the freeway.

The phone on the nightstand rang. It was Larry King. I had known King for years and had been on his show several times. Whenever I was involved in a high-profile case, he'd try to reach out to me.

King said he heard that I might be working on the Simpson case. So, he tracked me down at the Beverly Hilton. The moment I said hello, I was on the air. The CNN talk show host was asking me questions as the Bronco traveled on the highway.

"My concern is that this could really wind up being a suicide," I told him.

A little while later, Simpson's car turned into the driveway of his home. Jason, his son from his first marriage, was there. He ran into the driveway, pleading with his father to give himself up. I don't know what he said to Simpson, but soon after, he surrendered. If his son hadn't run to meet the car, I think Simpson might have shot himself.

Simpson was taken into custody. Now, Lee and I could settle into our work, analyzing the evidence. Shapiro had called the Los Angeles County Coroner's Office to see if we could examine the bodies. He was told that they had already been released to the funeral parlors and the families did not want a second autopsy. (If the family didn't give authorization for a second postmortem examination, we couldn't legally do it.) So, we visited the crime scene and then went to O.J.'s home. We looked at many pairs of his shoes to see if any matched the bloody shoeprints we saw at the scene. They did not.

Now that criminal charges had been filed, O.J. was in serious legal trouble. When I'd flown out to Los Angeles, I thought I'd analyze evidence at the scene and the coroner's office and then leave. Maybe I'd come back to testify if there was a trial. I thought that would be the extent of my involvement.

But it turned out, this was just the beginning.

◆ ◆ ◆

It was July 1994, and once again, I was on a flight to Los Angeles, my third trip in the last month. And it surely wouldn't be my last. The O.J. Simpson case kept getting bigger and bigger, a blend of real-life crime and fizzy celebrity entertainment. The cable news networks couldn't get enough. Simpson's face was on magazine covers and newspaper front pages everywhere.

A few of my colleagues at the New York State Police questioned why I wasn't working for the prosecutors. In their world, prosecutors were the Good Guys. Simpson was the suspect, which made him the Bad Guy. In their eyes, anybody helping him was a Bad Guy, too.

I didn't believe that—and I said so. Whether testifying for the prosecution or defense, experts should use forensic science to find the facts. Either the fingerprints or tire tracks or genetic markers match, or they don't.

When I work on a case, I always ask myself a simple question: If I'd been hired by the other side, would I come to the same conclusions? If I determine that a man died from a chokehold in police custody, would I reach the same conclusion regardless of who I was working for, the district attorney or the victim's family? The answer should always be yes.

It didn't matter who hired me—the defense or the prosecution. My forensic science opinion would be the same. We are all working for justice, and therefore, in theory, we should all be friendly colleagues. Of course, that "kumbaya" approach doesn't work in real life. Prosecutors and defense lawyers have egos, and the "win or lose" system encourages them to see each other as the enemy. And that animosity often extends to the experts the other side uses.

Lawyers serve a different function than criminalists or forensic scientists. They look out for their client—no matter what the evidence says. That's what Shapiro was doing for Simpson. That's why he hired me and Henry Lee. And that's why he was adding more attorneys and experts to the Simpson team. With each new batch of hires, Shapiro would ask me to fly to Los Angeles to update them on the science of the case. When he asked me to recommend DNA experts, since the science was becoming important in the investigation, I suggested Barry Scheck and Peter Neufeld. The two civil rights attorneys had founded the Innocence Project, a nonprofit group that used DNA to free prisoners wrongly convicted of crimes. Shapiro hired them.

Using DNA was still a relatively new forensic technique in 1994. The structure of deoxyribonucleic acid was discovered in 1953, but it was only in the late 1980s that scientific advances allowed it to be used to identify an individual. A person's unique genetic code is present in their blood, skin, hair, semen, and saliva. During criminal investigations, criminalists could collect items at a crime scene that might have been touched or worn by a suspect. Scientists at police labs then could extract these biological materials from the items and create what they called a DNA profile.

When investigators identified a suspect, they'd compare that person's DNA to the DNA found at the crime scene. It was a technique that was incredibly accurate. Police used DNA matching to identify criminals. Others, like Scheck and Neufeld, were using it to exonerate innocent people convicted of crimes.

There was a specific chain of custody, or protocol, that went along with collecting DNA. You had to be careful not to contaminate the evidence with your own DNA, or that of others you might have come into contact with, so you had to take extra precautions, like wearing gloves and bagging each item individually. Investigators were still learning the correct way to collect and handle DNA evidence.

Along with Scheck and Neufeld, Shapiro recruited F. Lee Bailey, a legendary criminal trial lawyer and flamboyant courtroom advocate. Bailey had represented some of the most notorious defendants in US history, including Samuel Sheppard, a doctor accused of murdering his wife. (The case was the inspiration for the television series and movie *The Fugitive*.)

Then there was Alan Dershowitz, a Harvard Law School professor and one of the top civil liberties attorneys in the nation. We had worked together on several cases, including the murder trial of Claus von Bülow, a socialite accused of attempting to murder his wife by injecting her with insulin. (It was my opinion that the evidence showed that von Bülow's wife ended up in a coma because of her own drug and alcohol use. He was acquitted in the second trial.)

The reason for my latest flight to Los Angeles was to brief the newest member of O.J. Simpson's legal team: Johnnie Cochran.

Since Cochran and I had worked together on the Settles case in 1982, his reputation had grown. If someone in the Black community was hurt or killed in a police encounter, they'd call Johnnie Cochran.

And why not? He was a smart, charismatic, talented lawyer who didn't seem to lose. He'd fight city hall and, more times than not, win big settlements for his clients.

Reporters were calling O.J.'s defense lineup "the Dream Team." The sobriquet had been coined for the US Olympic men's basketball team in 1992, which included superstars Michael Jordan, Larry Bird, Earvin "Magic" Johnson, and Charles Barkley.

A star-studded legal team didn't mean O.J. Simpson was going to be acquitted. Shapiro was still trying to create a coherent legal strategy.

Lee and I knew our roles: to analyze the forensic evidence for the defense. Shapiro had asked me to brief each of the new attorneys and their staffers on the latest forensic findings. Now, it was Cochran's turn.

When the Boeing 757 landed at Los Angeles International Airport on July 23, 1994, I was ready. A driver from the Cochran law firm drove me to his office.

I was thinking about how far Cochran had come since we met in 1982. On the plane I'd read a New York *Daily News* story that listed his famous clients. When football great James Brown was accused of rape in 1985, Cochran got the charges dropped. Four years later, when former TV child star Todd Bridges was charged with shooting a drug dealer, Cochran won an acquittal. When pop star Michael Jackson was accused of sexually abusing a thirteen-year-old boy, Cochran worked out an agreement with the accuser and his family to drop the charges.

I was also thinking about Simpson's arraignment. I was there in Los Angeles just one day after Simpson, looking grim and haggard, had pleaded not guilty to charges of murdering his ex-wife and Goldman. But at this point, I had to block out everything, including theories about Simpson's role in the murders, and focus on one thing: the scientific evidence.

The driver pulled up to a Wilshire Boulevard address, a new, ten-story, red-brick office building with dark windows. The receptionist waved me through to a conference room at the end of a long hallway. As I moved closer, I could hear voices. When I stepped inside, Cochran was there, sitting at the head of a rectangular table, flanked by six attorneys, their assistants, and reams of papers and documents. I was the only white person there. Cochran took pride in having an all-Black office.

Cochran stopped in mid-sentence. He stood up, stepped over, and hugged me. "Doctor Baden, good to see you again," he said.

"I'm glad to be here," I told him.

He pointed to the table. "Sit down. We were wrapping up a few things."

I sat down next to his assistant Carl Douglas, but Cochran continued to stand. He didn't waste any time. "Doctor Baden is one of the best forensic scientists in the country. He helped me a long time ago, with Ron Settles. And I'm glad he's here now, because he's a fighter."

Some of the lawyers nodded their heads. Cochran commanded the room, and he was prepared. He had talked to Simpson and investigators. Now, he wanted to go over the nuts and bolts of the autopsy reports and other forensics with me.

"A lot of things weren't done right," I said.

I knew Los Angeles's chief medical examiner, Lakshmanan Sathyavagiswaran, who everyone referred to as Lucky. When he was in medical school in New York City, he'd come down to the medical examiner's office and help with autopsies. At the time, he was considering becoming an internist. But like me, he enjoyed autopsies so much, he changed his mind and became a forensic pathologist.

I told Cochran and the others that Lucky was a good medical examiner. But I said critical mistakes were made when evidence was collected during the crime scene investigation. No one from the medical examiner's office had responded to the scene quickly enough to examine the bodies there and evaluate the time of death based on the postmortem changes. When they did come, it was just to take them to the morgue.

I had examined the outdoor crime scene photos taken before Nicole's body was removed. There were many blood spatters on her prone back. Most were small cast-off drops from the knife's blade. But I said there were a few large drops that probably came from the killer. Blood is very slippery. And after multiple stabbings, the attacker's palm sometimes slips down the handle onto the upper blade, cutting the hand and leaving behind the big drops of blood apparent in the photographs. If swabs of those potentially incriminating blood drops had been taken for DNA, the person they came from might have been identified. Instead, Nicole's body was turned over onto her back, placed in a heavy plastic bag, and transported to the morgue, where it was washed by autopsy technicians before it was examined by a medical examiner. Any trace evidence on the body—blood, saliva, semen, hair, fibers—was cleaned away.

Those plastic body bags were also a problem. When a body is put in a bag, some trace evidence—such as the blood drops on Nicole's back—rubs off and is lost. And because the bags are often used more than once owing to their cost, DNA from previously transported bodies can contaminate newer evidence.

The murder weapon hadn't been found. But Lucky said one knife was probably used on both victims. He said that Simpson's wife was ambushed, hit on the head, and incapacitated when the killer slit her throat. He thought Goldman was caught in a small garden area outside the house and injured himself flailing against the trees. Lucky said that was how Goldman ended up with bruises on his hands.

But the forensic evidence didn't support that theory. There were bloodstains on Goldman's lower pants and the tops of his shoes that indicated he was standing, facing the attacker and fighting with him, while he was being stabbed.

"It shows that she and Goldman fought for their lives and took longer to die than the coroner contends," I told Cochran and his associates. "They didn't die quickly. She had injuries on her hands that were consistent with defensive wounds. And Goldman's knuckle was bruised, indicating that he struck the suspect. When we examined O.J., he didn't have any bruises on his body."

After an hour, Cochran had heard enough.

"What's really interesting is what wasn't done. All the mistakes they made," Cochran said.

By the time I finished my report, I later learned, Cochran had already mapped out a good portion of what would become Simpson's defense strategy. The team would raise questions about all the mistakes police made collecting forensic evidence. But Cochran wasn't finished. He planned to focus on something else that he knew would resonate loudly with jurors—race.

Chapter 13

• • •

IF IT DOESN'T FIT...

In early January 1995, a jury of four men and eight women was empaneled by the prosecutors and defense attorneys for O.J. Simpson's trial. One juror was Hispanic, one was white, two were of mixed race, and eight were Black.

The trial was expected to last from six to eight months. I was practically living in Los Angeles by then, advising Simpson's attorneys on forensic evidence that was expected to be presented in court.

Henry Lee and I had examined it all. We had gone over Simpson's house, clothing—particularly his shoes—to find any evidence there. We were surprised to learn that even though a bloody shoe print was found at the crime scene, no one from the prosecution had visited Simpson's house to look for a match. We didn't find a shoe at Simpson's home that matched the crime scene imprint.

Dr. Lee and I also spent a long time working out the time of death. When did the victims actually die? Prosecutors kept pushing for 10:15 PM, citing the barking dog. We pushed back, saying using a dog to determine the time of death was not supported by science.

I believed the criminalist's and medical examiner's failures to collect blooddrop swabs from Nicole's back and their sloppiness in the crime scene investigation could raise serious questions about the reliability of the prosecution's evidence.

The trial began on January 24, 1995, and it seemed that everyone in America was watching.

In their opening statement, Marcia Clark and Chris Darden, the lead prosecutors, laid out their case to the jury. Nicole and O.J. had been married for seven years and divorced for two, they reminded jurors.

"He killed her out of jealousy. He killed her because he couldn't have her, and if he couldn't have her, he didn't want anybody else to have her," Darden argued.

In Cochran's opening statement, he made it clear that race would be the cornerstone of Simpson's defense. He would portray Simpson as another Black man in America being framed by white cops and prosecutors.

Addressing the jurors, he invoked the words of the Reverend Martin Luther King Jr.: "He said it best when he said that 'injustice anywhere is a threat to justice everywhere.' So, we are now embarked upon a search for justice, this search for truth, this search for the facts."

He said the prosecutors weren't interested in the truth—they were only interested in punishing Simpson, a successful Black man.

"This case is about a rush to judgment, an obsession to win at any cost," he said, adding that the jurors were the "conscience of the community."

"Your verdicts set the standards of what we should have and what should happen in this community. You have this rare opportunity, it seems to me, to be participants in this search for justice and for truth," he said.

In effect, Cochran was telling the court—and the nation—that the Simpson case was as much about racial justice as it was about murder.

It was ironic that race was the foundation of Simpson's defense. For most of his career as an athlete, actor, and sportscaster, Simpson had shied away from the topic. He was one of the first crossover stars, someone who appealed to both white and Black audiences. He was likable and nonthreatening to white people.

Although he played college football at the University of Southern California in the late 1960s—a time of social unrest—Simpson never spoke out against racial injustice like Muhammad Ali, Bill Russell, Kareem Abdul-Jabbar, or other Black athletes. Instead, he focused on marketing himself and considered his skin color irrelevant. As Simpson liked to say, "I'm not Black. I'm O.J."

But Cochran knew what he was doing. He understood the landscape in Los Angeles. He knew how Black and Hispanic residents felt about the LAPD—how they had been targeted by law enforcement for years.

This was a period of simmering racial unrest not only in Los Angeles but also the rest of the country. The animosity of the 1990s was different from the discrimination of the 1960s. Back during the civil rights movement, the protests largely centered on desegregating the South. Activists conducted sit-ins to integrate schools and restaurants. They organized large, peaceful protests to make sure Black people were able to vote.

But discrimination had become more nuanced. It was illegal to tell a Black family they couldn't move into a white neighborhood, but banks, real estate agents, and school districts found quiet ways to keep communities segregated.

Much of the current racial unrest focused on the police.

Police departments were integrated, but it didn't halt racial profiling. Officers continued to stop Black and Hispanic people in their cars or on the street without probable cause or on the slimmest pretext.

It was still potentially fatal for a Black person to walk or drive through a white neighborhood. The police would arrive, a confrontation might ensue, and a suspect could end up injured—usually a Black or Hispanic citizen at the hands of one or more white cops. If the suspect died, the police often blamed the victim. White officers were rarely charged. If they were, they were usually acquitted. That only built up anger and frustration in communities of color.

What happened to Rodney King proved the point.

In March 1991, King, who was on parole for robbery, had led police on a high-speed chase through Los Angeles. When he finally stopped, King was ordered out of the car.

LAPD officers then beat him with batons and kicked him repeatedly for a reported fifteen minutes. But there was a difference between this police brutality case and others: a bystander with a camera filmed the confrontation. The video showed that more than a dozen cops watched and commented on the beating. King sustained facial fractures and a broken leg and teeth.

Ultimately, four officers were charged with excessive use of force. A year later, on April 29, 1992, a jury consisting of twelve residents from the distant suburbs of Ventura County—nine white, one Latino, one biracial, one Asian American—found the four officers not guilty.

Los Angeles exploded. Residents set fires and looted and destroyed liquor stores, groceries, shops, and fast-food restaurants. Light-skinned motorists were pulled out of their cars and beaten.

The uprising in South Central Los Angeles was particularly violent. More than half of the population was Black. Unemployment stood at 50 percent, a drug epidemic was ravaging the area, and gangs and violent crime were rampant. The unrest was an outlet for the frustrations of people without hope.

During the five days of rioting, more than fifty people died, including ten shot and killed by LAPD officers and National Guardsmen. More than two thousand people were injured, and nearly six thousand alleged looters and arsonists were arrested. More than a thousand buildings were damaged or destroyed. In all, approximately $1 billion worth of property was lost.

But it wasn't just King. There were other police brutality cases across the United States that hadn't been documented by cameras, including a high-profile one in Detroit that I had examined a few years before Simpson's. That case had been a harbinger of things to come.

On November 5, 1992, a pair of white plainclothes Detroit police officers approached Malice Green, a thirty-five-year-old Black man they said they knew was a drug addict, who was sitting in a car in front of a known drug house on the city's west side.

When officers Walter Budzyn and Larry Nevers asked Green for identification, he did not respond. Instead, he walked around to the passenger side of the car and got it. When Green opened the glove box, the officers said, something fell to the floor, which Green quickly grabbed. The officers yelled for him to open his hand and let them see, but Green didn't comply.

So, there on the busy street, Budzyn and Nevers began beating him. Nevers used his heavy metal flashlight as a weapon, hitting Green more than a dozen times on the head. Soon more police officers arrived. But by then, Green was unconscious.

There was disagreement about what was in Green's fist. Police said they thought it was drugs. Bystanders said it was a piece of paper and his keys. Green wasn't clutching drugs in his hand, but police said they found crack cocaine in his car. It didn't matter. Green was dead on arrival at Detroit Receiving Hospital.

Green, an unemployed steelworker, instantly became a national face of police brutality. His deadly encounter with police stirred racial tensions in the region.

It came out that Budzyn and Nevers, who had called themselves "Starsky and Hutch" after the TV series about two detectives who played by their own rules, had a history of disciplinary problems.

In a move that was even more unusual then than now, the city took action against the officers. Detroit's police chief condemned Budzyn and Nevers, along with other cops at the scene who didn't step in to stop the violence. He suspended seven officers without pay.

Meanwhile, an autopsy by Wayne County assistant medical examiner Kalil Jiraki called the death a homicide. It said that Green died of blunt-force injury to the head and brain. The prosecutor's office presented the case to a grand jury, which returned second-degree murder charges against Budzyn and Nevers.

Assistant Wayne County Prosecutor Kim Worthy handled the case. As Worthy was preparing for trial, she saw that the officers' defense lawyers had hired three medical examiners who strongly disagreed with Jiraki's finding. They said the head and brain injuries did not cause Green's death—drugs and heart disease did.

So, Worthy asked me to review the records. I said yes. This was an important case—the first time I had been involved in legal proceedings where white police officers were on trial for the death of a Black man.

The records showed Green's drug use and his health were emerging as crucial elements for the defense. The three defense experts said the autopsy was flawed because the blows to the victim's head alone were not enough to kill him. They maintained that Green died from a heart condition exacerbated by a deadly mixture of crack cocaine, alcohol, stress, and adrenaline. I had to reread their findings to make sure I had them right. This was just a variant of psychosis with exhaustion—that bogus diagnosis some medical examiners had been using to exonerate police officers for decades.

After a thorough review, I agreed with Jiraki's analysis.

As expected, during the trial, the defense experts told the jurors that cocaine and alcohol in Green's blood, combined with the blows to the head and stress, had triggered a fatal heart attack—a natural death.

"I feel very strongly that in this case, cocaine has a lot to do with the demise of this young man," Haresh Mirchandani, chief medical examiner for Philadelphia, testified. "You have a person that is literally saturated with adrenaline because of cocaine. Then you add stress and blows to the head; it is flooding the body with adrenaline, and the heart can stop beating."

When I testified, I told the jury that the cocaine level was high enough to cause bad behavior but not death, and that Green did not die of a heart attack. No, he died of severe brain concussions from multiple blows to the head. Homicide.

I explained that the pounding from the flashlight caused massive bleeding across the surface of Green's brain and jostled the brain tissue underneath, disrupting the nerves controlling his breathing.

Nevers's defense lawyer John Goldpaugh was visibly annoyed by my answer. "How do you know that he died from a concussion when concussions can't be seen?" he asked. He noted that a concussion can cause a loss of consciousness and death without leaving a visible injury on the brain. It interferes with how your brain works and doesn't show up on X-rays.

I shook my head. My analysis, in part, was based on common sense. I reminded the jurors that both sides agreed about one thing: the officers repeatedly hit Green in the head with a heavy flashlight until he lost consciousness. He never regained it. The cops said they did it because Green was out of control, a threat to their safety.

Without warning, Judge George Crockett III turned to me. He handed me his open Bible and directed me to read Hebrews 11:1. This was the first time a judge had ever asked me to read a Bible in court. I glanced at the passage, took a deep breath, then read it so everyone in the court could hear: "Faith is the substance of things hoped for, evidence of things not seen."

"Like concussions, for example," Crockett said. Fatal injuries, he was implying, are not necessarily visible at autopsy.

Budzyn and Nevers were convicted a month after the trial began. Nevers was sentenced to serve twelve to twenty-five years in prison and Budzyn was sentenced to eight to eighteen years.

Later, however, their convictions were overturned, because while the jury was waiting to be sequestered, they were shown the movie *Malcom X*. The officers' attorneys claimed that had influenced the jury because it showed scenes of police brutality. In subsequent trials, the officers were convicted on a lesser charge of involuntary manslaughter.

Cochran knew about the Green case and told me that he was concerned that police racism wasn't any better in Los Angeles. He knew all about the LAPD's long history of police misconduct and he planned to bring it up during Simpson's trial. Cochran had experienced it himself.

In 1979, he was driving his three daughters in his car when several police cars "squealed to a halt around him." They leaped out of their cars with their guns drawn.

"Get out with your hands up," an officer said through a bullhorn.

The cops then aggressively searched his car—a Rolls-Royce with Cochran's initials on the license plate. Back then, Cochran was already a successful attorney who fought racial profiling. He still had his badge from when he worked for the district attorney's office, and when the officers saw it, they stopped searching the car and left. Cochran didn't file a complaint, but he knew why they targeted him in the first place: as he'd quipped during my work on the Settles case, he was a Black man driving an expensive car in a white neighborhood.

Cochran wasn't anti-police. His father was a cop. Cochran had worked for the prosecutor's office. But he knew that law enforcement was a hotbed of racism, and that communities of color were paying the price. He said minority communities were entitled to the same rights as white Americans. Tactics the police used in Black and Hispanic neighborhoods would never be tolerated in suburban white communities.

Cochran's view was that Simpson was the victim of racist law enforcement officials who had fabricated evidence to frame him for a crime he did not commit.

O.J. Simpson was a star. He drove expensive cars, wore good suits, lived in a tony neighborhood. Maybe most galling of all to the bigoted mind, he was a Black man who had married a beautiful white woman.

"Race plays a part of everything in America," Cochran said when asked about bringing the subject up in the trial.

Cochran knew he had a receptive audience, since eight of the jurors were Black. And he felt certain that many of them, like him, had been stopped and harassed by police for no other reason than the color of their skin. So, as the case unfolded, whenever Cochran got the chance, he'd remind jurors of the LAPD's sordid racist past.

◆ ◆ ◆

The prosecutors went first. It was their job to prove that Simpson committed the murders. They started by showing jurors many crime scene photos with gruesome shots of the victims.

Cochran objected, arguing that they were "more prejudicial than probative." But Prosecutor Clark said it was critical that jurors see the evidence for themselves.

Judge Lance Ito decided that about ninety color photographs could be shown—with a caveat. He wanted to keep the disturbing images from everyone except the jury. So, before discussing a particular photograph, prosecutors would post it on a big screen facing the jury box. Ito allowed one member of the defense team to view the images in question.

Cochran designated me as that person. So, after each picture went up, I headed to a spot next to the jurors, looked at the photographs with the jury, then later described the images to the defense.

As I spent time standing next to the jury box, something strange happened. I couldn't speak to the jurors, but through eye contact and body language, we began to form a bond. We were all forced to look at the same photographs, often showed many times by the prosecutors. Some would nod or smile at me when I approached them. That familiarity helped later when prosecutors tried to shred my credibility. I had already developed a rapport with the jurors, so they didn't think I was such a bad guy.

The pictures posed another unintended—but more critical—problem for the prosecutors. The first few times the pictures went up, I could see the jurors' shock and revulsion. A few struggled to maintain their composure. Others fought back tears. But the images, with repetition, lost their shock value and began to have the opposite effect. Some jurors became numb. At times they seemed annoyed that they had to look at them again.

As the trial continued, prosecutors pinned their hopes on evidence collected from the crime scene. But there were issues with this strategy from the start. The first detectives to arrive noted a bloody fingerprint on the gateway at Nicole's house. Somehow, the fingerprint was not properly collected. Detective Mark Fuhrman listed it in his notes, but no further action was taken to secure it. The detectives who took over after Fuhrman's shift at the crime scene apparently were never told about the print, and it was either lost or destroyed.

Other important items of evidence were also not logged or entered into the chain of custody, which made the forensic collection procedure look sloppy.

That led to other questions. Prosecutors said they found blood on a pair of socks in O.J. Simpson's bedroom, blood that contained his former wife's genetic markers. They said blood found in Simpson's Ford Bronco was a mixture of genetic markers of Simpson and his victims.

But a prosecution witness acknowledged the evidence was often mishandled. Photos were taken of critical evidence without rulers in them to aid in measurement. Items were photographed without being labeled and logged, making it difficult, if not impossible, to link the photos to any specific area of the scene. Most crucially for the reliability of DNA evidence, separate items were bagged together instead of separately, causing cross-contamination.

Police used a blanket that came from inside the house to cover Nicole, contaminating the body and the area surrounding it. Police didn't only use poor evidence-collection protocols; the officers' bloody shoe prints may have obliterated any prints the perpetrator left behind.

Throughout the investigation, there were also issues with how evidence was secured. About two milliliters of Simpson's blood were missing from a vial of evidence—maybe. Investigators didn't know for sure. There was no documentation of how much blood was taken from Simpson in the first place. The person who drew the blood could only guess he had taken eight milliliters. LAPD could only account for six. Worse, the blood was not immediately turned over as evidence but was carried around by a detective for several hours before it was entered into the chain of custody, allowing for speculation as to when and how the two milliliters of blood may have disappeared.

The security of the LAPD's storage and labs was brought under scrutiny as well when it was discovered that some pieces of evidence had been accessed and altered by unauthorized people. Simpson's Bronco was entered at least twice by unauthorized people while in the impound yard.

Maybe evidence was mishandled, Cochran posited. But maybe something more nefarious happened—maybe evidence was planted.

Enter Fuhrman, the first detective on the scene. Cochran called him a racist cop who was out to get Simpson.

Kathleen Bell, a real estate agent, testified that Fuhrman had used racial slurs while speaking to her a decade earlier. Laura McKinny, a writer who was composing a screenplay and novel about the experiences of female police officers, had thirteen hours of taped interviews with Fuhrman between 1985 and 1994. On the tapes, Fuhrman used the N-word and described police brutality perpetrated against Black suspects. Clips from the tapes were introduced as evidence, including Fuhrman making a reference to the planting of evidence—thus implying that police brutality and evidence planting were common practices in the LAPD.

Investigators said they found a single bloody glove at the crime scene. Fuhrman said a few hours later he found the matching glove about a mile away, outside Simpson's house. Fuhrman was alone when he made the discovery.

Prosecutors believed the gloves were among the biggest pieces of evidence against Simpson. DNA tests showed blood on the glove found at Simpson's house contained genetic markers from Simpson, Nicole, and Goldman. Cochran argued that the glove was planted there by Fuhrman, because the racist police officer wanted to frame Simpson.

Under oath, Fuhrman recounted what he saw and did after arriving at the crime scene. But during cross-examination, Bailey methodically tore down his testimony. Fuhrman recounted to the jury that he had once answered a domestic violence call at the Simpson house in 1985. Bailey implied that Furhman was angry to find the Black celebrity was married to a white woman.

Cochran said Fuhrman wanted revenge.

When asked if he had falsified police reports or planted evidence in the Simpson case, Fuhrman suddenly and unexpectedly invoked his Fifth Amendment rights against self-incrimination.

Bailey suggested that Fuhrman was a suspiciously overeager investigator. His discovery of the glove on Simpson's property when he was by himself made him indispensable to the prosecution's case.

Months later, the controversy over the gloves reached a crescendo. During testimony by an executive from a glove manufacturer, Darden asked that

Simpson try the gloves on. Cochran didn't object, and Judge Ito allowed it. First, Simpson put on thin surgical gloves first to protect any trace evidence inside the leather ones. He grimaced as he struggled to pull on one leather glove, and then, after approaching the jury box, tried to don the other. He shook his head and pinched the ends of his fingers showing he couldn't squeeze his hands in all the way. "Too tight," he whispered.

Darden complained that Simpson wasn't trying. But Simpson shrugged, leaving little doubt that he considered the gloves hopelessly undersized. Cochran later uttered a phrase that would become etched into pop culture: "If it doesn't fit, you must acquit."

Darden had violated a cardinal rule of courtroom law: don't demonstrate something in front of a jury unless you know the outcome. That was the moment I could feel the jury begin to swing toward acquittal.

◆ ◆ ◆

Eight months after the trial began, on August 10, 1995, I was finally called to testify. I had reviewed the evidence countless times and had consulted with Lee and the defense team. I was more than ready.

When I got up that morning, I put on a solid light-gray suit, a white button-down shirt, and a navy-blue tie with several vertical wiggly gray lines. By now, my hair, long in the back, was gray. So were my moustache and sideburns. With my round glasses, I felt I looked like a scientist. I knew this was going to be a rough couple of days. The prosecution would try their best to poke holes in my findings, which disagreed with their experts' version of events.

I had one goal: make my testimony understandable to the jurors. Break down the complicated scientific findings so that ordinary people would know what I was saying.

One of the major hurdles for the prosecution was how to present the relatively new forensic science of DNA in layman's terms. Prosecutors had called in experts to explain it, but they came across like university lecturers. I could tell some jurors were lost. Others struggled to stay awake.

In contrast, defense experts Scheck and Neufeld were able to explain DNA in clear terms. They also didn't challenge the reliability of DNA testing methods, which were fast becoming the gold standard in forensic science. Instead, they attacked the way the LAPD had gathered and processed the evidence, arguing that it had rendered the DNA evidence presented in this case unreliable. In essence, law enforcement had used twenty-first century technology, but nineteenth-century evidence-collection methods. To me, the highlight of the trial's testimony was when Neufeld, in cross-examining the state's highly credentialed statistician, got him to admit that he had made a significant mistake in his statistical DNA calculations, which created a false anti-Black bias.

At trial, much is scripted. Because of discovery, both sides have already seen all the evidence. They have a list of all potential witnesses. This way, everyone has a chance to prepare.

But for the jurors, all the evidence and testimony are new. A lawyer, after calling an expert, always begins by asking them to explain to the jury why their opinion has merit by citing their education, teaching appointments, publications, and experience.

So, at Shapiro's prodding, I talked about my role in investigating the murders of the Reverend Martin Luther King Jr., Ron Settles, and Medgar Evers. As I recounted a few details of the Settles case, Cochran leaned forward, his chin in one hand, listening intently and smiling at me. The jurors seemed to take note, scribbling in their pads. I gave a tour of my career, pausing to mention particularly important autopsies and exhumations, including some for Los Angeles prosecutors. I also told them that I had testified as an expert on behalf of the Los Angeles district attorney's office.

Once I had established my credentials and the judge accepted me as an expert, Shapiro began questioning me about the coroner's report. I told him I found problems that called into question some of the prosecution's evidence.

I said that the injuries on Nicole Simpson and Goldman indicated that both had put up significant struggles before they died, fighting hard enough to have left marks on their killer and occupying him long enough to make the prosecution's timeline unlikely.

Nicole had struggled before she lost consciousness. Goldman could have fought for many minutes before and after he was stabbed, I said.

Prosecutors had theorized a quick double murder of almost surgical precision, one that would have allowed O.J. to enter Nicole's yard between 10:15

and 10:40 PM, kill two people too stunned to resist for very long, exit, shed his bloody clothes, and meet a limousine driver five minutes away at his home by 11.

Each killing could have taken less than a minute, Lucky had testified.

But I suggested that the struggle was more protracted. Both victims were conscious, resisting, and capable of screaming, which would tax the skills and nimbleness of a sole perpetrator.

Multiple defensive wounds on Nicole Simpson's body suggested that she was a moving and persistent target, I told the jurors.

"My opinion is that she struggled with the assailant or assailants prior to succumbing when her neck was cut," I said.

Goldman put up even more of a fight, suffering twenty-two stab wounds or more on his face and neck, chest, and abdomen. A cut on his right shoe indicated that he even kicked the assailant.

While blood flowed rapidly from Nicole Simpson's carotid artery, blood only oozed slowly from Goldman's severed jugular vein, leaving him more time to stand and fight for his life.

Lucky had testified that on the basis of the autopsy findings, there was a single killer who was tall, muscular, and right-handed, similar to O.J. But I testified that no one could say how many killers were involved, their height and build, or whether they were right-handed or left-handed from an autopsy.

After questioning me for two hours, Shapiro yielded to Brian Kelberg, the deputy district attorney. Kelberg suggested in his opening questions, as prosecutors often do, that defense experts are hired guns because they are paid for the time they spend on a case. The prosecution witnesses—police, medical examiners, laboratory experts—do not get paid for each case. What prosecutors don't mention is that the work these witnesses do on those cases is part of their job; they get full salaries and benefits. Kelberg wanted to make sure that the jury knew I had been paid a total of $100,000 for the time I had spent reviewing materials and preparing reports.

Kelberg and I went back and forth on a number of other issues, too, including the cut on Simpson's hand. Simpson told me and Lee that he had hurt his hand on a glass he broke in Chicago after he was told of Nicole's death. But Kelberg suggested that Simpson cut himself while committing the murders.

I told the jurors that we had examined Simpson a few days after the murders and that he didn't have any other cuts or bruises on him—nothing that would indicate he had been in a violent struggle.

Kelberg continued his offensive, attacking my assessment that Goldman could have stood and fought after he was stabbed. I told him that I based my opinion on the flow of blood from the stab wounds. It flowed downward toward the ground, consistent with my finding that Goldman had been standing during the attack.

Kelberg asked, wouldn't it be illogical for someone to keep stabbing a victim after their jugular vein was cut?

"Murder and struggles are not logical, Mr. Kelberg," I replied. "If they were logical, there'd be fewer of them."

After hours of testimony and cross-examination, it was over. For me, it had been like a forensic fencing match. When testimony ended for the day, I believed I had helped the jurors to better understand how Nicole and Ron Goldman were murdered.

"They listened to everything you said," Cochran told me when I got off the stand.

Now, it was time for me to head back to New York.

◆ ◆ ◆

For the next few months, I handled most of my consultation with the defense team over the phone. I was at state police headquarters in New York when the attorneys began closing arguments in late September.

Like millions of others, I watched both sides sum up nearly nine months' worth of testimony as they tried one last time to sway the jury. Prosecutors focused on Simpson's violent relationship with his ex-wife. Darden described Simpson as a man with "a short fuse" that burned every day toward the climactic moment when he grabbed a knife and released his rage.

Cochran's summary was heartfelt and visceral. He launched an all-out attack on Detective Fuhrman, whom he called a "perjuring, genocidal racist." He claimed that Fuhrman set out to get Simpson by planting evidence, including the glove.

But Cochran also focused again on a bigger theme, one that he hoped would connect with the eight Black jurors. He talked about corruption in the LAPD. Cover-ups. Evidence tampering. Acquitting Simpson would send a powerful message that police corruption and racism would not be tolerated.

The trial had begun on January 24, 1995. Jurors had heard 134 days of testimony. And on October 2, after only four hours of deliberation, the jury announced it reached a verdict.

Everyone was stunned. Assuming deliberation would take more time, almost no one was in the courthouse when the jury reported it had decided. So, Judge Ito decided to reconvene court the following day at 10 AM Pacific Daylight Time to read the jury's decision.

On Tuesday, October 3, Americans all over the nation gathered around their TV sets for the live broadcast. Los Angeles braced itself for another possible onslaught of racial violence. The police and sheriff's departments put officers on modified tactical alert and set up an emergency operations center. I was attending a lecture with about a hundred troopers at state police headquarters in Albany, but everything had been stopped so we could watch the verdict.

On the television screen were the people I had spent so much time with in and out of the courtroom that past year: Simpson, Cochran, Shapiro, Kardashian, Darden, Clark, and others. They all appeared nervous. The tension was palpable.

Then, the verdict was read out: on both counts of murder, not guilty. I saw Simpson exhale, visibly relieved. He mouthed "thank you" in the direction of the jury. But others in the courtroom, especially the victims' families, looked on with shock and disbelief. The cameras cut away to the streets and various gatherings around the country. Reaction was divided down racial lines. White viewers were stunned, but Black ones cheered.

In my state police meeting, everyone groaned. They were ticked off at the verdict. A few were ticked off at me. They believed that Simpson had gotten away with murder, and that I had violated the "blue code": police officers stick together no matter what. Of course, I knew that both the New York State Police and the NYPD were almost all white—I had eyes, I could see that. But I had never thought about how that affected their policing. That day, it hit me how deeply race affected how officers behaved.

At the meeting, McAuliffe shook his head, angry. "Michael, I can't believe you defended him."

"No. I didn't defend him. I evaluated the evidence as I would for either side. Tim, they screwed up," I said, referring to the prosecution.

"You know he did it. He got away with murder," he said.

What could I say? Everyone had an opinion about Simpson, and they weren't going to change it.

For Simpson himself, it wasn't over. In February 1997, a civil trial found him liable for the murders. He was ordered to pay $33.5 million in compensatory and punitive damages to the victims' families. With few assets remaining after his long legal battles, Simpson paid very little.

In 2007, while in Las Vegas for a friend's wedding, Simpson led a group of people who broke into a hotel room to take back sports memorabilia he said had been stolen from him and was about to be sold. A member of the group had a gun. Simpson was arrested, convicted, and sentenced to nine to thirty-three years in prison for armed robbery and kidnapping. He was released from prison in 2017.

The O.J. Simpson murder case spawned a cottage industry of books, movies, and videos. In interviews after the trial, jurors said they were swayed by Cochran, who had raised enough reasonable doubt in their minds about the evidence, especially after Fuhrman's testimony and his refusal to answer questions by invoking his Fifth Amendment rights.

I felt that some Black viewers cheered that day because they believed Simpson had nothing to do with the murders. That he was framed. Others celebrated not necessarily because they believed Simpson was innocent, but because he had come to represent every Black person who had ever been beaten or falsely accused of a crime or unjustly killed by a cop. They cheered because of the way Johnnie Cochran, a brilliant Black attorney, beat the system against all odds.

Black people in Los Angeles and the rest of the nation were tired of the racial bias they witnessed every day in the criminal justice system. To white people, the Black community's reaction to the verdict should have been a wake-up call that there were serious racial problems in this country.

The Simpson verdict was a cathartic moment. But I was worried. If things didn't change soon, America's deep racial divide—now even more clearly exposed—would continue to deepen and metastasize. And in the years that followed, the cancer continued to spread.

Chapter 14

. . .

JUSTICE DELAYED

On a narrow bridge in the middle of the night, Willie Edwards Jr. was trapped. Four Ku Klux Klan members blocked his way and backed him up against the edge of the span. Behind him were only open air and a 125-foot drop to the cold, rocky water below.

A few hours earlier, Edwards had been sitting in his Winn-Dixie delivery truck in a Montgomery, Alabama, parking lot. It was just after midnight on January 23, 1957, and he was getting ready to start his shift for the grocery store chain. But then, without warning, four men, guns in hand, approached the truck, grabbed Edwards, threw him in the back of their car, and sped away.

As they drove down a two-lane stretch of rural Alabama road, the men said they'd kidnapped him because they'd been told he had harassed a white waitress. "Now, you're going to pay," one said. Edwards said they had the wrong man, that he was filling in for another driver, that he'd never spoken out of turn to any white woman. He pleaded for his life, on behalf of his pregnant wife and children. The men laughed.

The car screeched to a halt on the Tyler-Goodwin Bridge, a rusty steel structure over the Alabama River. The men dragged Edwards out of the vehicle. Edwards was scared, surrounded, and unable to run.

One Klansman pointed his gun at Edwards. "Hit the water," he said. Edwards went screaming over the edge and into the river.

The four men then drove back to their favorite café and joked about the Black man who'd "jumped in for a swim."

Three months later, in April 1957, two fishermen found what remained of Edwards's body.

Edwards's wife, Sarah, was left to raise their two young daughters and, later, the son she'd been carrying when Willie died. In 1997, the oldest child, Malinda, reached out to me.

Malinda was three years old when her father was killed. When she called me, she said she had just watched an old episode of my show, *Autopsy*, on HBO. The 1994 episode from the series' first season included my role in the Medgar Evers investigation.

"I'm hoping you can help me the same way," she said.

Malinda, who was then living in Buffalo, New York, said nothing had been done to prosecute the people involved—even though one of the suspects had given a full confession as to his role in the murder and had expressed a willingness to testify against the others. Charges had been filed sometime in the 1970s, and hearings scheduled.

"But a judge threw out the charges because the coroner said he didn't know how my father died," Malinda said. "I saw how you conducted the re-examination of Medgar Evers. Could you do the same for my father? Find out his cause of death? We have nowhere else to turn."

I had never heard of Willie Edwards, but the story his daughter shared with me was harrowing and compelling. He was killed in 1957, a place and a time when the KKK and other segregationists had all but declared war on Black people. Lynchings and other murders were still being used to terrorize and control Black people in the South. And if everything Malinda said was true, Willie Edwards was openly murdered with impunity. The criminals were known but remained unpunished.

Lynchings had spread across the United States after the Civil War, mostly in the South. A lynching usually involved the assembly of a white mob, followed by the seizure and murder of the victim. Many occurred because a Black man was accused of looking "improperly" at a white woman. The overwhelming majority of victims were Black and subjected to extreme brutality before being hanged. Torture, mutilation, and castration were not uncommon.

Extrajudicial lynchings were often public spectacles attended by the white community. Photos of hanging bodies were sold as souvenir postcards. From

1882 to 1968, the NAACP documented 4,743 lynchings in the United States. The great majority were of Black men. It was impossible to know for certain how many occurred because there was no formal tracking system. Many historians believe the true number was much greater.

I wanted to help Malinda. "Send me what you have and I'll see what I can do," I said.

The Edwards case was coming at a difficult transitional period in my life. After the Simpson trial, I had settled back into my routine with the state police, investigating homicides, lecturing, setting up conferences, and, since 1993, working on my HBO show.

Meanwhile, my personal life was a mess. After thirty-eight years of marriage, Judianne and I agreed to divorce in 1996. I knew we should have done this much earlier; we had been living separate lives for years. It took a world-shattering event for me to finally push for our separation: my son Jud's tragic death in May 1996.

I was in Chicago, changing planes on the way to a conference in Texas, when I heard myself paged on the airport public-address speaker. I picked up the call at the Delta ticket counter. It was my boss at the state police, Major McAuliffe. My heart raced. Why would he be calling?

"Michael. I have bad news," he began. "It's your son, Judson . . ."

I don't remember the exact words he used. But I remember the way I felt the moment I realized what he was saying: that Jud, my brilliant, troubled son, was dead.

Of my four children, Jud had, in some ways, the most potential. Jud was smart; he'd attended Phillips Exeter Academy in New Hampshire and graduated from Columbia College. He could have been whatever he wanted to be. But his heroin addiction proved to be too much. Despite having two physician parents who knew a great deal about drug addiction—or maybe because of it—he couldn't beat his habit. Nothing we did worked.

There had been happy periods in his life when he was clean, but then something would happen and he'd start using again. We got him treatment, the best drug programs. But you can't force someone to go straight. They have to want to. And even then, it's a long, difficult process.

I had talked to Jud just a few days earlier. He'd said things were good out in California. He was still attending out-patient treatment at Daytop and even had started playing chess again. I'd taught him how to play when he was young, and he became really good. But as a teenager, he gave it up. Now he was on the treatment center's chess team, playing against other teams.

"Dad, don't worry about me. I'm doing well," he said.

And I believed him.

I stood at the airline counter and struggled to regain my composure. I called home to Judianne to get more details, but she didn't know any more than I did.

I knew it was probably an overdose. We'd thought Jud was turning his life around. He was thirty-two years old and had a new girlfriend. I had just talked to him about law school. He said he wanted to apply, and I said I'd help him. Now, I had to go to California to arrange to bring his body back to New York.

I changed tickets. I boarded the plane to California and took my seat. I felt like screaming but was able to control myself. Jud's death felt like my fault. I was filled with guilt over the many things I could have done to prevent it. I feel this guilt to this day. And his death still hurts.

I knew Jud's death would have a profound effect on his siblings. All of them had looked up to him. He was their protector. His sister Trissa and brother Lindsey had become doctors. His younger sister, Sarah, was a student at Brown University. They were all still close to one another—all but inseparable. Judianne and I were working all the time when they were growing up and our children had learned to lean on one another.

Though I had worked long hours and traveled extensively, I'd tried to be there for all my children (even if I wasn't always successful). This was especially true with Jud, because he was the one who got into trouble at school and with drugs. For his part, he'd always understood the kind of work I did and encouraged me to do what was right, not what others wanted. Staying in touch with Jud had always been a priority for me. I tried to talk to him at least once a week and to see him as much as I could. And he always would tell me, *Dad, don't worry*. But I always did. And now he was gone.

The next few days were a blur. When we buried his body, a part of my soul was buried with him.

McAuliffe, always the deacon, tried to comfort me. He listened and offered sage advice. "Nothing I say can ease your pain. But with time, it will get better. This too shall pass," he said. "This too shall pass." It hasn't.

Johnnie Cochran was among the friends who called to offer condolences on Jud's death. By that time, he had become the most famous lawyer in America. He had a television talk show, and his autobiography was on the *New York Times* bestseller list.

Lately, Cochran had been encouraging me to devote more time to social justice cases. He knew that I agreed with him that some medical examiners ignored the science because they felt that they were part of the prosecution team. Although I was one of the founding members of the National Association of Medical Examiners, I had resigned around the same time I became New York City chief medical examiner because I thought it was becoming too biased toward police.

Cochran felt the problem had ballooned. Police were stepping up enforcement of their stop-and-frisk policy targeting Blacks and Hispanics, especially since 1994's sweeping new crime law that gave cities more money to hire police officers. More confrontations involving police were becoming fatal for suspects. Cochran believed that officers were getting away with murder. He felt that I could help victims' families hold bad cops accountable.

Maybe Cochran's advice was why I was so intent on taking on the Edwards lynching case. Yes, relatively speaking, it was old—a 1957 hate crime. But it also raised troubling questions about district attorneys and the role they play in moving cases forward, an issue that continues to fuel social unrest to this day.

Malinda sent me the files. I learned that Willie Edwards was listed among the names of forty-one civil rights martyrs inscribed in granite at the Southern Poverty Law Center headquarters in Montgomery, Alabama. But no one had faced justice in connection with his death.

Edwards had been a twenty-four-year-old truck driver just trying to eke out a living to support his children and pregnant wife. And in 1957, in the deeply racist South—especially in Alabama—that was enough to get you killed.

I read the death certificate. The cause of death was "undetermined." That's a problem in any investigation. It means the coroner couldn't say for certain whether the death was natural, accidental, or homicide. For prosecutors, "undetermined" gives them cover if they don't want to launch an investigation.

And so it was with Edwards.

I'd have to do another autopsy to determine the cause of death. There were a lot of questions that could only be answered by reexamining the body. I asked Malinda if the family would agree to exhume Edwards's body. A few days later, she said yes.

While studying the documents, I realized the FBI had contacted me about this case back in the mid-1970s when I was working in New York City. They wanted to know if I would perform an autopsy in a civil rights case in which the attackers threw a Black man off of a bridge. The body had remained in the water for three months before it was found. The FBI agent asked, "Could the cause of death be determined after twenty years?"

"Yes," I said. "And I'd be available to do the autopsy. Just let me know the details."

But I never heard back from the investigator. And now, here the case was, in front of me again.

When Edwards didn't come home after his shift, his wife had called the police, who initially classified Edwards as a missing person. On January 26, 1957, Montgomery Police Captain E. P. Brown told a newspaper reporter that Edwards was the "subject of a wide police hunt." He didn't think foul play was involved.

Edwards's death certificate was signed by Coroner Vann Pruitt. I found his name in the Montgomery phone directory and called the number. To my surprise, Pruitt was still very much alive and couldn't have been nicer or more helpful. He said that in Alabama in the 1950s, you didn't have to be a doctor to issue death certificates. He'd been a criminalist, head of the Huntsville Alabama Crime Lab, as well as the county coroner. He was not a physician but he knew how to find bullets in a dead body to give them to the crime lab.

"I'm an expert on explosives," he said, adding that he helped with the police investigation into the 1963 bombing of a Birmingham, Alabama, church that killed four girls.

Pruitt said he hadn't felt confident giving a cause of death in the Edwards autopsy because he wasn't qualified to make such a decision. So he marked it "undetermined." I thanked him. Then I called James Lauridson, the chief medical examiner for Montgomery, Alabama. He agreed that it was an important case and said he'd help.

We also agreed to do an exhumation and autopsy together. He was the only person who could issue a new death certificate with a corrected cause and manner of death.

I called Malinda to let her know, and, in November 1997, headed to Montgomery. Lauridson met me at the airport. He said he had already arranged the exhumation.

Edwards was buried in the New Pleasant Valley AME Zion Church in nearby Hope Hull, Alabama. His casket would be brought from the cemetery to the Alabama Department of Forensic Sciences in Montgomery. We would do the autopsy there.

Lauridson gave me a quick tour of the area, to provide context for Edwards's death. It was an eye-opening drive.

During the tour, we talked about the region's troubled racial past. Lauridson said Alabama was a different place now: "Those days are behind us."

Maybe, I thought.

When I glanced out the window, I saw a wide expanse of land dotted with white. It was a cotton field.

"You know, I've never seen a cotton boll," I said.

He smiled, then stopped the car by the side of the two-lane road. "Let me show you what cotton looks like."

We walked into the field. I bent down and touched one of the plants.

"Ouch!" I said.

Each round, fluffy clump had five or six little thorns around it. I'd pricked my finger, drawing a little blood. It made me think about slavery, and how the South—and northeastern banks—grew rich because of the labor of slaves, picking this thorny crop.

We got back in the car.

As we drove to the hotel, Lauridson shared more details. The murder had remained unsolved for nearly twenty years until the FBI, investigating another case, uncovered the names of four KKK members who were allegedly on the bridge that night with Edwards. The FBI passed along the information to then–State Attorney General Bill Baxley, who reopened the case in 1976.

Four people were subsequently arrested and charged with Edwards's murder: Sonny Kyle Livingston Jr., Henry Alexander, James York, and Raymond Britt Jr.

Britt was the one to break his silence and describe the details to investigators. It all began, he said, when a white woman, a waitress, said that a Black truck driver for Winn-Dixie had "harassed or smiled" at her. That night, the four men decided to hunt him down. They didn't know the man's name. They just knew they were looking for a Black man in a Winn-Dixie truck.

The men armed themselves, piled into a car, and drove down the highway until, at around 11:30 PM, they spotted a truck with the Winn-Dixie logo parked near a grocery store. Edwards was behind the wheel. This was not his normal route. He had been called in to substitute for a sick driver.

When Edwards turned his dome light on to fill in his log book, the Klansmen had a clear view inside the cab. Henry Alexander turned his car around and pulled up in front of Edwards's truck. It was about ten minutes before midnight. They grabbed him and drove off.

Britt told investigators that Edwards "was very frightened and pleaded with us not to harm him." Over and over, Edwards denied having said anything to any white woman. Pointing his gun at Edwards, one Klansman threatened to castrate him. On the bridge, Edwards was "sobbing and begging for his life," Britt said. Then, he said, they forced Edwards to jump off.

Britt had received immunity in exchange for his affidavit, but Livingston, Alexander, and York were indicted on first-degree murder charges.

But in a surprise decision, Judge Frank Embry dismissed the charges—even with Britt's sworn testimony—because no cause of death was listed on the death certificate. He concluded that "merely forcing a person to jump from a bridge does not naturally and probably lead to the death of such person."

Embry's ruling was stunning—an example of pure Southern racial "justice." It was hard to understand his justification. But if prosecutors really wanted to move forward, they could have done another autopsy in 1976 when the FBI agent called me. Why hadn't they called me back? Clearly, there was no desire to prosecute the case. Or maybe there was something else going on.

Then came another twist. In 1993, the wife of one of the suspects, Diane Alexander, contacted the Edwards family. She said her husband Henry had confessed his role in the murder shortly before he died of cancer. She was overcome with remorse, because she was the waitress whose accusation led to Edwards's death.

With this new information, they could have reopened the case. Two of the four suspects were still alive, and Britt was still willing to testify. But nothing happened. While I was there to do the autopsy, I learned that one of the suspects, Livingston, had become a prominent bail bondsman with a very big advertisement directly opposite the police station. I saw the advertisement myself when Lauridson gave me a tour of the area. Still, I wasn't sure why prosecutors didn't want to hold anyone accountable for the crime. But if Lauridson and I could find a cause of death, there would be one less obstacle to doing so.

Inside the autopsy room at the Alabama Department of Forensic Sciences, we opened the casket. Unlike Medgar Evers's, it contained only skeletal remains. Edwards's skull was missing, too. Pruitt told me that he had removed it for "evidentiary purposes" in 1957 in case there was a trial, but no one could find it now.

We X-rayed the body and carefully examined the bones. We had pictures of the old autopsy so we could see the skin. Lauridson was terrific, competent, and open minded to whatever the science found. Working slowly and methodically, we saw there were no gunshot wounds and no stab wounds, but there were fractured bones from the fall.

When it was over, we both agreed that the cause of death was drowning and blunt-force injuries. Lauridson then issued a new official death certificate, with the manner of death listed as a homicide. Then, he sent it to Montgomery County district attorney Ellen Brooks, who was being urged by Edwards's family to reopen the case.

With a proper death certificate in place, the Edwards family once again sought justice. In a letter dated January 30, 1998, Malinda and her mother formally appealed to Brooks to officially reopen the case. They wanted her to present the evidence to a county grand jury.

"Our family is still hopeful that we may see some action before the principals in this case are deceased and any hope of justice disappears," the letter said.

But things didn't go as planned.

Lauridson and I had called Brooks before we exhumed the body to explain what we were doing. "This might turn out to be a homicide. If that's the case, would you be willing to try the case?" I'd asked.

She'd said yes, she'd do it. And she presented the case to a grand jury, which concluded Edwards's death was a homicide caused by the Ku Klux Klan. But they declined to indict anyone specific for the murder.

I was angry. I knew they had strong evidence, including Britt's confession. But I knew prosecutors control what a grand jury hears and how the evidence is presented. The adage that "a prosecutor can indict a ham sandwich" is true. So I couldn't help wondering: What had Brooks shown the grand jury? What had she told them? Grand jury proceedings are secret. The Edwards family was in the dark.

The prosecutor decides what evidence is presented to the grand jury and how, and who should be considered for indictment. And law enforcement officers are rarely indicted. I thought of the Arthur Miller case, where the Brooklyn district attorney had presented the evidence against the police officers. From my perspective, it had been a slam-dunk. Yet, the evidence was presented to the grand jury in such a way that no one was indicted.

And forty years after Miller's death in Brooklyn, that trend continues. Just look at Breonna Taylor.

Shortly after midnight on March 13, 2020, Taylor, a twenty-six-year-old Black emergency medical technician, was shot and killed by police in her Louisville, Kentucky, apartment after officers smashed through her front door with a battering ram.

Taylor and her boyfriend, Kenneth Walker, had been asleep in bed. Walker, who later stated he feared an intruder had broken in, used his legally owned gun to fire one shot, wounding Sergeant Jonathan Mattingly in the leg. Mattingly and Officers Myles Cosgrove and Brett Hankison, all white and in plain clothes, returned fire, blindly shooting thirty-two times into the dark. Breonna Taylor was shot six times.

Louisville police had received a court-approved "no-knock" warrant to search the apartment for signs of drug trafficking while investigating Taylor's ex-boyfriend, Jamarcus Glover. Those orders were changed to "knock and announce" before the raid. The police involved stated they complied with the warrant, but Walker said he heard no announcement.

The three officers were placed on administrative leave pending an investigation. Walker was arrested for attempted murder of a police officer, a charge that was dropped as the FBI, Department of Justice, and Kentucky attorney general began their own investigations. Neither Taylor nor Walker had a criminal record. No drugs were found in the apartment. Following an internal investigation, Hankison was fired by the Louisville Metro Police Department for violating procedure.

After Kentucky attorney general Daniel Cameron, a Black Republican prosecutor, presented the case, the grand jury only indicted one person, Hankison—and that was for a minor charge, "wanton endangerment." The reason? Some of the bullets he fired entered a neighboring apartment, where they didn't strike anyone.

The NAACP investigated the grand jury's action and made a troubling discovery. The civil rights group said Cameron presented a biased view of the case—one that favored law enforcement. Contrary to statements he made during a September 23, 2020, press conference, Cameron did not present charges of homicide for consideration by the jurors or explain when police were justified in using self-defense. Instead of providing the grand jury with all relevant evidence, the NAACP said, Cameron and the Kentucky attorney general's office only permitted the jurors to vote on whether Hankinson should be indicted for shooting into the neighbor's apartment.

The NAACP also said Cameron failed to present body camera video or audio evidence and omitted critical information about how the police violated their own protocol.

Taylor's death and the grand jury ruling led to massive nationwide protests against police brutality. But I knew nothing would change unless prosecutors were held accountable for their actions. They had been hiding behind grand jury secrecy for too long. That had to end.

In my experience, many prosecutors are blatantly biased in favor of police. They work closely with officers and are reluctant to file charges against "one of their own." Law enforcement, after all, is a big bloc of important voters for district attorneys who want to move up the judicial or political ladder. This short-sighted, self-serving policy only builds more anger and resentment in all communities—Black, white, and Hispanic. Police misconduct should be punished, not condoned. Otherwise, it will continue.

With Edwards, the decision not to charge anyone was flat-out wrong. Brooks said the grand jury declined to indict because of "insufficient evidence" and the previous immunity agreement with Britt.

No one was held accountable for Willie Edwards Jr.'s murder. Not in 1957. Not in 1976. Not in 1998. In the end, the Alabama criminal justice system failed—from the police to the prosecutors. Lauridson thought things had changed in Alabama. But Willie Edwards's family knows better.

Chapter 15

• • •

POSITIONAL ASPHYXIA

It was past midnight, and the case on my desk was troubling. I stared at the documents—police reports, witness statements, medical records. This was another in an increasing number of deaths I had reviewed that shared a similar narrative. Police were called by a family member about a loved one in a mental health crisis, usually wanting the emotionally disturbed person taken to a hospital. The person hadn't committed any crime. They weren't armed. But after police arrived, the officers' use of force caused serious injuries or the mentally ill person's death.

This new case was just as disturbing as the others. On the night of March 25, 1999, Olivia Graves called the Anaheim California Police Department to report that her fiancée, Brian Drummond, was hallucinating. She said she was afraid that he'd hurt himself.

"He has bipolar disorder and schizophrenia, and he's out of medicine," she said.

Graves asked for help. The four officers who arrived that night asked a few questions, but left without offering any help at all. Then, the following night, the police returned. This time Drummond's neighbor, David Kimbrough, called them. Kimbrough said Drummond claimed to be seeing "snakes at his feet," and he was afraid that Drummond was going to dart out into traffic on the busy street.

Officers Christopher Ned, Kristi Valentine, and Brian McElhaney found Drummond in a 7-Eleven parking lot. Ned and Valentine recognized Drummond from the night before.

They reported that Drummond was agitated, seeing things that weren't there. He wasn't armed. The officers called for an ambulance to take him to a hospital. Before it arrived, however, they decided to take Drummond into custody "for his own safety."

Witnesses said they saw Ned "knock Drummond to the ground." The officers cuffed his arms behind his back as Drummond lay on his stomach. McElhaney "put his knees into Drummond's back and placed the weight of his body on him."

Then, witnesses said, Ned knelt on top of Drummond's body, too, with one knee pressing down on his neck. Drummond weighed 160 pounds. The combined weight of Ned and McElhaney was nearly 400 pounds. With the two officers leaning on his neck and upper torso—and laughing, according to one witness—Drummond gasped for breath, then passed out. Doctors were able to revive his heart but it was too late to save his brain. He fell into a coma. A year later, he remained in a permanent vegetative state with no hope of recovery.

The police department said Drummond's coma was caused by drugs in his system—not the actions of the police officers. His family felt otherwise and hired an attorney to sue the department. The attorney asked me to review the case.

Drummond's fate raised important issues. In 1999, police departments were handling more and more calls involving the mentally ill. Much of this rise was due to the nationwide closure of state psychiatric hospitals between 1955 and 1994. With the debut of new psychiatric drugs, the assumption was that the mentally ill could be taken care of in the community. Five hundred thousand patients with mental illnesses were discharged during this period. But the communities did not provide sufficient support. And former patients who couldn't take care of themselves became the police's problem.

In the cases I was now receiving, police, instead of calming the person in a mental health crisis, were often restraining them because they weren't obeying officers' orders. What police didn't seem to understand was that people with mental health issues often can't comprehend what officers are asking them to do. People were being placed in the prone position so police could handcuff them behind their backs. Sometimes officers would sit on the supine suspect or kneel on their back to make it easier to cuff them. They would even hogtie them or place a so-called spit hood over their head. These strong-arm tactics can turn routine calls into deadly police encounters—ones in which "emotionally disturbed persons," who should be brought to the emergency room for medical help, are restrained in ways that hinder their breathing.

Drummond's case was disconcerting on so many levels. As officers pinned his body to the ground, bystanders said Drummond uttered a phrase I remembered witnesses reporting they'd heard Arthur Miller say, too, as he lay dying by a Brooklyn police car in 1978—a phrase that would later come to symbolize police brutality: "I can't breathe."

By this point in my career, I had been a forensic pathologist for more than thirty years. I had done thousands of autopsies. And I had worked all over the world for human rights groups and private attorneys. I was still working for the New York State Police, but I was also seeing more cases as a private consultant. Many of the calls came from families who had lost a mentally ill husband, mother, brother, or daughter during a police encounter.

This increase in calls appeared to stem in part from the popularity of my HBO show *Autopsy*, but Johnnie Cochran had also recommended me to a number of civil rights attorneys seeking second opinions in cases involving police violence.

I had gravitated over the years to civil rights and social justice cases. These allowed me to address issues that were largely hidden from the public—like police mishandling of the mentally ill. Unless you had a family member or friend with mental illness, you wouldn't know much about how America's broken mental health system fed into the likewise broken criminal justice system.

In a just world, mentally ill people would get treatment long before an encounter with law enforcement was required. But that wasn't happening in 1999. Insurance companies didn't adequately cover mental illness. Quality psychiatric services were almost impossible for disadvantaged people to access. Psychotropic medicines came with spectacular price tags. People whose mental illness was complicated by addiction or substance abuse couldn't find help for both at once. Beyond that was another critical problem: most mental health professionals in America were white. There were few Black or brown psychiatrists.

I'd been working to raise public awareness of these issues for a long time, yet it was hard to see any signs of change. The long grind of fighting injustice sometimes left me drained. But then, I met a woman I could talk to about the issues in American life that troubled me so.

Linda Kenney was a prominent criminal defense, civil rights, and employment discrimination attorney in New Jersey, a tough, street-smart brunette from Red Bank I had first read about in an employment discrimination case involving Black police officers in her state.

Linda had been hired by the family of a Hispanic man fatally shot by a Union Beach, New Jersey, police officer. The Monmouth County medical examiner was going to do the autopsy, but Linda wanted another independent forensic pathologist to be there to observe. She had been a Monmouth County prosecutor and was concerned about the pro-police bias of medical examiners. One of the partners in her firm recommended me. So, she called and asked if I could be there the very next day.

I told her I was scheduled to testify in a case that morning in a small town about a hundred miles north of Albany, and that later that night, I would be flying from Newark Airport to the Gambia, where my son Lindsey, a medical student, was helping train health workers how to immunize against childhood disease.

She was persistent. She said she'd arrange a helicopter to take me from the New York courthouse, after I finished testifying, to the New Jersey medical examiner's office. So, I agreed to do it.

As I exited the helicopter at the hospital where the examiner's office was located, I was greeted by Linda: a beautiful woman in a designer suit, matching high heels, and red lipstick. I quipped that she was overdressed for the morgue. She said that after the autopsy, she was giving a lecture at an important conference of judges.

We hurried inside the building. When we got to the door of the autopsy room, I turned to her.

"Why don't you get some coffee? I'll come out when we're finished," I said.

It was unusual for a lawyer to watch an autopsy. They usually wait outside the room. But Linda shook her head—she'd promised her client that she'd be at the autopsy. There was no time to argue. The body was on the table.

"You'll have to change in the bathroom," I said, handing her a pair of green scrubs.

She squinted and pointed her right index finger at me. "You want me to wear that?"

I told her yes, otherwise she would ruin her clothes.

She was firm. She wasn't going to change. And she didn't. So, Jay Peacock, the Monmouth County medical examiner, and I began the autopsy.

According to police, the man on the table—thirty-two-year-old Eric Montalvo—had been shot by a cop after a foot chase. The officer said that, as Montalvo turned to face him, he spotted a "silver object" in the suspect's hand. The officer said he believed the man had a gun, so he shot him. But witnesses said that when the officer fired, Montalvo's back was to the officer and his hands were lifted over his head to surrender.

As Peacock examined the body, I noticed there was an irregular half-inch exit-type bullet hole in the chest near the right nipple. When we turned the body over, I saw another hole in the back: a small, round perforation with a surrounding abrasion collar, typical of an entrance wound.

I turned to Linda. "What the officer said was wrong. What the witnesses said was accurate."

Now, autopsy completed, I just had to get Newark Airport. It was a mad dash, but the driver made it there in time for my flight to the Gambia.

Peacock and I both agreed that Montalvo had been shot in the back, but despite our autopsy findings, which showed that the officer's statement was wrong, prosecutors did not bring criminal charges. So, Montalvo's family filed a civil lawsuit. I didn't know what would happen because I knew how difficult it was to sue police. Before you can even file the lawsuit, you have to clear a very high bar called *qualified immunity*—a doctrine that shields government officials from personal liability for violations while doing their jobs. You have to show that the police clearly violated established law. Then, if your case makes it onto the docket, you still have to overcome community bias in favor of law enforcement.

The difficulty involved is frustrating, especially for the minority communities most affected. When police misconduct has clearly taken place, yet no one is held accountable, it only reinforces their belief that the system is stacked against them.

In Montalvo's case, however, the county agreed to settle the lawsuit. They awarded money to the man's young child.

A few months after the autopsy, a young attorney I had met at Linda's firm decided to play matchmaker. He called and said Linda had a "crush" on me. I didn't know it at the time, but he had already told Linda I felt the same about her.

I wanted to call her, but I had some reservations. I was in my early sixties. Asking a woman out on a date made me feel like I was back in high school. My divorce wasn't quite finalized. Also, while Linda was already divorced, she was at least a decade younger than me. She had a son; I had three living children.

I overcame my doubts, and we hit it off. (On our first dinner date, she disclosed that she'd had to dispose of the clothes she had worn at the autopsy because she couldn't get rid of the odor.) After dating for a while, we moved in together. We later bought an apartment on the eighteenth floor of a New York high rise in Midtown Manhattan. We leaned on each other and I started having fun again—I hadn't gone out to a leisurely dinner in years. We'd entertain family and friends at our apartment. My life was less chaotic. I still had to go to the state police in Albany once a week but I didn't mind. I felt like I had a home again.

That helped in those dark moments when I thought of Judson. I was good at compartmentalizing things in my life. Otherwise, I would have broken down. As a forensic pathologist, you see so many horrific things. The worst of humanity. With Jud, I tried to remember the good times. But I missed him very much. And I knew his siblings did too. Without Jud, there would always be an empty place in our hearts.

Linda was busy with her cases. She joined Johnnie Cochran, Peter Neufeld, and Barry Scheck in a high-profile civil rights lawsuit. They each represented one of four young Black men—the Jersey Four—shot at by state troopers who stopped their van on the New Jersey Turnpike in April 1998.

The men had been on their way to basketball tryouts at North Carolina Central University. The troopers said they only opened fire, wounding three of the men, after the vehicle had rolled back toward them. When the police searched the vehicle, they found no weapons and no drugs—nothing but basketball equipment and a Bible.

Cochran charged that the men were victims of "driving while Black." The incident generated protests and demands for state and federal investigations of the New Jersey State Police. It opened an intense national debate about racial profiling, a law enforcement tactic that targets certain groups because of their race or ethnicity.

While Linda worked on that case, I was drilling down on the Drummond matter. I found that law enforcement encounters with the mentally ill cut across socioeconomic and racial lines. I already knew that the government didn't keep any records when someone was fatally shot by an officer or killed while being restrained. But I discovered that they didn't track whether the victim was mentally ill, either. Drummond was white, but I was seeing a disproportionately larger number of victims with mental health issues who were Black or Hispanic.

Most people with mental illness are not violent. Using law enforcement as a blunt instrument against them contributes to the stigma that they are. In fact, people with mental illness are much more likely to be victims of crimes than perpetrators.

Yet many police departments don't train officers on how to handle someone who's having a mental health crisis. If a person runs into traffic nude because they haven't taken their psychiatric medication, and a family member calls 911 for an ambulance to take him to the emergency room, police will usually show up and tell the person to put their hands behind their back to be cuffed. The person doesn't because they're hallucinating and can't understand what's happening. So, police sweep them to the ground. And when they're prone on their abdomen, police put pressure on their back so they can handcuff the person. But police don't realize that by exerting pressure this way, they're cutting off the person's ability to breathe. And when they says they can't breathe, officers don't believe him. In a few minutes, the person is dead.

Or, as in Drummond's case, they are alive but in a permanent coma from brain damage caused by lack of oxygen.

When Drummond's attorney, Kent Henderson, first contacted me, he said Drummond's was one of the worst cases of police brutality that he had seen. And the police department hadn't acknowledged the officers' misconduct, even though they had clearly mistreated a mentally ill man.

"The city is trying to get the case dismissed," he said.

Henderson sent me Drummond's file. I had police and sheriff reports, hospital records, statements of police and civilian witnesses, and audio and video interviews. I also had a medical assessment of Drummond from doctors and staff at San Bernardino Community Hospital.

As I reviewed the materials, I shook my head. From the moment the police encountered Drummond, everything they did escalated the situation.

At the time of the incident, Drummond was thirty-two years old, a Navy veteran, and the father of four children. The night his girlfriend, Olivia Graves, called police, she was hoping they'd help her take him to the hospital to get his medications. He had prescriptions for bipolar disorder and schizophrenia, but because he was uninsured and couldn't afford to refill them, he hadn't taken the medications for five days.

Graves said police refused to transport him the first time they were called, saying Drummond wasn't a danger to himself or others. She said the officers acted unprofessionally and cracked jokes during the encounter.

Later that evening, Graves took Drummond to a medical facility, but they didn't have health insurance, so they couldn't afford to refill his prescriptions. They left without any medicine.

The Anaheim police were called again the next night by Kimbrough, the neighbor who was worried about Drummond's safety.

Officers Ned, Valentine, and McElhaney found Drummond at the 7-Eleven and decided to take him to a medical facility. They moved to restrain him. Witnesses said Drummond offered no resistance, but the officers knocked him to the ground, handcuffed him, and pinned him under their weight.

Witnesses further said Drummond began gasping for air and begged the police to stop, saying the same words over and over: "I can't breathe." The officers laughed. Another officer arrived and applied handcuffs and a "hobble restraint" to Drummond's ankles. About a minute later, they noticed that Drummond had become limp. When the officers realized he was unconscious, they removed the restraints, turned him over onto his back, and attempted to perform CPR.

Drummond's heart was revived approximately seven minutes after both it and his breathing had stopped. But his brain was severely damaged, and he was in an irreversible coma.

In my report, I concluded that Drummond's coma was "due to anoxic encephalopathy which resulted from diffuse brain damage caused by decreased oxygen supply to his brain." The coma's cause was the way police restrained him: *positional asphyxia.*

"The brain has only a ten-second oxygen supply at any given time and requires a constant flow of oxygen to prevent cell death," my report said. "When Mr. Drummond was sat upon with pressure applied to his back, the ability of his diaphragms [*sic*] and rib cage to move air into and out of the lungs was compromised. The pressure on his back and neck diminished the ability of air to move through the windpipe and of oxygenated blood to flow in arteries going to his brain." I added that the obstruction to his nose and mouth against the ground also compromised his ability to breathe.

The Anaheim city attorney's position was that Drummond's brain damage and coma were his own fault.

For years, I was among a few forensic pathologists who had been warning police not to place suspects in prone position. That's because a person lying face down on the ground will have trouble breathing if pressure is applied to the back. The more weight on their back, the more their breathing will be compromised. As a result, their body might not get enough oxygen to fuel their organs, leading to brain damage and death.

It was basic science. But more and more medical examiner reports, I noticed, were downplaying positional asphyxia because the obstruction to breathing leaves no marks on the body. Some blamed other factors for a suspect's death, like drug use, obesity, sickle cell trait, or heart disease. Too many forensic pathologists were calling the manner of death in fatal police encounters natural or accidental or undetermined instead of homicide.

Over the next few years, Henderson kept me updated on the Drummond case as it worked its way through the legal system. One judge dismissed it because of qualified immunity, but then the Ninth Circuit Court of Appeals reinstated the lawsuit and criticized the Anaheim Police Department.

"The force was not only severe, but it was also, on the facts asserted, wholly unwarranted," wrote Judge Stephen Reinhardt.

The case did eventually go to trial, but an Orange County jury ruled that police had not used excessive force. In 2009, the city paid $145,000 to Drummond's family to halt any further legal action.

None of that benefited Drummond. He died in 2006—seven years after his police encounter and three years before the case was settled. No officer was ever charged.

After Drummond's death I amended my original report with Drummond's family. I said that, in my opinion, his death was due to the brain damage caused by the positional asphyxia he suffered while being restrained by police on March 26, 1999.

The legacy of the Drummond case lives on. The Ninth Circuit's decision in *Drummond v. City of Anaheim* is often cited in police brutality cases to argue against qualified immunity.

Judge Reinhardt's opinion noted that the Anaheim Police Department was concerned enough about positional asphyxia to warn its officers in training bulletins about the dangers of kneeling on a detainee's back or neck, including a bulletin issued nearly a year before the Drummond incident. The officers ignored the warning.

History has a way of repeating itself.

Chapter 16

• • •

SICKLE CELL TRAIT

Fourteen-year-old Martin Lee Anderson was a bright young man, a real handful for his single mom. He talked his way into and out of trouble, and sometimes took things that didn't belong to him. His grandmother stepped in to help out. She started taking the boy and his younger sister with her to church services.

But Anderson pushed her too far one day when he skipped out of Sunday school and took his grandmother's Jeep for a joyride. His grandmother decided it was time to teach him a lesson. She pressed charges. Anderson was sentenced to probation—which he then violated.

So, on a sunny morning in January 2006, Anderson stepped out of his mother's car and into a special "boot camp" program designed to help youths like him turn around their lives through hard exercise and "tough love."

The facility in Panama City, Florida, was run by the Bay County Sheriff's Office. Florida legislators had given sheriffs money to create five of these "boot camps" in the state. Teenagers were rousted from bed every morning by 5 AM for exercise before breakfast and class time.

Guards dealt out verbal harangues and demanded dozens more push-ups if a teenager stepped out of line. The teens were seen as slack, spoiled kids in need of clear directions and harsh discipline. Boot camp would help them "shape up," it was believed, and build their self-confidence and fitness for adult life.

When Anderson arrived at boot camp with a group of other teens on the morning of January 5, 2006, they started out with a run around a 1.5-mile track. But he slowed, then stopped. He was having trouble breathing, he said. He was out of breath.

The sheriff ordered Anderson to keep running. He staggered and fell to the ground, panting. Guards swarmed him, lifted him onto his feet, and shoved him face first against a wooden fence by the track. "Go on! Keep going!" they shouted. He pleaded with them to stop, saying he couldn't run any more.

The guards pushed Anderson back onto the track. He staggered. They kicked him, kneed him, choked him—supposedly all in an effort to keep him running. When he fell face down into the dirt, they sat on him and applied pressure to a pain-sensitive area of his head, a technique used to restrain criminal suspects. When Anderson passed out, they waved ammonia capsules under his nose to snap him back to consciousness.

A camp nurse stood by. On one occasion she checked his vital signs, but she didn't do anything to stop the beating.

Forty minutes later, Anderson's limp body was whisked into an ambulance and taken to the hospital. He remained comatose for a few hours, then died with his parents at his side—the same day he'd been taken to boot camp.

Nearly two months later, Bay County chief medical examiner Charles Siebert released his autopsy findings. He said the teen died of "complications from sickle cell trait"—in other words, natural causes.

He died of natural causes? Anderson's parents and the local Black community were outraged. A video from the boot camp clearly showed the boy being restrained, tormented, and beaten to death.

The family hired Benjamin Crump, a local civil rights attorney, to help them seek justice for Anderson. Crump called me to do a second autopsy. He said the family didn't have any money. But I said I'd do it pro bono.

I had heard of the case and seen the video. And I knew that sickle cell trait—when someone has a single sickle cell gene—does not cause death or infirmity. If someone has two sickle cell genes, it causes sickle cell *disease*, which can have severe medical consequences. But a person with sickle cell trait could live their whole life without ever knowing they're carrying the gene. The medical examiner's ruling seemed clearly at odds with the scientific evidence.

This was my first case with Crump, part of a new generation of civil rights lawyers. Like Johnnie Cochran, he was fearless. He challenged the status quo and filed lawsuits to hold police departments accountable for misconduct.

Crump was born and raised in Lumberton, North Carolina—one of the poorest areas in America. The oldest of nine siblings, he received his undergraduate and law degrees from Florida State University. He was a devout man, often quoting Bible passages during community meetings and news conferences. In the years that followed he would earn the nickname "Black America's attorney general." His clients would receive millions of dollars in settlements from cities with problem police departments—although offending police would usually remain unpunished.

In January 2006, at the time of Anderson's death, Crump was known in Florida, but the Anderson case would bring him to national prominence. The case appeared to have exposed another false diagnosis that police officials, medical examiners, and district attorneys could use to shield officers from criminal and civil charges related to in-custody deaths.

By that point, I was being asked to review an increasing number of fatal police encounters. Meanwhile, I was still working for the New York State Police. I had also remarried. In November 2000, Linda Kenney and I wed in our apartment. My brother Robert was best man. There were six wedding officiants: Johnnie Cochran, Major Timothy McAuliffe, Rabbi Itchy Herschel, Chicago judge Haskell Pitluck, Henry Lee, and former New York State inspector general Joseph Fisch— the only one there who actually had the authority to legally marry us.

About 150 guests, many in tuxedos and evening dresses, crowded into our three-bedroom apartment. They drank small, individual-sized red bottles of Piper-Heidsieck champagne through straws and ate hors d'oeuvres. We had a spectacular view of the city, including Rockefeller Center with its decorated Christmas tree below. Trissa, Lindsey, and Sarah were there, each of us missing Jud very much.

The party broke up at 2 AM. Linda and I weren't going on a honeymoon. So, when everyone left, we sat on a couch and looked out the window at the city below, lit up for the holiday season. We didn't have to say a word. We held hands as we sat in silence, staring at the red, yellow, blue, green, and white lights dangling from windows and hanging from trees. At that moment, I felt optimistic about the future. We didn't know how much time we had. We both knew how precious life was. So, we vowed to live life helping each other.

In May 2003, Judianne died of metastatic breast cancer. She was sixty-eight. After our divorce, she had lived in Westport, Connecticut. We'd had good times together. She was the mother of my wonderful children. And I had nothing but great respect for what she had accomplished in her work with drug addicts. She had single-handedly created a groundbreaking drug treatment program that was still helping thousands of addicts all over the world. Yes, we had our differences and fell out of love. But I had only wanted the best for her. I felt for our children and the many other people she had left behind. But I had already begun a new life's journey with Linda, and I felt reinvigorated.

Then, in March 2005, Johnnie Cochran died of a malignant brain tumor at age sixty-seven. I'd known he was ill, but his death was a real blow to Linda and me. With his colorful suits and ties, his gift for courtroom oratory, and a knack for coining memorable phrases, Cochran had been a vivid addition to America's legal pantheon. His catchphrase from the Simpson trial—"If it doesn't fit, you must acquit"—would be quoted for years afterward. Legal experts called that the turning point in the trial.

But more than that, Cochran had been a friend. I admired his grit and tenacity, his drive to make a difference in the world—and not only for Black Americans. For years, he was a voice of reason, fighting against police use of excessive force before it became a mainstream cause.

He took cases with racial themes, championing the causes of Black defendants. Some of them, like Simpson, were famous, but most were ordinary people.

Although he frequently took on police departments in court, Cochran wasn't anti-police. Like me, he believed that most cops are good, honest people who do their job the right way. They put their lives on the line every day to protect the public.

But Cochran also believed that too many police officers were crossing the line, especially when they interacted with Black and Hispanic people. It wasn't just "one bad apple." And when cops got out of hand, too many other people stepped up to shield them from the just consequences—their fellow officers, district attorneys, medical examiners, even judges and the laws themselves, like the ones that created qualified immunity. He knew that if bad cops were not held accountable for their actions, nothing would change.

Police routinely pulled over Black and Hispanic drivers with little or no probable cause—traffic stops that sometimes led to shooting or restraint deaths. They used excessive force without justification against minority suspects and confused, mentally ill people who didn't put their hands behind their back as quickly as ordered. They were not held accountable for violating the civil rights of thousands of people, so anger and resentment continued to build in communities of color, leading to civil unrest.

That's what happened with Anderson. Thousands of people protested his death. The demonstrations were peaceful, but most of the protesters were angry. They accused the state of covering up the excessive force they could clearly see the guards using on the video.

"They're getting away with the murder of a child," said Charlene Howard-Gammage, president of the Florida State University chapter of the NAACP. "Nobody is doing anything. They're just writing it off as another death."

Anderson's parents, Gina Jones and Robert Anderson, led the fight for justice. After I talked to Crump, I called Anderson's mother, Gina, to find out more about her son.

"Did he have any health problems?" I asked her. "What did he like to do? Why was he at the boot camp?"

She sighed. Then, she recounted her son's life. "He was a good boy. He was a smart boy," she said.

When Anderson and his sister were young, Jones had gotten a divorce from their father, a long-distance truck driver. She then set out to raise her children in a hardscrabble neighborhood in Panama City, a tourist destination on the Florida Panhandle.

Anderson showed intellectual promise early on—but he also began getting in trouble, mostly for shoplifting. In the ninth grade, he was accepted at a prestigious school that helped children with behavioral problems. He excelled. He made the honor roll and joined the chess team.

"His teacher called and said he was the best chess player in school," Jones said.

I smiled, remembering the chess games I'd played with my brother in our Brooklyn housing project and how I'd taught the game to my son, Judson.

Anderson's good behavior didn't last. He fell in with a bad crowd. When he got in trouble, his father came over to discipline him, but the punishment had little effect. "We tried," Jones said.

There wasn't much money. Jones worked at a fast-food restaurant.

That's when her mother started taking the kids to church. When Anderson stole his grandmother's Jeep one day in June 2005, driving it to a nearby shopping center rather than attend Sunday school, she called the police.

"She just wanted to teach her grandson a lesson—that you just couldn't take a car without permission," Jones said.

Anderson was charged with auto theft but got probation. He was placed under house arrest and could only go to school and work—nowhere else. When he violated the terms of his probation, the judge gave him a choice: juvenile jail or boot camp.

"I wasn't sure about that place, but he said, 'Mom, I'll be all right,'" Jones said.

She dropped him off that morning. A few hours later, she and Anderson's father were called to Sacred Heart Hospital, where they found him hooked up to machines, brain dead.

"A nurse came in and said we had to make a decision . . ." She paused for a moment, her voice breaking. "We decided to take him off life support." They talked to their son and prayed. They held his hand and whispered their love to him, hoping that he could hear them. Then the doctors came in and removed the life-sustaining equipment. Within an hour, her boy was declared dead.

"Doctor Baden, what they did to him . . . It's hard for me to think about it. It's too painful," she said.

After the funeral, Jones started calling attorneys to see if anyone would help them hold the boot camp guards accountable. Several lawyers turned her down, saying the case would never see the light of day because of qualified immunity. But when Jones found Crump and told him the story, he said he'd take the case.

Crump reviewed the videotape. At first, Jones said she didn't want to see it. But when she did, it only strengthened her resolve to get justice for her son, she told me.

"I understand," I said, and told her I planned to review her son's case.

"Everything from your son's medical history to the way the medical examiner conducted the autopsy."

I explained that a forensic pathologist's job is to assess whether a death was the result of injury or disease. "I am going to figure out if what we saw in the video was what caused his death," I said.

Then, I told her about my work with the New York State Corrections Commission's Medical Review Board—how we had come up with ways to prevent suicides in jails, and put a stop to some practices that permitted prison guards to brutalize inmates for decades. Her son's death didn't have to be meaningless.

Jones was quiet for a moment. "Doctor Baden, we don't want anyone else to go through this pain. I'd like to do something to make sure this never happens again."

"That's why I'm coming to Florida," I said.

At the time, I thought I was going to perform a second autopsy. But things changed between my first conversation with Crump and when I boarded a plane to Florida.

I had gotten a call from the corrections chief in Florida. He knew me from his former job at the New York Department of Corrections and was familiar with my work on that state's medical review board, which investigated jail and prison deaths.

He asked if I could conduct a second autopsy on Anderson. I said yes. But a short time later, he called me back. He said Governor Jeb Bush had appointed a Florida forensic pathologist to perform the second postmortem examination: Verne Adams, the medical examiner in neighboring Hillsborough County.

I was still going to Florida. Crump had asked me to attend the second autopsy, as well as interview people and examine Anderson's medical records.

When I got off the plane in Tampa on March 12, 2006, I was greeted by Crump and several members of his law firm. It was the first time we had met in person.

"Thank you for coming," he said.

"I'm glad to be here."

We made some small talk as we walked to the car that would take us to the autopsy. On the way, we talked about sickle cell trait, which Siebert had listed as the teenager's cause of death.

I explained to Crump that this wasn't the first time a medical examiner had misattributed an in-custody death of a Black person to that entirely benign genetic condition.

Sickle cell trait, a symptomless blood condition that overwhelmingly occurs in Black people, was rarely fatal. When it was, it happened in cases of extreme low-oxygen conditions. "You'd have to climb Mount Everest where there is very little oxygen to die from sickle cell trait," I said.

I told him that sickle cell was widespread in Africa and those of African descent because the sickling of red blood cells prevented the malaria parasite from developing. Malaria is still a major cause of death in Africa.

What concerned me was that medical examiners were now citing it as a cause of death for Black people who had been forcefully restrained by police.

No one was keeping statistics as to how many times sickle cell trait had been used to improperly exonerate police in restraint deaths. But I had seen it a few times and was worried about the practice spreading.

When I was a medical resident at Bellevue Hospital, I treated a number of patients with sickle cell anemia. The disease causes great pain, especially in joints, whenever oxygen levels go down, such as in an acute pneumonia. When patients do die of sickle cell disease, it takes time—usually days—of painful symptoms as the number of sickled cells increase. They do not die, lose consciousness, or go into a coma in minutes, as happened to Anderson. It does not cause sudden death.

When I arrived at the autopsy room, Adams was there. So was Pam Bondi, a smart prosecutor also from Hillsborough County. I knew her from Fox News in New York City where she and I were sometimes guests together discussing the latest high-profile murder. Siebert, who had performed the first autopsy, was also in the room, as was the exhumed body of Martin Lee Anderson.

Everyone acted professionally. We knew that each of us was there to help answer medical and legal questions surrounding Anderson's death.

While I was in the autopsy room, I called Sacred Heart Hospital, where Anderson had been taken while he was unconscious but still alive. I spoke to one of the doctors, who said he had examined Anderson's blood. He said that all of the red blood cells in the samples drawn before Anderson's death were normally shaped—there was no sickling. The microscopic slides that I had reviewed from the first autopsy did show sickling. But it was postmortem sickling—sickling that occurred after he died—and therefore had nothing to do with his cause of death. In order to diagnose a death from sickling, the sickling had to be observed while the person was alive.

After the autopsy was completed, I called Crump at the hotel.

"Siebert made a mistake," I said.

Anderson didn't die of natural causes. No, he died because of the way the guards restrained him. With the pressure to his back while prone, his lungs, heart, and diaphragm couldn't move. That prevented him from breathing and stopped oxygen from reaching his brain.

Crump said this would go a long way to help with the family's push for justice. Then, he asked me for a favor. Because the official findings might not be released for many weeks or months, he wanted me to explain my opinion at a community meeting he was holding the next day in a church. Crump said he was going to update everyone about the case.

This was not how I usually worked. Normally, I would give my findings to family attorneys or state officials and then, months later, testify about them in deposition or court. Still, I agreed to speak to the community because of its interest in the case.

The following day, Crump drove me to the church in the Panama City neighborhood where Anderson had lived with his family. There were 250 people waiting for us there, almost all Black. Gina Jones, Anderson's mother, approached me from the front of the sanctuary. She smiled and hugged me.

"Thank you, Doctor Baden," she said. "Thank you for everything."

I smiled back. "Gina, I'm glad I came. I'm so sorry for your loss."

She nodded. "But now, we're going to do something about it."

When everyone was seated, Crump began. He was a charismatic man with a remarkable talent for connecting with everybody. He said this was just the beginning of the journey, that they would have to fight hard for justice. There would be marches and protests. National civil right leaders would fly in to help.

And then, he introduced me. He went over my résumé and said I was helping free of charge. The audience stood and applauded.

I was overwhelmed. I had spent years being cross-examined during trials, sitting quietly while my work and character were picked apart and criticized. I'd been demoted, fired, mocked, and denounced for telling the truth about the deaths of Black and brown victims. Hearing applause was a bit of a shock.

I didn't speak for very long. The crowd was quiet and listened to every word.

"Martin Lee Anderson's death had nothing to do with sickle cell trait. He died because he was physically punished by guards at a boot camp. He died because he couldn't breathe," I said.

Afterward, people in the crowd shook my hand and thanked me. All that the people in that audience wanted was the truth—something I had been preaching for years. In too many similar cases I had seen, public officials twisted the facts or outright lied about what had happened. But people often know when public officials are not telling the truth. This case was a perfect example. The video showed a wiry young teenager being brutalized for more than forty minutes. Common sense said Anderson didn't die of sickle cell trait. The Black community knew that no one dies of sickle cell trait.

Crump walked over. "You ready?"

I nodded. He drove me to the airport.

I didn't know how the case would end, but I knew the Anderson family was in good hands. Crump was an incredible attorney. As we drove, he asked if I would be available to come down again, to talk to officials and testify. He hadn't sued yet. He was still collecting evidence. I told him I'd do whatever he needed.

A few days later, I got a call from the head of a Florida legislative committee looking into boot camps. He asked if I would testify to that committee the next day. I didn't have to fly there; I could do it over the speakerphone. I agreed.

After I was sworn in remotely from my New York City office, I explained my findings: Anderson had died because he couldn't breathe, not from sickle cell trait. I warned them that certain kinds of restraints—like sitting on someone in the prone position—could cut off a person's supply of oxygen and suffocate them.

I wasn't sure if they would take any action, but days later, the head of the state's law enforcement agency resigned and legislators enacted a law to eliminate military-style boot camps. All of the Florida boot camps were closed. The legislature also paid Anderson's parents $5 million to settle civil claims. Jones told me she was pleased that the state had shuttered the boot camps. "They were operated like bad prisons," she said. "They were brutalizing children."

But the case was not over yet.

When Adams's autopsy report was released four months later, he agreed that Anderson had not died of sickle trait, that he was suffocated. But Adams shifted blame away from how the guards restrained the teenager. Instead, he created a new cause of death. He said the attempt of the guards to revive Anderson by forcing him to inhale the fumes of the ammonia capsule had caused his vocal cords to go into spasms, closing his airways and preventing breathing. I didn't agree that the use of ammonia played a role in causing his death. And I knew that that ruling would be used to excuse the guards' intentional use of force.

Sure enough, that's what happened.

In November 2006, seven guards and the nurse at the scene were criminally charged with aggravated manslaughter for Anderson's death. They faced up to thirty years in jail.

When they went on trial in late 2007, Bondi was the prosecutor and Adams, with his unique and exonerating opinion on Anderson's cause of death, was her main medical witness. During the trial, defense attorneys got Adams to admit that no death from ammonia capsule suffocation had ever been reported before, or after, Anderson's death. But it didn't matter. The all-white jury came back in ninety minutes with not-guilty verdicts for all eight defendants.

The media noted that the prosecution's two medical experts said the ammonia capsule caused the boy's death. That would have raised doubts with the jury as to whether the physical restraint by itself would have caused Anderson's death. Investigators with the Civil Rights Division of the US Justice Department said they'd make a "thorough and independent review" of all of the evidence. But they eventually decided that there was insufficient evidence to pursue federal charges. Neither state nor federal prosecutors contacted me for my opinion. If they had, I would have told them that the cause of Anderson's death wasn't ammonia capsules, but unnecessary intentional prone pressure on his back by the guards that prevented him from breathing.

Three years later, Bondi was elected the state's attorney general with major support from law enforcement.

Meanwhile, Crump called the jury's verdict a "tough pill to swallow."

"You kill a dog, you go to jail," he said at a news conference, in an apparent reference to Black NFL quarterback Michael Vick, who had pleaded guilty to federal dogfighting charges a few months earlier and had faced up to five years in prison. "You kill a little Black boy, nothing happens."

After the verdict, I began thinking more about the important role that video had played in even getting the officers charged. Without the video, would there have been a second autopsy? Would there have been a financial settlement? Would anyone have been charged?

I thought about how many Black or Hispanic people had died in police encounters where there was no video record. At a traffic stop on a road outside a city or town. Any time no one was around and the police version of events was the only version available.

How many thousands of times had something happened? To how many lives?

Chapter 17

• • •

EXCITED DELIRIUM

After serving for twenty-five years, I retired from the New York State Police. I loved the job and the people there. But by 2011, most of the people I had worked with since becoming a physician were retired. Still, I wasn't ready to play golf. So, I decided to continue investigating civil rights cases.

Linda was supportive. "This is what you love. Go for it. It will keep you young," she said.

"I still feel like I have a lot to offer. If I didn't, I'd stop," I told her.

After the Martin Lee Anderson case, I saw an increase in calls for help from families who lost a son or daughter in a police encounter. I knew how painful it was to lose a child, and I didn't want to turn anyone away. I reviewed every request. I had been a forensic pathologist for more than fifty years and I knew the red flags in these encounters that indicated a mistake might have been made—determinations like excited delirium, sickle cell trait, drug overdose, and "pending" diagnosis. If there was anything questionable in the police narrative or autopsy, I'd take the case to the next step: a deeper dive into the available medical and autopsy information.

I had of late noticed a disturbing trend: more and more medical examiners were using excited delirium to explain police restraint deaths. It was a diagnosis that supported a particular conclusion: that police officers on the scene, restraining the victim, were not responsible for their death.

Somehow, most of the excited delirium victims were Black or Hispanic.

The cases were spread all over America, involving police departments in small towns and big cities as well as county sheriff's offices in rural areas and suburbs.

There was something else that troubled me. Some of the forensic pathologists conducting these suspicious autopsies were prominent members of the National Association of Medical Examiners, a group I had helped found in 1965 and resigned from in the 1970s. NAME was meant to educate and set standards for medical examiners but had rapidly become more pro-prosecution and quick to defend forensic pathologists who made mistakes. NAME embraced excited delirium as a proper diagnosis—even though it had been criticized by major national medical associations and civil rights groups.

The Kenwin Garcia case in New Jersey is a perfect illustration of what I believe is wrong with using excited delirium to explain a death in police custody.

In 2011, I received a call from attorney Mitchell Perlmutter, who had filed a federal suit on behalf of the Garcia family. He wanted me to conduct a second autopsy and review medical and police records to determine how Garcia died. He sent me the autopsy and toxicology reports, police audio transcription, death certificate, and hospital and medical records. He also included witness statements and police reports as well as one filed by a defense expert, Dr. Vincent DiMaio.

I'd known DiMaio since he was in medical school in Brooklyn. I had worked with his father Dominick when he became chief medical examiner of New York City. DiMaio had developed into one of the best medical examiners in the country and was chief medical examiner of San Antonio, Texas. He had testified in cases all over the country. He also was a proponent of excited delirium.

Garcia's case proved to be a troubling example of excessive use of force by police, one where better police training on how to handle the mentally ill—and some empathy for the victim—could have prevented a death.

Garcia was born in Trinidad in 1983. His family said he was a quiet, humble man who stayed away from alcohol and drugs. He was tall and strong, six-foot-four and 180 pounds, and worked at a nursing home. He didn't go out much after work. He liked to listen to reggae music and styled his hair in dreadlocks.

In 2005, when Garcia was twenty-two years old, something changed. Garcia lost his job for yelling at and threatening his boss. A doctor prescribed medicine to calm him down, but he still occasionally "acted erratically," his family said.

In 2006, he was charged for shoplifting from a retail store when he tried to exchange an open package of cigarettes for a Hershey bar. Later that year, he was caught jumping a turnstile at Newark Penn Station. When he failed to appear in municipal court, a bench warrant was issued.

Garcia enjoyed taking long walks, sometimes to neighboring towns in northern New Jersey. On July 15, 2008, a state trooper spotted Garcia—a tall Black man with dreadlocks—walking on the shoulder of busy Interstate 287. The trooper pulled over to ask him questions. Garcia was cooperative. He gave the officer his name.

The police computer showed that Garcia had an outstanding warrant, so at 6:18 PM, the trooper cuffed Garcia's hands behind his back, placed Garcia in the back of the police car, and closed the door. Backup police units pulled up.

It was the hottest hour of a mid-July day. The car's air conditioning was not switched on.

At about 6:25 PM, Garcia kicked out the rear window of the police cruiser.

Officers pulled him out of the car and pushed him face down into the grass along the highway. They cuffed his ankles together, hogtied his wrists to his ankles, pepper-sprayed him, struck him repeatedly, and knelt on his prone back.

When an ambulance arrived at 6:27 PM, Garcia was comatose.

Garcia's voice is calm throughout the nine minutes of police audio recorded between 6:18 and 6:27. He says "please" sixteen times. It was hot outside—and even hotter in the back of the closed police car. Garcia asked for water seven times, but was refused. When he kicked out the window to get air, an officer shouted, "What's the matter with you? Are you, are you retarded?"

The beating started. Police told him to "say his prayers" two times. Garcia said over and over: "Please don't beat me again." During that same nine minutes, police officers said "fucking" or "fuck you" eighteen times. There was no suggestion the handcuffed man was delirious or fighting back or a danger to anyone.

Troopers mocked him as he lay dying on the ground. "You're not laughing no more, are you?" one officer said.

"Stop moving your legs. I'm gonna fucking break them!"

"He looks like a filthy animal."

"Piece of excrement."

Garcia arrived at Morristown Memorial Hospital comatose, without a heartbeat. He was pronounced dead seven days later, on July 22, having never regained consciousness.

In their reports, officers on scene said they never punched, hit, or struck Garcia. They said he attacked them, kicking out the window in the first cruiser and banging his head against a passenger window in a second before the ambulance arrived.

The autopsy told a different story. Garcia had suffered severe internal injuries. His breastbone and several ribs were broken, a kidney was torn, and extensive internal bleeding had poured three pints of blood into his abdomen. He'd suffered multiple blunt-force injuries to his head and brain.

Toxicology showed no recreational or psychiatric drugs or alcohol in his blood.

Dr. Lyla Perez, who performed the autopsy, concluded that the cause of death was "excited delirium associated with blunt force trauma that occurred during a violent struggle while resisting arrest."

Perez said she based her finding of excited delirium in part on a book coauthored by DiMaio. New Jersey State authorities then hired DiMaio to "look into" the case. He attributed Garcia's death entirely to excited delirium and said Garcia died of "natural causes."

I shook my head when I read his report. Natural causes? They severely beat Garcia while he was restrained on the ground, and DiMaio said the young man just happened to die of natural causes?

Clearly this "excited delirium" diagnosis had spiraled out of control.

For years, I had been explaining to my colleagues at law enforcement conferences that excited delirium is junk science. It's not a concept recognized by the American Medical Association or the American Psychiatric Association. It isn't a valid diagnosis; it's a misappropriation of medical terminology. It's used to justify police violence, mostly against people of color.

So, how did excited delirium become the go-to diagnosis for medical examiners explaining deaths in police custody?

The term's origins can be traced to Florida medical examiner Charles V. Welti in the early 1980s. As cocaine flooded the streets of Miami, Welti, then deputy medical examiner, found himself in the trenches of the epidemic. He noticed that cocaine users were having strange and violent outbursts during confrontations with police, then dying for reasons he struggled to understand.

In 1984, a twenty-eight-year-old Miami jeweler who led police on a high-speed chase died suddenly after they handcuffed his wrists and legs. Wetli believed the man died not due to the subduing actions of law enforcement, but as the result of a cocaine-induced psychotic episode. He decided to take a second look at deaths of other cocaine users dating back to 1983 to see if there was a pattern.

The term *excited delirium* was first used in 1985 in a paper by Wetli and David Fishbain, a psychiatrist and professor at the University of Miami, titled, "Cocaine-Induced Psychosis and Sudden Death in Recreational Cocaine Users."

The paper was based on the deaths of five white men, one Black man, and a white woman. Five of the seven died in police custody, but the paper dismissed the violent police confrontations or restraints as the causes of death. The victims' toxicology showed the presence of cocaine, but at levels too low to be fatal. The authors concluded that even traces of cocaine could trigger what they called "excited delirium."

A year after the study was published, Wetli began using this theory to explain the mysterious deaths of Black women who were suspected prostitutes.

By late 1988, Wetli had either performed or supervised the postmortem examinations of more than a dozen Black women whose bodies were discovered naked from the waist down in empty lots or abandoned buildings. He noted that all the women had been using cocaine, and that they had died during or after sex. He told a Miami newspaper reporter in 1988 that under the influence of cocaine, "for some reason, the male of the (Black) species becomes psychotic, and the female of the species dies in relation to sex."

"At that time, that was true," he would say years later in a sworn deposition. "That's what our perception was. We were just beginning to find out about cocaine-induced excited delirium, which was very rare in women but was very common in males. And then we had this cluster of females who were dying with low levels of cocaine and sexual activities . . ."

In December 1988, the body of fourteen-year-old Antoinette Burns was found under a shade tree in a Miami neighborhood known for drug activity. Burns was found lying on her back with her skirt pulled up around her waist and her underpants near her ankles. Everything Wetli saw at the scene fit the pattern of the other women: a young Black female who appeared to have recently had sex. Wetli noted no obvious signs of trauma. Here was another Black woman driven to death by drugs and sex.

But the toxicology report called into question Welti's theory: there was no cocaine in the teenager's system.

Wetli's boss at the Miami-Dade County Medical Examiner's Office, Joseph Davis, reexamined all of the excited delirium autopsies. What he found was stunning. There were neck injuries and petechial hemorrhages in the women's eyes—evidence of strangulation. So Davis reclassified all of Wetli's autopsies—nineteen women, including Burns—as homicides.

After Davis's ruling, police homicide detectives began investigating the women's murders. They determined that the nineteen women had died at the hands of a serial killer—and they quickly turned their attention to Charles Henry Williams, a Black man, who had been seen with some of the victims. He was arrested in 1989 on two rape charges unrelated to the murders. A year later, he was convicted of one count of rape and sentenced to forty years in prison.

Investigators believed Williams killed as many as thirty-two women. They were still gathering evidence when Williams died in prison of AIDS in 1994.

Wetli's pushing of excited delirium as cause of death might have allowed Williams to keep killing. But the bogus diagnosis didn't derail Wetli's career. In 1996, he left Miami and became chief medical examiner in Suffolk County, New York.

By then, his theory on excited delirium and Black drug users had taken root in Miami and spread around the country. In the early 1990s, "excited delirium" began showing up in autopsy reports in other states—California, Rhode Island, and Wisconsin—and even Canada.

After a decade as Suffolk County chief medical examiner, Wetli had participated as a medical expert in more than one hundred excited delirium cases, nearly all of them as a defense expert in fatal police encounters.

Wetli also began to use the term *agitated delirium* interchangeably with excited delirium ("It's the same thing," he said in a deposition) and started attributing the condition to causes other than cocaine, including alcohol.

Excited delirium remains controversial to this day. Groups like Physicians for Human Rights, which was awarded the Nobel Peace Prize in 2018 for its efforts to stop the use of sexual violence as a weapon of war, are quick to point out the term's racist past. In 2022, the organization released a report sharply criticizing excited delirium, saying the term "cannot be disentangled from its racist and unscientific origins."

"Excited delirium has come to rest on racist tropes of Black men and other people of color as having 'superhuman strength' and being 'impervious to pain,' while pathologizing resistance to law enforcement, which may be an expected or unsurprising reaction of a scared or ill individual (or anyone who is being restrained in a position that inhibits breathing). Presently, there is no rigorous scientific research that examines prevalence of death for people with 'excited delirium' who are not physically restrained," the group wrote.

In my opinion, the "superhuman strength" stereotype meshes with excited delirium to give police an excuse to use excessive force when subduing Black men. How else are police going to restrain someone with that kind of strength?

At first, I really didn't know what to make of Wetli's theory of excited delirium. He described three major components: the presence of cocaine in a person's system, a temperature of 105 degrees or higher, and bizarre or crazy behavior. These three things supposedly resulted in very rapid deaths.

But then, Wetli and others began adding other components, including the presence of any drug in the victim's system, as well as removing some. Now, he declared, excited delirium could be caused by the presence of alcohol or different drugs in a person's body—methamphetamine, marijuana, even Benadryl and antihistamines—not just cocaine. And you didn't need a high temperature, either.

There was one signature constant, however: the presence of police.

If a person died suddenly while being restrained by the cops—especially if the person was Black—it had to be excited delirium. Very few deaths were attributed to excited delirium outside of police encounters. It was the chase, the struggle, and the ensuing excessive release of adrenaline that caused the cardiac arrest.

A person's behavior before an altercation with law enforcement was supposedly a good indicator of whether they would suffer excited delirium. They say an individual with the disorder is usually in an acute state of confusion marked by intense paranoia, hallucinations, and violence toward objects and people.

Wetli and I had been friends. I also knew his wife, Dr. Geetha Natarajan, the Chief Medical Examiner of New Jersey. When they got married, I was one of the "best men" at their wedding.

So, I told him about my concerns directly. We'd approached each other at a conference to say hello before his retirement in 2006, and during our conversation, we discussed excited delirium. He said he was thrilled that it had been accepted as a diagnosis by some parts of the medical community. But I responded that I believed excited delirium was a speculative diagnosis without any scientific foundation—one that was very biased toward police.

I noted the fact that the police who chased down and struggled with the suspect never died of excited delirium bothered me. "How come it's only the suspect and not the police, who are doing the same thing, who dies?" I asked.

Wetli started getting defensive. "Well, the police aren't on drugs."

"But you said you don't always need to be on drugs to die of—"

He turned and walked away. He didn't want to hear any criticism.

It reached a point where we no longer spoke.

The year 2006 saw another development in the history of excited delirium. That's when DiMaio and his wife Theresa published *Excited Delirium Syndrome: Cause of Death and Prevention.* The book was dedicated to "all law enforcement and medical personnel who have been wrongfully accused of misconduct in deaths due to excited delirium syndrome."

DiMaio had often been called as a defense expert for police accused of misconduct. Now, in 2011, he was testifying in the Garcia case as an expert for the defense.

DiMaio's testimony added a new element to the excited delirium theory: he claimed that the absence of drugs didn't matter. Drug use, especially cocaine, had been a critical part of the "excited delirium" formula. But Garcia had no drugs in his system. DiMaio's theory was that excited delirium was caused by a rush of adrenaline produced by the body during a struggle with police. These heated altercations led this supposedly dangerous chemical to spike. That caused the heart to race, inducing cardiac arrest. So, in DiMaio's opinion, Garcia's manner of death was natural—he died because his body made too much adrenaline.

Except no one has shown that adrenaline is higher than average in anyone who is said to have died of excited delirium.

I reviewed all the evidence in the Garcia case and wrote my report for the attorney, Perlmutter. I advised him that I disagreed with Perez's conclusion.

"It is my opinion that the direct cause of Mr. Garcia's death was the violent manner in which police improperly restrained him utilizing pepper spray, hogtying, multiple blows that caused laceration of his kidney and internal hemorrhage, and pressure on his back that interfered with his breathing. It is my opinion that the manner of Garcia's death is homicide," I wrote.

A few months after I wrote the report, the state paid $700,000 to the family to settle the lawsuit. As part of the settlement, the Garcia family agreed not to discuss the case in public. They were forbidden to speak negatively about the police.

Despite the evidence, no criminal charges were filed. A grand jury found that the New Jersey troopers' use of force was justified. As in other grand jury cases, there is no way to know what evidence the prosecutor presented to the jury and how it was presented. The transcripts are not public record.

The state police denied any wrongdoing, as law enforcement always does when they settle cases.

Why would a police officer taunt and mock someone who is mentally ill or refuse water to a cooperative prisoner on a hot afternoon? Was it racism? Macho posturing? Only the officers who were on the scene know the answer to that. But the audio recording of that day shows a clear lack of concern as to Garcia's well-being. Couldn't the officer have turned on the air conditioning in the car? Couldn't someone have given Garcia some water?

Police involved in these cases also show a troubling lack of remorse. So many deaths like Garcia's could be prevented with effective training. Officers don't need to be so militaristic, especially when dealing with the mentally ill. Most in-custody deaths aren't life-or-death situations. No one is pointing a gun at the officers. But time and again, the police act like they're in a war zone, and the suspects are the enemy.

I investigated another excited delirium case the same year involving a twenty-nine-year-old Black man with a history of schizophrenia. It was another death that could have been prevented.

At 8:50 PM on July 8, 2008, Samuel De Boise's mother called 911 from the front yard of her suburban St. Louis, Missouri, home. Her son, who had run out of the house naked the night before, had just returned home. Still nude, he was walking around the house breaking things, talking nonsensically and threatening to kill her. She said she'd left her house unharmed.

The St. Louis County Police arrived at about 9:00 PM, stationed themselves outside the house, and ordered De Boise to come out. De Boise came outside with nothing on, empty-handed and cooperative. Police told him to lay face down on the grass with his hands behind his back.

He wasn't immediately handcuffed, so he stood up. When he did, he was tasered about ten times—first in the front of his body, then in his back—for a total of 53 seconds.

De Boise fell down. When EMS arrived and examined him at 9:19 PM, De Boise was face down, hands cuffed behind his back, with "one officer kneeling over him holding him down." Although De Boise wasn't moving, other cops were also "pressing on his lower extremities, arms and shoulder blades while a paramedic injected Ativan and Haldol into his left hip." Ativan treats anxiety, while Haldol is for schizophrenia and causes drowsiness and dizziness.

Minutes later, as they were moving De Boise into the ambulance, the paramedic noticed De Boise was in full cardiac arrest. An electrocardiogram showed no electrical activity. He was dead.

At autopsy, Chief Medical Examiner Mary Case found four Taser probes from two discharges embedded in his torso: two in front and two in back. All of his organs, including his heart and brain, appeared normal. Case listed his cause of death as "Excited delirium due to acute psychotic episode (schizophrenia)" and the manner of death as "Natural."

In other words, she concluded that De Boise was killed by mental illness, not Taser electrocution or police pressing on his back.

In the report I sent John Burton, the attorney for the De Boise family, I wrote that excited delirium was an "invented syndrome to protect police" and not recognized as a valid diagnosis by major medical associations. After reviewing all the information, I said, my conclusion was that De Boise died of "cardiopulmonary arrest due to repeated Taser applications during police restraint. The manner of death is homicide because it occurred at the hands of another."

But in the end, a federal judge dismissed the lawsuit that claimed police used excessive force and ignored De Boise's medical needs.

When I look at the case, I can't help thinking about how it could have been handled differently. What the family needed that night was a mental health professional to talk to—not a police officer to give orders that De Boise wouldn't understand.

De Boise had struggled with mental illness since he was seventeen years old. He had worked in construction, operated a tow truck, and was a rapper, poet, and musician.

His family told police that, in the days before his death, his behavior had become increasingly erratic and that he was researching "weapons of mass destruction, Hitler, and the Iraq war." He clearly needed to be in a mental health facility.

Police arrived at the house believing he could be dangerous. They surrounded the house carrying pistols, a rifle, shotgun, and Tasers. But when De Boise walked outside naked and unarmed, he wasn't a threat.

The police claimed that after De Boise initially agreed to lie down, he jumped to his feet and began charging officers. And US magistrate Terry Adelman of Missouri wrote in 2013 that he believed that this made tasing and applying prone back pressure to a mentally ill man having a mental health crisis reasonable.

"While the evidence also shows that he was naked, unarmed and surrounded by six police officers, testimony from the officers indicates that Samuel was physically strong and challenging," Adelman said.

So many police fatality cases had unhappy legal endings—judges dismissing medically well-founded lawsuits, police officers not being held accountable for what were unjustifiable deaths, police versions of events repeatedly judged more reliable than witnesses'. Little did I know that the increasing use of smartphones and social media would slowly start to change the narrative.

His body was left in the

Chapter 18

• • •

SUMMER OF DEATH

On a sweltering summer day in 2014, New York City police officers approached forty-three-year-old Eric Garner, whom they suspected of illegally selling single cigarettes in his very poor neighborhood near the Staten Island Ferry.

Three weeks later, as eighteen-year-old Michael Brown Jr. and a friend were walking in the middle of a two-lane street in the St. Louis suburb of Ferguson, Missouri, an officer stopped and told them to use the sidewalk.

Neither Garner nor Brown survived their encounters with the police.

Their violent deaths in American neighborhoods a thousand miles apart triggered national demonstrations against police brutality as well as debate about policing in communities of color and racial discrimination in the criminal justice system. It became the tipping point for many who had complained for decades about police treatment of Black and Hispanic people.

Garner and Brown were both killed by police in bright daylight, their deaths witnessed by people in their neighborhoods. And smartphones would play a critical role in both cases, illustrating just how important video was becoming in documenting police encounters and—sometimes—helping to bring officers involved to justice.

Smartphones have made it easy for bystanders to record such encounters in real time. In Garner's case, the videos contradicted the official police narrative of the incident. Videos from Brown's killing showed how callous the police department was in the aftermath of his death. His body was left in the hot, sunny street, uncovered for hours in full view of all who passed by, blood from bullet wounds leaking onto the ground while the police refused to let his mother go to him.

I was involved in both cases. They showed me that if things didn't start to change, race relations in America would continue to deteriorate. And if that happened, I wasn't sure how they would play out.

My wife was worried about me. I was busier than ever at an age when I should have been slowing down. Every night she'd see me sitting at my desk, going over documents or writing reports. But I always had her support. And I made sure I was there for her, too. She was still practicing law and was a host on the Law & Crime television network. We made a good team. And that meant a lot as I dove into an increasing number of civil rights cases.

I had learned about Eric Garner from television reports. Then, the day after his death, Sanford Rubenstein, the attorney for his family, phoned me, saying they wanted a second autopsy. They were worried that the medical examiner's office would protect the officers. I agreed to help.

Garner was a big man, six-foot-two and 395 pounds. He stood out on the streets of Tompkinsville, Staten Island, a working-class neighborhood where he hawked single cigarettes, or "loosies."

In early July 2014, officers had spotted Garner as he was selling loosies. When they approached him, Garner became agitated, and shouted at them to back off. The officers didn't engage him that day. They just warned him to stop selling.

On July 17, two plainclothes officers in an unmarked police car were circling Garner's block when they saw him on the street. Justin Damico and his partner Daniel Pantaleo suspected he was dealing loosies again. They radioed for backup, got out of their vehicle, and walked toward Garner, ready to arrest him.

"We're taking you into custody," they told him.

"For what, what did I do?" Garner said.

"For selling cigarettes," Damico replied.

Garner denied it. A neighbor said Garner had just come down to break up a fight. He had no cigarettes. An eleven-minute video taken by a neighbor, Ramsey Orta, shows that one of the officers tried to grab Garner's arms, but

Garner shrugged him off. "Don't touch me. Please, do not touch me," he said. He made no hostile move toward the officer.

But they'd had enough. Pantaleo wrapped his arms around Garner's neck in a carotid sleeper-type chokehold. Four more officers arrived and helped wrestle Garner to the pavement. They exerted pressure on his back, with Pantaleo's arm pressed against his neck and Garner uttering, eleven times, "I can't breathe." Police pressed his nose and mouth onto the sidewalk, obstructing his breathing. The video shows that he was on the ground lifeless less than fifty seconds after the police first touched him.

He was pronounced dead at a hospital an hour later.

The neighbor who captured the incident on his smartphone, including Garner's many cries of "I can't breathe," uploaded it to a social media site. It went instantly viral, unleashing a tidal wave of anger. Not only was the Black community incensed at the unnecessary and needless brutality, they were also angry that the police and responding EMTs delayed in providing CPR when Garner became unresponsive.

As I reviewed the Garner case, I couldn't help but think about the state of race relations in America. By the summer of 2014, President Barack Obama, the first Black president, was well into his second term. When Obama took office in 2008, some politicians and pundits said it was time to stop talking about racial disparities and injustice. But as reports of deaths during police encounters continued to increase, it was clear that such discussions were still needed.

Most of white America wasn't paying attention to these cases. Newspapers and television networks in the predominantly white media usually ignored the deaths of Black people, especially those who died suddenly after being restrained by police. When the media did cover them, they often only reported law enforcement officials' version of events.

With smartphones with cameras becoming more commonplace, making individuals better equipped to document police and victim interactions, I had hope that maybe the tide was starting to turn. When witnesses recorded a police encounter on their phone, they could immediately share it with a news outlet. Or they could just post it themselves on a social media platform, like Facebook or Twitter. If it went viral, millions of people could quickly see the altercation themselves—as they did with Garner's.

In addition, some police departments had started using body cameras, pager-sized devices that clipped onto an officer's uniform and recorded audio and video of their interactions with the public. This record was intended to restore faith in the community that the police department's version of an incident was accurate.

Video was becoming an important tool for medical examiners, too. There are injuries you can't see clearly on the autopsy table because they leave no marks. For example, you can't see the damage done by pressing on the back of a suspect in the prone position. But the video of Martin Lee Anderson's killing clearly showed heavy guards pressing on his back, which prevented the slender teenager from breathing. That was critical in being able to prove that he had died of traumatic asphyxia. The autopsy always begins at the scene. Medical examiners who do not include findings from the scene and do not consider the pre-death activity before completing an autopsy report can make serious mistakes in determining the cause and manner of a death. Video made avoiding these mistakes easier.

As I drilled into Garner's case, I was worried about the police narrative. Their initial report contained no mention of police using a chokehold to restrain him. The video, however, clearly showed Pantaleo placing Garner in a chokehold—Pantaleo's left arm around Garner's neck—which the NYPD had banned in 1993.

Even after the video went viral, police claimed Pantaleo didn't use a chokehold. "It was bringing a person to the ground the way we're trained to do to place him under arrest," said Pat Lynch, the president of the Patrolmen's Benevolent Association.

I called the medical examiner, Floriana Persechino, and told her that the family wanted me to do a second autopsy. Was there anything she could tell me about her findings from the first one?

She agreed that the family had a right to know what her findings were and said that the body was still at the Manhattan Medical Examiner's Office. If I came there, I could examine everything retained at the office, including all the external and internal photographs of the body, the microscopic slides, and the toxicology results. So, I went there to examine the photographs and records.

We both agreed that there were no injuries to the skin of the neck, but that

there was prominent hemorrhage in the neck muscles and petechial hemorrhages in the eyes that were evidence of severe compression from a chokehold.
She said that she was going to release those findings the next day and would
rule the manner of death a homicide.

After reviewing the photographs and microscopic slides, I told Rubenstein that I agreed with Persechino's conclusion that Garner's death was due
to asphyxia, obstruction of breathing—a homicide. So, he went outside the
building at First Avenue and Thirtieth Street and held an impromptu press
conference.

I told reporters the same thing I said earlier to Rubenstein, that the medical examiner and I had both concluded that Garner's death was caused by the
way he was restrained by police.

"There was hemorrhaging around Garner's neck and petechial hemorrhages in the eyes, which are indicative of severe neck compressions. The compression of the neck that prevented his breathing trumps everything else as
cause of death," I told reporters.

I added that compression of the chest and face that were documented in
the video also contributed to his death.

The police union's spokesman disagreed. Once again, he insisted the officer
didn't use a chokehold. Instead, he called that a "seatbelt" takedown maneuver
and said that Garner's neck was likely injured when EMTs intubated him.

There was something else about this case that disturbed me—something
on the video that had become a rallying cry for justice. Garner kept saying, "I
can't breathe." And the police officers ignored his pleas. Time and again I had
heard police officers say, "If someone can talk, they can breathe." But that's
wrong. You can talk without actively inhaling or exhaling—without breathing. You can speak while being suffocated.

When someone is pleading that they can't breathe because officers are on
top of him, the officers need to get off. The person is already restrained; there
is no danger to them or anyone else. Police have to be taught that when someone says "I can't breathe," it is not some sort of manipulation. It means they
should immediately stop pressing on the person's neck or back and remove any
obstructions to the nose or mouth. Doing so would prevent most of the deaths
that are now occurring during police restraints.

The aggressive police tactics exposed by Orta's video, including neck holds designed to render a person unconscious, pressing or laying on a person's back while cuffing them from behind, and pressing the nose and mouth against the ground, all increase the risk of death. Other strategies, like using spit masks, restraint chairs, and repeatedly tasing someone to comply, can also cause death. Did the officers know these tactics could be deadly? Did they believe the tactics were appropriate for arresting people for minor offenses, such as selling loosies?

Chokeholds had been controversial for years. The US Supreme Court ruled in 1983 they could be used, but Justice Thurgood Marshall gave a blistering dissent on the issue.

In 1976, Los Angeles police officers pulled over Adolph Lyons, a Black man, for a broken taillight. The officers met him with guns drawn even though he offered no resistance. They ordered him to face the car, spread his legs, and place his hands on top of his head.

When Lyons complained of pain, one of the officers wrapped his arm around Lyons's neck and began to choke him. Lyons blacked out. He woke up face down on the ground, lying in his own urine and feces. The officers released him with a citation for the broken taillight.

Angry about the way he was treated, Lyons brought a federal lawsuit against the city and the officers who assaulted him.

Lyons's attorneys showed that their client was not the only man who'd been choked by a Los Angeles police officer. Between 1975 and 1980, LAPD cops had used chokeholds on at least 975 occasions.

When he sued, Lyons didn't only want money compensating him for his injuries. He sought an injunction—a formal court order that would forbid the LAPD from using chokeholds "except in situations where the proposed victim of said control reasonably appears to be threatening the immediate use of deadly force."

But the Supreme Court ruled 5–4 against Lyons, holding that he could not obtain such an injunction unless he could show that he was personally likely to be choked by a Los Angeles police officer in the future.

Justice Byron White, who wrote the opinion for the majority, went even further. To obtain an injunction, Lyons would also have to show that *all* police officers in Los Angeles routinely choke any citizen they arrest, question, or cite, and that the city approved of it.

Justice Marshall strongly disagreed. He said the ruling made it too difficult to obtain an injunction preventing police misconduct—that "if the police adopt a policy of 'shoot to kill,' or a policy of shooting 1 out of 10 suspects, the federal courts will be powerless to enjoin its continuation." And in fact, the court's ruling is still a great obstacle to attorneys challenging police brutality.

Marshall noted that Los Angeles instructed its officers that use of a chokehold does not constitute deadly force, but no less than sixteen people had died between 1976 and 1980 following the use of a chokehold by an LAPD police officer. Twelve of the victims were Black. The Los Angeles chief of police, Darryl Gates, said it was because Black necks were weaker than white necks. But Marshall was incensed. He said the carotid sleeper chokehold was a lethal police tactic, and that it was used more commonly against Black men that white ones. Further, he said the evidence showed that the city's official policy permitted police officers to employ chokeholds in a variety of situations where they faced no threat of violence, especially against Black men.

With Garner, the case against Officer Pantaleo was sent to a Staten Island grand jury. The borough, New York City's smallest, was also likely its most conservative. Seventy-five percent of the 476,000 people who lived on Staten Island were white, and it was home to many police officers.

For six weeks, Staten Island district attorney Daniel M. Donovan Jr. empaneled the grand jury to weigh evidence; it heard testimony from the officers involved and twenty-two civilian witnesses. Donovan granted all the officers except Pantaleo immunity. Michael Graham, a St. Louis forensic pathologist and past president of the National Association of Medical Examiners, also testified at the secret proceedings.

The grand jury deliberated for only a few hours before clearing Pantaleo of criminal wrongdoing. In delivering a vote of "no true bill," jurors determined there was not probable cause that Pantaleo had committed a crime.

The Black community was outraged. They believed that, once again, a white police officer had gotten away with murder. US attorney general Eric H. Holder Jr. was among the people stunned by the grand jury.

"Mr. Garner's death is one of several recent incidents across the country that have tested the sense of trust that must exist between law enforcement and the communities they are charged to serve and protect," Holder said.

Waves of angry but generally peaceful demonstrators took to the streets in New York and all over the nation. Protesters chanted, "I can't breathe."

Five months later, District Attorney Donovan, with full police endorsement, was elected to Congress, representing a sliver of Brooklyn and all of Staten Island, by an overwhelming majority.

A Staten Island judge refused requests to release the grand jury testimony even to New York City's Civilian Complaint Review Board. And even though it was revealed that Pantaleo had been investigated for misconduct seven times in the five years before Garner's death, he kept his job.

Holder decided not to bring any charges against the officers or the department, and five years later, Donald Trump's attorney general William Barr ordered the case dropped.

After the federal government officially dropped the case against Pantaleo in 2019, the New York Police Department opened disciplinary proceedings against him. Michael Graham, the same St. Louis forensic pathologist who testified before the grand jury, was a witness at the disciplinary hearing—which, unlike the grand jury, was public. He said Garner had died of "heart problems and not from choking. I didn't see anywhere in here that he was unable to move air."

Really? I thought. Did he not see the videos and hear Garner plead "I can't breathe" eleven times? Did he not see the neck, back, and face pressure obstructing his breathing?

Then, Persechino testified—and she downplayed the role of the police restraint. She told the panel that Pantaleo's action set into motion "a lethal sequence of events" that "triggered an asthmatic attack." She said "even a bear hug" could've hastened his death, given Garner's fragile health. Under cross-examination, she said a person in good health might have survived the confrontation. But I knew there was no microscopic evidence in Garner's lungs of an asthmatic attack.

At that point, I wondered what she might have told the grand jury five years earlier. The autopsy findings showed that Garner's health issues had nothing to do with his death. Besides, the central issue at this disciplinary hearing was whether Pantaleo used a banned chokehold, not whether Garner was physically capable of withstanding one.

In the end, five years after Garner's death, Pantaleo was fired. And the city paid $5.9 million to settle the wrongful-death lawsuit filed by Garner's family.

Still, I wondered if justice was actually done. Even with explicit video as evidence, Pantaleo wasn't criminally charged, by either the city or the US Department of Justice. And I couldn't stop wondering about the role the prosecutor and medical examiner might have played in preventing that from happening.

◆ ◆ ◆

While I was involved in Eric Garner's case, I received a call from Benjamin Crump, who had been hired to represent Michael Brown Jr.'s family in Ferguson, Missouri. Crump asked me to do a second autopsy on the teenager.

"Doctor Baden, I need you out there as quickly as possible. I wouldn't ask you if it wasn't so important," he said

He said the St. Louis County medical examiner had just conducted an autopsy, but hadn't released her findings. That worried Crump and Brown's family. They wanted me to do an independent autopsy because they did not trust local authorities to conduct an unbiased examination.

A policeman had shot the teenager multiple times in circumstances that remained unclear, and the lack of transparency had led to anger and frustration in the Black community. Crump didn't have to tell me this was a volatile case. I had seen the disturbing images of Ferguson in newspapers and on television.

On August 9, 2014, Brown and a friend were walking in the middle of Canfield Drive, a two-lane street in the St. Louis suburb of Ferguson, when officer Darren Wilson drove by and told them to use the sidewalk.

Words were exchanged, and the white officer left his car to confront the teenaged Brown, who was Black. The situation escalated, and the officer shot and killed the unarmed Brown.

Brown's bloody body remained uncovered in the street for four hours in the summer heat. People in the neighborhood who gathered at the scene lashed out verbally at police, angry not only about the shooting but also about the mistreatment of the boy's body.

The next day, after a candlelight vigil, some people in the crowd protesting Brown's death started smashing windows and looting items from local stores. Other protesters stood on police cars and taunted officers.

The destruction spread. A QuikTrip convenience store just blocks from where Brown was shot was looted and burned. Other businesses were damaged or destroyed. The people's frustration was boiling over.

I told Linda I was going to Ferguson. She understood but was worried because of the violence. I promised I'd be careful, but I had no plans to slow down—all these videos of fatal police encounters and broken families were adding up to a national showdown. And at this point, St. Louis law enforcement wasn't sharing any information with the victim's family or the public.

On Sunday, August 17, I boarded a flight to St. Louis.

The FBI had already opened an investigation into Brown's death. New contradictory information was coming out quickly—mostly from witnesses. Two white men working nearby told the media that they saw that Brown's hands had been raised when the officer fired repeatedly.

The protests continued and were getting more destructive. The Missouri State Highway Patrol took over security from Ferguson and St. Louis County officers after images showed many officers equipped with military-style armored vehicles, body armor, and assault rifles. For many in the Black community, they were no longer police departments. They were an occupying military force.

Police released surveillance video, taken shortly before Brown was spotted walking in the street, that showed him appearing to take some cigarillos from behind the counter of the Ferguson Market and then pushing a worker who confronted him as he left the convenience store. Police said Brown took almost $50 worth of cigarillos. Protesters said police were now trying to shift the narrative from the officer to the victim. They said the cops wanted to paint Brown as a "bad guy" who deserved to be shot.

Governor Jay Nixon declared a state of emergency and imposed a curfew in Ferguson. He called the National Guard to help keep order.

Once I had landed in Ferguson, I was taken to the Austin A. Layne Mortuary, where Crump was waiting with Brown's mother, Lesley McSpadden, and father, Michael Brown Sr. I wanted to talk to Brown's parents first to ask them about their concerns, which I could then address in the autopsy. I wanted to know about his health and any prior surgeries, whether he had a history of drug use they were aware of, or a seizure disorder. As I approached, I could see the pain on their faces.

"I'm sorry for your loss," I said to them.

They nodded. I sensed that they weren't sure if they could trust me at first. I was a stranger. They were angry at the police and the city—all government officials, especially everybody involved in their son's death.

But when I started asking them about their son, they opened up.

They said that because of Michael's size, six-foot-five and nearly three hundred pounds, people often thought he was older than he was. Everyone called him a "gentle giant." He didn't have any health problems.

Michael Brown Jr. was twelve when his parents had split. At first, he had lived with his mother, but by the age of sixteen he'd moved in with his father. Michael Brown Sr. was tall, with a bald head, moustache, and beard. He said he had briefed his son about dealing with police. His advice: Just follow orders. Be respectful. Listen and follow directions.

"There was no way he was going to attack that officer. He was a good person. He would never harm a police officer," he said.

Brown had struggled academically and switched schools several times. He had just completed the summer course he needed for his high school diploma. He was supposed to start vocational school for heating and cooling in the fall.

"But now, I'm planning his funeral," his mother said.

They talked about how their son's body was treated after he died. The police just left his body to rot in the street, they said, like the days of public lynchings, when white mobs left mutilated Black bodies hanging from trees to serve as a warning: *We have complete control over your lives. One wrong move and you could end up like this.* That was the message the police were sending by leaving Brown's uncovered body there for so long.

When Lesley arrived at the scene, her son's body was still there on the ground, but the police kept her away. They would not let her touch her son; they told her she could stand behind a police line with everyone else. No one called an ambulance. The police treated him like dirt, she said.

But leaving his body there had unintended consequences for police.

After the shooting, people in the neighborhood rushed out of their homes and apartments to see what was going on. They took video of the scene and posted it online. The fact that the cops didn't respect Brown enough to move his body off the street or shield it from the hot sun outraged people all over the nation and drew additional attention to the shooting.

A ten-minute video posted on YouTube taken on a smartphone by someone who identified himself as a neighbor captured Brown's body, the yellow police tape that marked off the crime scene, and the residents standing behind it. "They shot that boy 'cause they wanted to," said one woman who can be heard on the video.

"He had his hands up and everything," said the man taking the video, speaking to a neighbor. At one point, a woman can be heard shouting, "Where is the ambulance? Where is the ambulance?"

I told Brown's parents I was angry. "There was no reason they should have left his body in the street. No reason." Any police procedures they might have done, like documentation with photographs and measurements, would have been completed in an hour or two.

When they saw that I was empathetic, they opened up more.

"It hurts. It just really hurts," McSpadden said. "Why did they kill him? I don't understand it."

It was still unclear what had happened—how the situation escalated so quickly, why the officer opened fire. Investigators had their work cut out for them.

Brown's friend Dorian Johnson said the two of them were walking down the street when Officer Wilson pulled up and ordered them to "get the fuck on the sidewalk." Wilson then got out of the car and grabbed Brown by the throat, Johnson said. Police claimed that Brown forced his way inside the cruiser and tried to grab Wilson's gun. That's when Wilson shot at Brown the first time.

Did Brown have his hands in the air when he was shot? How many shots were fired? No one could say for sure. Or no one would say. The autopsy might help answer those questions.

"Doctor Baden, we just want to know what happened to our son," Lesley McSpadden said. "We want to know if he suffered. If he was in any pain."

Another attorney had hired someone to assist with the autopsy, so everything was ready for me when I walked into the autopsy room. Three hours later, after I'd finished, I was ready to discuss my initial findings with Brown's family, Crump, and the other attorneys.

I told them these were just preliminary findings that could change as more information became available. The family members would have to steel themselves. Some of it would be hard for them to hear.

"He was shot six times, including twice in the head. He was bending his head forward when the last shot was fired. That last shot was the fatal one." He would have lost consciousness immediately following the last shot, I explained. If an ambulance had come, they wouldn't have been able to provide any help.

They listened to every word. Then, with her voice full of tears, McSpadden asked: "He wasn't in any pain after that?"

"No pain," I responded.

Overcome, she started sobbing.

Crump wanted to let the community know about the private autopsy, so we drove to the Greater Saint Mark Missionary Baptist Church for a news conference with media and community members.

I repeated everything I had told Brown's family.

Brown was shot six times, I said, the last two in the head and brain. One of those bullets shattered his right eye and facial bones. The head shots would have caused him to fall, where he was left on the ground for all to see.

The wounds were catastrophic. Brown would not have survived even if he had been taken to a hospital right away, I said.

There was no gunpowder residue around the bullet holes, indicating the shots were not fired from very close range.

My preliminary autopsy results were the first time that critical information concerning Brown's death had been made public. As with other cases I had worked on with racial overtones, I felt it was important that I address the issue of transparency. I believed that the victim's family and community had the right to know the facts as soon as possible.

"I'm hoping that this will calm the community," I told the reporters. "The community and family wanted to ask certain simple questions. They have been asking from the beginning: 'How many times was he shot?' This information could have been released on day one. When the medical examiner or police didn't release it, that contributed to the community feeling that something was being covered up."

As I answered reporters' questions, I stressed that the autopsy didn't assign blame for or justify the shooting. "We need more information. For example, the police would be examining the automobile to see if there is gunshot residue or blood in the police car," I said.

I didn't want to speculate. I took each question as it came, and stuck to the facts.

"Are any of these wounds inconsistent with the witness accounts that Michael Brown was shot while rushing the police officer?" one reporter asked.

I replied that, at this point, it was hard to say for sure if he was moving forward or backward when he was shot. The bullet wounds indicated his head was bent forward, I replied, but the autopsy couldn't tell his direction of motion.

"How far away was Brown from the gun when he was shot?" another asked.

"We can tell certain distance," I answered. "We can tell the distance from the muzzle of the gun to the body, and the body's clothing. The closer the weapon is to the body, the more powder residue there will be on the body and the skin and the clothing. In this instance, there's no gunshot residues on the skin surface, so the muzzle of the gun was two or more feet away at the time of discharge."

Still, I said, it could have been just two feet away, or it could have been thirty feet away. "We also have to look at the clothing, which we haven't had the opportunity to do yet. Sometimes clothing can filter out gunshot residues."

"Can you get access to the clothing, and was there any signs of struggle?"

I said I'd have access to the clothing at some point. It was currently in the hands of Mary Case, the chief medical examiner who had handled the autopsy of Samuel De Boise in 2008.

Brown's autopsy had shown no signs of a struggle. But I knew that didn't mean a struggle hadn't occurred.

"One of the things that the attorneys have also asked for is records from the medical examination of the officer who shot Brown. Signs of injury to the officer, and to Michael Brown, are both needed before making that determination," I said.

The reporters also asked me questions about myself. Crump had introduced me as a well-known New York–based medical examiner, one of only about four hundred board-certified forensic pathologists in the nation. He said I had reviewed the autopsies of both President John F. Kennedy and the Reverend Dr. Martin Luther King Jr., and had performed more than twenty thousand autopsies. And he mentioned that I hosted the HBO show *Autopsy*, calling me a "celebrity medical examiner." I told the reporters I didn't like that title because 99 percent of what I did had nothing to do with celebrities.

They asked me about my fees. And I told them that I had waived my usual $7,500 fee for this autopsy—and acted likewise in other cases where families couldn't afford it. "Families should have the opportunity to know what happened to their loved ones. Money shouldn't be an obstacle in trying to get justice."

After Crump announced the results of my autopsy, US attorney general Eric Holder said the Justice Department would conduct a third autopsy. It was an unusual move, but multiple examinations sometimes occur when there is distrust of the authorities involved. (The DOJ released the results of its autopsy on December 14. Its findings mirrored those of my postmortem examination.)

I stressed that my examination was not meant to determine whether the shooting was justified. "In my capacity as the forensic examiner for the New York State Police, I would say, 'You're not supposed to shoot so many times.' But right now, there is too little information to forensically reconstruct the shooting." Also, too many contradictory witness statements were still being analyzed. "From the science point of view, we can't determine which witness is most consistent with the forensic findings," I said.

Crump showed no similar restraint when he gave his statement. The officer simply opened fire at an unarmed man, Crump said. He recklessly fired ten shots. Six bullets hit Brown's body.

"The sheer number of bullets and the way they were scattered all over his body show this police officer had a brazen disregard for the very people he was supposed to protect in that community," Crump said. "We want to make sure people understand what this case is about: This case is about a police officer executing a young unarmed man in broad daylight.

"Michael Brown's mom had the same question as any mother would have, which is 'Was my child in pain?' And Doctor Baden said that in his opinion he did not suffer.

"His mother also wanted to ask a question that neither Doctor Baden nor the lawyers could answer: 'What else do we need to give them to arrest the killer of my child?'" Crump said.

The crowd in the church erupted in applause.

Then a reporter asked me the last question: "All of us here know what happened to Michael. Why hasn't Officer Wilson been arrested?"

"As you know, who gets arrested is a district attorney decision, not a medical examiner decision," I said.

And with that, the news conference was over.

As I was leaving the room, I knew the district attorney would have to decide whether this was or was not use of justifiable deadly force. A police officer is entitled to use deadly force to protect themselves or a third person from serious physical bodily harm or death in the conduct of their duties. But I also knew, from my years of experience, that many decisions DAs make are based on politics—not witness statements or forensic science.

Returning home, I was leaving behind a community in chaos. This case risked becoming a political football. No matter what conclusions could be drawn from my work, Brown's death had been marked by shifting and contradictory eyewitness accounts that continued for more than a week after it had occurred. The autopsy findings could tell that he was shot six times but not if he was moving forward or backward.

For many, Ferguson was a tipping point. Brown represented more than one death. He represented all the unarmed Black men who had died in police confrontations. And in almost all of them, despite thousands of deaths and thousands of witnesses, white police officers were not held accountable. It was rare to see an officer charged, and even rarer to see any of them go to prison—I could not recall a single conviction.

How could that be? Were all those killings justified? No way. But I knew who was responsible: the police, district attorneys, and medical examiners who were part of the good-old-boy system. They knew how to evaluate cases to make sure police officers are not charged criminally.

Maybe that's why groups like Black Lives Matter were becoming so important. Black Lives Matter was founded in 2013 in response to the acquittal of George Zimmerman, a neighborhood watch group volunteer who killed

Florida teenager Trayvon Martin. The movement gained additional prominence as an increasing number of Black men—and some Black women—were shown to be victims of police use of excessive force, their deaths whitewashed by the systemic racism in our criminal justice system. In Ferguson, I saw the Black and white community marching in solidarity and demanding answers to Brown's death and the way his body was treated. I wasn't sure how this would all play out, but I was glad that civil rights groups were letting public officials know they would fight loudly for justice.

A few days later, Attorney General Holder visited Ferguson to offer assurances about the investigation into Brown's death and to meet with investigators and Brown's family.

Meanwhile, a grand jury began hearing evidence to determine whether Wilson should be charged. And in November, I was called to testify. It was unusual to call someone who had conducted a private autopsy for a victim's family, but Crump believed it was a good move.

In the months between my autopsy and the grand jury hearing, new evidence had surfaced. A witness named Tiffany Mitchell said she saw Brown and officer Wilson "wrestling" through the open police-car window. A shot went off in the car. Then Brown ran away from the car, followed by the officer, who kept firing shots at the fleeing teenager. Another witness said Brown was hit in the back, then his body jerked forward and he put his hands up. Brown said, "I don't have a gun. Stop shooting." Two people working outside said they saw Brown raise his hands, as if to surrender. But Wilson kept firing, and Brown crumpled to the ground.

In mid-September, Ferguson police chief Tom Jackson, a white man, released a video apology to Brown's family and attempted to march in solidarity with protesters. The move backfired. Ferguson officers scuffled with demonstrators and arrested one person moments after Jackson joined the march.

When I entered the grand jury room at the Buzz Westfall Justice Center in Clayton, Missouri, I noticed that all but two of the jurors on the panel were white. The way the room was set up, they sat in a semicircle around me.

That day, I was permitted to read Mary Case's autopsy report, which still hadn't been released to the public, to the grand jury. It stated that, when she had removed some tissue from Brown's thumb to examine under the microscope, she found foreign material "consistent with products that had been discharged from the barrel of a firearm." If true, it would support Wilson's claim that the gun discharged when Brown grabbed his weapon in the police car. But I suspected the foreign material might actually be dirt from the ground near where Brown's had fallen.

I hadn't received all the information I would have needed to complete my investigation, including Wilson's medical records from his visit to the hospital after the shooting. He said Brown had injured him—and that he feared for his life. But I hadn't seen the evidence of his injuries. If he had been injured, were his injuries consistent with a struggle? I couldn't say.

Robert McCulloch, the St. Louis County prosecutor, introduced me to the jurors and asked me to discuss my findings. I recounted what I had found: Brown had been shot at least six times, with none of the shots appearing to be from very close range.

I had no idea how the prosecutor had presented the case to the jury before I went in. In these proceedings, the prosecutor has total control of what evidence is shown to the jury and what is excluded. But I testified that it was my opinion that Brown was facing Wilson when the officer repeatedly fired his weapon. Even if they had been scuffling in the car, Brown wasn't a threat when he was killed. He didn't have a weapon. He was a distance away from Wilson when the officer shot him.

Following my testimony, I returned to New York. A few days later, the grand jury declined to return an indictment against Wilson.

Sure enough, their decision sparked another round of violent protests. At least a dozen buildings and multiple police cars were burned and police officers were peppered with rocks and batteries. Reports of gunfire on the ground forced some St. Louis–bound flights to be diverted. A day after the grand jury announcement, Officer Wilson resigned from the Ferguson Police Department.

A few months after the grand jury ruling, a member of the panel filed a federal lawsuit seeking an exception to the state law requiring secrecy on grand jury service. She said she wanted to "speak publicly about her experience on the grand jury" and "contribute to the current dialogue concerning race relations." She claimed that McCulloch's handling of the case was poor. "The prosecutor released an unprecedented amount of information that was presented to the grand jury as well as his own editorializing of that content, and that greatly diminished the interest in secrecy," the plaintiff's attorney later said in a hearing. But years later, a federal appeals court ruled against the woman.

In March 2015, the Justice Department decided not to press civil rights charges against Wilson, but did find systemic racial bias at the Ferguson Police Department. Local authorities had been targeting Black residents for years, arresting them disproportionately and fining them excessively. A year later, Ferguson and the Justice Department reached an agreement that required sweeping reforms of the city's police and court systems. In 2017, a federal judge in St. Louis approved a wrongful-death lawsuit settlement that ultimately awarded Michael Brown's parents $1.5 million. Because of qualified immunity, Wilson paid none of it. The city's insurance company paid instead.

For many, it was all too little, too late. Once again, no charges were filed against a white police officer who killed an unarmed Black man.

I had handled too many of these cases over the years. I knew everything that went on behind the scenes—how police, prosecutors, medical examiners, and current laws were biased toward shielding officers from charges arising from on-duty deaths. It seemed to me that making officers potentially liable financially would make them more careful about causing unnecessary civilian deaths. So what would it take for police officers to be held accountable?

There would be another prominent, well-publicized death of a Black man—and a global pandemic—before I'd get the answer.

Chapter 19

• • •

THE MORE THINGS CHANGE

I awakened to a gentle voice on the airplane intercom announcing our approach to the Minneapolis–Saint Paul International Airport. I yawned, adjusted my facemask over my ears, then stretched my arms over my head. I didn't know what to expect when I landed, but I braced myself for the worst.

George Floyd's death had struck a raw nerve. Over the years, I had witnessed protests after the deaths of Arthur Miller, Eric Garner, Michael Brown, and other unarmed Black men and women. But those were nothing like this.

Since Floyd's death on May 25, 2020, demonstrations and unrest had rocked Minneapolis and spread to at least 140 communities across the United States as well as other countries. Tens of thousands of people had filled the streets to express their outrage and sorrow. The daytime marches, unfortunately, sometimes descended into nights of disorder, with shootings, looting, and vandalism in some places. The National Guard had been activated in nearly two dozen states. In Minneapolis, protesters burned down a police station and the businesses near the site of Floyd's killing.

It wasn't just Black people marching, angry that police had killed yet another Black man. This time, many of the demonstrators were white—young and old, socially active, and fed up. Mere months into a deadly pandemic, they were risking their lives to stand in solidarity at last with groups like Black Lives Matter, which had been trying to draw attention to police brutality for years. The racial diversity of these protesters contrasted sharply with the clear divisions between Black and white opinions twenty-five years earlier when O.J. Simpson was tried for murder.

Smartphone video recorded by bystanders to Floyd's death showed white America exactly how police were treating their Black counterparts. It showed Floyd, lying face down in the street with his hands cuffed behind his back, a police officer's knee on his neck, as bystanders shouted at the cops to stop.

Officer Derek Chauvin pressed his knee into Floyd's neck as the man cried out in pain to his mother. He kept his knee on Floyd's neck while the man said, "I can't breathe. I can't breathe." He kept his knee there even after Floyd stopped moving. For nine and a half minutes, Chauvin stared back at the crowd in arrogant defiance, with his knee on Floyd's neck, seeming to enjoy what he was doing. It felt like he was sending a message: *Shut up or you're next.*

This wasn't my first case in Minneapolis. Ten years earlier, I had investigated the death of another unarmed Black man who died suddenly in police custody.

David Cornelius Smith was a twenty-eight-year-old Black man with mental health issues. He was on the sixth-floor basketball court at the downtown YMCA, where he was a member, on September 9, 2010, when he began behaving strangely. Staff members called police. When the two officers arrived, they asked Smith to leave. When he refused, they tased him several times, then wrestled him to the ground.

During the struggle, police kneeled on Smith's back. As captured on security video, after four minutes they realized he wasn't breathing. They called paramedics, but by the time they arrived, Smith was comatose. A week later he was pronounced dead.

Andrew Baker, the Hennepin County chief medical examiner, performed the autopsy and concluded that interference with Floyd's breathing produced extensive brain damage due to a lack of oxygen. He listed the cause of death as "anoxic encephalopathy due to cardiopulmonary arrest (resuscitated) due to mechanical asphyxia" while Smith was in the prone restraint position. He classified the manner of death as a homicide.

Minneapolis police chief Tim Dolan defended the actions of officers Timothy Gorman and Timothy Callahan, saying "a tragedy can ensue" even when officers "act appropriately."

A Hennepin County grand jury seemed to agree, clearing Gorman and Callahan of any criminal wrongdoing. Fred Bruno, the officers' attorney, said Smith had only himself to blame for his death, because he was "out of control."

Smith's family was upset and filed a wrongful-death lawsuit, which focused on the officers' use of prone restraint. They claimed that Gorman and Callahan had suffocated Smith by putting excessive weight on his upper back.

Their attorney, Robert Bennett (who ten years later would be one of George Floyd's lawyers), reached out to me to help in the investigation.

I reviewed all of the pertinent materials, including the autopsy report, video, police reports, depositions, and medical records.

The autopsy showed that Smith, who was six feet tall and 169 pounds, had no health problems that could have caused his death. The toxicology report showed that Smith had not been taking his psychiatric medications, but there was a high level of dextromethorphan, an ingredient in over-the-counter cold medicines, in his blood. That, together with his psychiatric problems, may have contributed to his bizarre behavior—but not to his death.

In my report, I agreed with Baker that the police restraint interfered with oxygen going to Smith's brain and that it was a homicide.

"Smith's death was due to chest compression during physical restraint by the police while he was prone on the ground, which prevented him from breathing and resulted in mechanical asphyxia," I wrote.

A few months after my report, the city settled the lawsuit with Smith's family for $3 million. As part of the settlement, the police department agreed to have all officers trained on the dangers of positional asphyxiation. On April 23, 2012, the Minneapolis chief of police ordered supervisors to show a video to all officers at roll call that "serves as a reminder that when a subject is restrained, there is a direct correlation between their ability to breathe and the position their body is in . . . persons on their stomach can't breathe" and should be turned on their side.

Yet here I was, about to land in Minneapolis, investigating a case involving the same cause of death in the same police department.

As the plane began its descent, I thought about Floyd's life and the video that had captured his death.

Floyd was born in North Carolina. His mother, Larcenia, a single parent, moved the family to Houston when he was two so she could search for work. They settled in the Cuney Homes, a public housing project of more than five hundred apartments south of downtown nicknamed "The Bricks."

Floyd was a good athlete, and Larcenia hoped that investing in her son's talent would help lift them out of poverty. At six foot, six inches tall, he was a star tight end for the football team at Jack Yates High School, playing for the losing side in the 1992 state championship game at the Houston Astrodome.

His friends called him "Big Floyd," but like Michael Brown, he was known in the neighborhood as a gentle giant. Floyd played basketball at South Florida State College for two years, then spent a year at Texas A&M University's Kingsville campus before returning to his mother's apartment in Houston. He worked in construction and security.

Between 1997 and 2005, Floyd was arrested several times on drug and theft charges. In August 2007, he was arrested and charged with aggravated robbery with a deadly weapon. He pleaded guilty in 2009 and was sentenced to five years in prison. By the time he was paroled, in January 2013, he was nearing forty and had five children.

A year later, Floyd moved to the Twin Cities as part of a church discipleship program that offered men a route to self-sufficiency by changing their environment and helping them find jobs. In Minneapolis, Floyd first worked as a security guard at the Salvation Army's Harbor Light Center—the city's largest homeless shelter. He left after a year, and began training to drive trucks while working as a bouncer at a club called Conga Latin Bistro. Floyd suffered a blow when his mother died in 2018. And he lost his job as a bouncer in 2020 when the coronavirus pandemic forced the club to close.

That May, on the evening of Memorial Day, Floyd was with two friends at a convenience store when employees accused him of paying for cigarettes with a counterfeit $20 bill, then called the police. A bystander's smartphone camera captured what happened next.

My immediate impression when I watched the video was that the police had done everything they shouldn't do. The officers had Floyd in the prone position with his hands cuffed behind his back; he was not a danger to anyone. Yet they were also pressing on his back while Derek Chauvin had his knee on Floyd's neck. People were yelling at Chauvin to get his knee off the man, that he was killing him. The smartphone captured in his expression the naked reality that Black people knew well: *I am a police officer. I am immune from criticism or punishment.*

I was watching a man die for nine and a half terrifying minutes as a direct result of being restrained by police. This wasn't a Hollywood movie; this was real life. It was slow and messy and horrifying.

I did not think the officer meant to kill Floyd. He didn't get up that morning and say, "I'm going to kill somebody today."

What would have happened, I wondered, if no one had recorded the killing? Would investigators or the district attorney have believed the bystanders? Or would they have accepted the cops' story of Floyd resisting arrest and thus deserving deadly force?

But I already knew the answer.

If I needed any more proof, all I had to do was read the statement released by the district attorney on May 29. He said the autopsy "revealed no physical findings that support a diagnosis of traumatic asphyxia or strangulation." And he noted that Floyd had underlying health conditions, including heart disease and drug abuse. That was why Crump had called me.

Floyd's autopsy was conducted by Andrew Baker—the same Hennepin County medical examiner who had performed the postmortem examination on David Cornelius Smith. His finding was stunning. The prosecutor and Baker were telling us not to believe our eyes—a textbook attempt at gaslighting.

Baker had to have known that injuries associated with positional asphyxia usually didn't show up on the victim's body. He had access to the video. Did he not watch it? Or was he giving in to police pressure? He was an appointed official, and his term was up in a few months. I didn't know what was going on behind the scenes. But it didn't really matter. I was there to perform a second autopsy and make an independent determination as to what killed Floyd.

I walked through the empty airport with a few dozen other masked people. The airport, like most large public places, now felt dangerous. Every day, more and more people were being hospitalized and dying from COVID, and we didn't yet have a vaccine or cure.

My son Lindsey, now a doctor, researcher, and professor at Harvard Medical School, was working with his colleagues to develop a vaccine for the drug company Moderna. Until they or someone else succeeded, traveling—being around large groups of people—was very risky.

Crump's driver took me to the hotel. The city streets were deserted, like the apocalypse had arrived.

I checked into the hotel. Crump had arranged a strategy meeting right there in the Hilton to minimize my exposure. He and cocounsel Antonio Romanucci, along with Allecia Wilson, a forensic pathologist and director of autopsy and forensic services at the University of Michigan who had also been hired by Floyd's legal team, would be there.

I unpacked, freshened up, and headed to the meeting. Crump shook my hand and introduced me to everyone.

"The family is very upset with what's happening. We think there's a cover-up," Crump said, noting Baker's preliminary findings.

We went over all the details. The next day, Sunday, we convened at Estes Funeral Chapel where Wilson and I would perform the second autopsy. Crump was there, too. We were all double-masked. Three of the younger lawyers, dressed in full personal protective gear, were also there. They wanted to watch the postmortem examination. The family agreed to let them.

It was fortunate that we all had taken extra protective-gear precautions because a day after our postmortem examination I learned from the media that Floyd had tested positive for COVID during the first autopsy. That information should have been disclosed to the funeral director so all of his people could have taken the proper precautions. Wilson and I should have been told, as well as the attorneys who would be in the room during the autopsy. Dead bodies could still transmit the virus.

When we entered the embalming room, Floyd's body was already on the table. Wilson and I changed into scrubs, put on thin plastic gloves, and began work.

She and I worked well together. We examined Floyd's body over a few hours, scrutinizing every organ and inspecting areas of the body that had not been previously dissected. There were abrasions on the left side of his face and shoulder showing how hard he was pressed against the pavement. We found hemorrhage in muscles in the right carotid area where Chauvin's knee had pressed into Floyd's neck—proof of pressure that had not been previously identified. Our autopsy showed no evidence of a death from natural disease. A portion of the coronary arteries had been removed and retained during the initial autopsy for further study, presumably because there were prominent arteriosclerotic plaques there. But there was no significant heart muscle damage. While there was a recreational level of fentanyl in Floyd's blood, it had not caused his death.

After we finished, Wilson and I cleaned up and met with Crump and the other attorneys to explain our findings. We said the video was the most important piece of evidence in this investigation. It showed that police pressure on Floyd's neck and back caused his death by interfering with his ability to breathe. Such lethal pressure would leave no marks on the body but still showed during our autopsy. George Floyd had suffocated. When he said he couldn't breathe, the officers should have listened. They also should have paid more attention to the restraint warnings that supervisors had repeated at roll calls over the last ten years.

The next morning, Monday, June 1, Crump held a televised news conference to discuss our findings. Wearing our masks, Crump, Wilson, and I explained what happened to Floyd—that he died because of the way police had restrained him.

Crump stated that the second autopsy and video showed that Floyd died because of Chauvin's knee on his neck and because two other officers pinned him down by applying pressure on his back, interfering with diaphragm movement and chest expansion. "His death was a homicide caused by asphyxia due to neck and back compression that prevented blood and oxygen from reaching the brain," I said at the news conference.

Our findings thus contradicted the publicly-announced Minneapolis medical examiner's findings.

Wilson and I elaborated, saying Floyd died because of the way he was subdued.

"The physical evidence showed that the pressure applied led to his death," Wilson said. "Some of the information I read states that there was no evidence of traumatic asphyxia. This is the point in which we do disagree. There is evidence in this case of mechanical or traumatic asphyxia"—autopsy and video evidence.

I agreed and stressed that any underlying health problems Floyd might have had did not kill him—did not contribute to his death. I also criticized the popular police misconception that being able to say "I can't breathe" means you can breathe.

By this point, four officers had already been fired—Chauvin, the two other officers pinning Floyd down, and a fourth who prevented upset civilian witnesses from getting closer to Floyd and Chauvin. Crump said Chauvin should be charged with first-degree murder rather than the lesser third-degree charge he was facing, and the other officers should be charged to the "fullest extent of the law."

He said that the family's distrust of the Minneapolis Police Department was based partly on the sanitized way it described how Floyd was restrained. The day after Floyd's death, the police statement described him as a suspected forger who "appeared to be under the influence," "physically resisted officers," and appeared to be "suffering medical distress." It never mentioned any officers' roles in his death.

The Floyd family was "encouraged," Crump said, that Minnesota Attorney General Keith Ellison was taking over the prosecution. That suggested the state didn't trust local officials.

At the end of the news conference, I realized that we were just confirming the obvious—what everybody had seen on the video. We told the truth about how Floyd had died. He didn't die of a bad heart. He didn't die of drugs. He died at the hands of police. His death, like so many others, could have been avoided if police had just stopped pressing on him when he said he couldn't breathe.

Later that day, Baker and the Hennepin County medical examiner's office agreed with the statements that Wilson and I made at the press conference: that Floyd's death was due to asphyxia while being restrained.

But the following day, the National Association of Medical Examiners issued a news release criticizing the value of second autopsy opinions by forensic pathologists. The release said the medical examiner who does the initial autopsy is more independent and credible than forensic pathologists hired by the family. There was an immediate backlash from the association's members and others, however—and NAME quickly withdrew that self-serving statement.

Before I headed to the airport, I called my wife. I told her everything went well. "We did the autopsy. I think we made a difference."

She was proud, but quickly warned me, "You better keep wearing your mask until you get back here!"

After we hung up, I said goodbye to Crump and the other lawyers. Then, I headed to the airport. By the time I boarded my flight that night, the media narrative had changed. It was no longer Floyd's heart disease and drugs that caused his death. Now, everyone was saying he died because of the way police restrained him.

What charges would be brought against the officers involved in Floyd's death would be up to the lawyers. I only knew that after all these years, something felt different. People were taking to the streets, across racial lines, to demand police reform. They wanted to ban chokeholds, prone back pressure, and other dangerous forms of restraint. They were demanding that cops stop profiling Black and Hispanic people and start treating them with respect and dignity. They wanted police to speed the release of bodycam footage and the disciplinary records of officers accused of brutality, and bring an end to qualified immunity that protected police misbehavior.

I was encouraged by the fact that that most of the protests were peaceful, and that so many people, of all races and religions and economic backgrounds, were fighting for change. And as I took my seat in the plane, I was filled with hope that we, as a nation, were moving forward toward racial justice.

I knew it wouldn't happen overnight. I knew we were still at the beginning. And I knew it wouldn't be easy. I had seen other protests for racial justice fizzle and fade. But this felt and looked different. No, after eighty-five years, I was convinced that things were changing. And I promised myself that I'd be there, doing my part.

EPILOGUE

Nine months after I left Minneapolis, Derek Chauvin, the white police officer charged in George Floyd's death, sat at a table inside a courtroom, flanked by his attorneys.

He looked different from the last time I'd seen him, on the smartphone video that had captured Floyd's death. Then, Chauvin had been in his police uniform, a knee on Floyd's neck, staring arrogantly at bystanders who were yelling at him to stop. They said he was killing Floyd, whose head was pinned against the pavement, as this unarmed Black man pleaded repeatedly, "I can't breathe. I can't breathe."

Now, on March 8, 2021, the forty-five-year-old Chauvin was wearing a suit and tie. He looked nervous as he waited for a Hennepin County judge to enter the courtroom. It was the first day of Chauvin's murder trial. Soon, prosecutors and defense attorneys would deliver their opening statements.

No one knew what would happen.

Six weeks later, the case was in the jury's hands. It only took ten hours for them to reach a verdict. They found Chauvin guilty of second-degree unintentional murder, third-degree murder, and second-degree manslaughter.

It was a stunning turn of events.

On June 25, Judge Peter Cahill sentenced Chauvin to twenty-two-and-a-half years in prison for Floyd's murder. Cahill acknowledged that Floyd's death had been a reckoning for the nation. The murder had triggered massive protests against racial injustice and also prompted debate about how much the law should protect officers when someone dies in their custody.

"Part of the Minneapolis Police Department's mission is to give citizens 'voice and respect,'" Cahill said. "Here, Mr. Chauvin, rather than pursuing the MPD mission, treated Mr. Floyd without respect and denied him the dignity owed to all human beings and which he certainly would have extended to a friend or a neighbor."

After the sentencing, Benjamin Crump said the sentence would help heal some of the pain.

"For once, a police officer who wrongly took the life of a Black man was held to account," he said.

Watching the trial unfold on television from my home in New York, I had hoped Chauvin's conviction would be a watershed moment in the fight to stop police brutality against people of color. The signs were certainly there. White people, Black people, Hispanic people, and more, of all ages, had been marching in the streets with longtime civil rights activists who viewed Floyd's death as a symbol of racial intolerance and injustice.

I knew it would take time before police departments changed their tactics and procedures. I also knew most police departments wouldn't do it on their own. Laws would have to be enacted to force them to change. That meant politicians would have to be engaged in police reform. But politicians didn't always have the will to do the right thing. They'd need to be pushed. Activists would have to keep up the pressure.

Meanwhile, every day it seemed that somebody was reaching out to me, asking if I could perform a second autopsy or review documents related to a family member who had died in police custody. Over the last year, my work had only increased, a sign that fatal police encounters were still a problem.

People didn't trust the criminal justice system, and I understood their concerns. I have had extensive experience working closely with police, prosecutors, and others involved in the law enforcement community, during which time I was exposed to many of the flaws in that system. I worked more than fifty years for the New York City Medical Examiner's Office and the New York State Police, but my work as a forensic pathologist extended beyond that. I headed many forensic panels, including the House Select Committee on Assassinations reviewing the deaths of President Kennedy and Dr. King. I have investigated deaths in many countries for human rights groups and private attorneys and taught homicide courses for police, judges, attorneys, and physicians all over the world. I've been a director on the boards of drug abuse and alcohol abuse treatment programs, where I applied what I've learned from the dead at the autopsy table for the betterment of the living.

I've done just about everything I had set out to do when I decided to follow my bliss so many years ago. I'm now in my late eighties. My three surviving children are all doctors, trying to make the world a better place. My wife, Linda, keeps me grounded. She's my rock, even as she continues her own work as a prominent criminal defense and civil rights attorney. At a time when most people my age are retired, I'm still going strong, fueled by the fact that I know I can still help people find justice.

And that's why writing this book was so important to me. We are at a pivotal moment in US history. I believe it's necessary to help the public understand how the criminal justice system really works—how prosecutors, medical examiners, and police sometimes work together to protect cops involved in fatal shootings or restraint deaths. If we are going to change the system, we have to understand the problem first.

Beyond that, *American Autopsy* is about some medical examiners' roles in helping law enforcement and prosecutors whitewash deaths—especially of Black and Hispanic people, the mentally ill, and other vulnerable citizens—at the hands of police. At the beginning of my career, I believed that most police officers and prosecutors were good. That there was no racism in the criminal justice system. That there was no racial bias in police departments. Prosecutors and police were the good guys and always did the right thing. They followed the law.

Yes, I reasoned, there were some bad cops. But they were few and far between. Besides, most professions had a few bad people—bankers who embezzled money, politicians who took kickbacks, doctors who sold prescriptions to drug addicts. But to me, a rogue cop was someone who took bribes—not someone who'd kill a Black or Hispanic person during a routine police encounter, then try to cover it up or justify the killing.

Then, the racial injustice of particular deaths—Eric Johnson's, Arthur

Miller's—made me begin to question my beliefs. These cases slowly slotted together, like pieces in a mosaic. And years later, when all the pieces were assembled, it revealed to me a disturbing picture of America's broken criminal justice system.

My faith in the criminal justice system continues to be shaken to this day as new information emerges in old cases where minorities were wrongly convicted of crimes.

In 1965, I sat in a Manhattan courtroom watching my boss at the time, Milton Helpern, testify at the trial of three men charged with killing Malcom X, one of America's most influential Black leaders.

I recalled that the Black defendants and their six Black attorneys were seated at one table, the three white prosecutors at another. When Helpern took the stand, he said Malcom X had died from multiple shotgun and bullet wounds to his chest and heart.

Back then, I thought the defendants were the bad guys and the district attorney, police, and medical examiners were the good guys. So, when the men were convicted, I didn't question the evidence.

Fast forward to November 2021. Manhattan District Attorney Cyrus Vance announced that a twenty-two-month investigation conducted jointly by his office and lawyers for two of the three men convicted in Malcom X's murder had found that the men were innocent.

Vance said prosecutors, the NYPD, and the Federal Bureau of Investigation withheld key evidence that, had it been turned over, would likely have led to the men's acquittal.

Yes, the system is broken—but it can be fixed. I still believe most police officers are good, hard-working, honest people who follow the law. Most of my friends are in law enforcement. There's no war on Black or Hispanic people. Most police officers are overworked, underpaid, and forced to deal—often without the proper training—with many of America's most serious social and mental health problems.

But I also believe that most of the bad cops aren't held accountable for their behavior. When that happens—when there are no consequences for rogue behavior—it corrupts the entire system, eroding trust in our institutions. Why should police departments change procedures when cops know they won't be punished if they make a mistake? For many police departments, settlements in wrongful-death lawsuits have become part of the cost of doing business. And the settlements are paid with taxpayers' dollars—not those of the person responsible for the death.

Over the years, I've come to the stark conclusion that the racial bias in the US criminal justice system is endemic. Just look at the facts. When a white kid gets caught with drugs, he's sent home or to a drug rehabilitation center. His Black counterpart, caught with the same amount of drugs, gets sent to jail. Police officers don't routinely stop vehicles with white drivers unless they are speeding or swerving on the road. But statistics show that Black and Hispanic drivers are stopped more often—sometimes for little or no reason. And it's during these traffic stops that bad things happen.

A white man walking down the street at 11 PM is not afraid of being stopped and frisked. But people of color live in fear, knowing they can be stopped by police at any time for any reason. White families don't have "the talk" with their children. But Black and Hispanic families do, going over a checklist of how to behave if a cop stops them. If they don't follow the rules— and even if they do—they could end up dead.

In 1968, during hearings of the National Advisory Commission on Civil Disorders—the so-called Kerner Commission—more than 130 witnesses testified about the events leading up to the urban uprisings that had taken place in 150 cities in the summer of 1967. One of the complaints that came up repeatedly was "the stopping of Negroes on foot or in cars without obvious basis." It was true then. It remains true now.

In fatal police encounters, it doesn't matter whether the victim was shot or choked. It doesn't matter if the person was unarmed. It doesn't matter if the person was mentally ill and running in the street naked. All a police officer has to say to justify a victim's death is three magic words that have been endorsed by the US Supreme Court: "I felt threatened."

It was like that when I started work as a medical examiner. It's like that today. Racial bias isn't a new phenomenon. It's part of law enforcement culture. Just look at the history of policing in the United States.

The origins of modern-day policing in the South can be traced back to volunteer forces of white men who quashed slave uprisings and pursued, captured, and returned runaway slaves to their owners. The earliest slave patrol was created in South Carolina in 1704, and the practice continued until the end of the Civil War. They were not designed to protect public safety, but rather rich slave owners' interests, and they used excessive force to control slaves and to stop anyone who might help them escape.

In the North, while the reasons for introducing policing were different, the practice had similarly racist roots, including returning runaway slaves to their Southern owners. As more and more immigrants arrived in the United States, they settled in cities, where they could find jobs. This influx was followed by a rise in "nativism"—the belief that native-born white Americans were "better" than immigrants. Someone needed to make sure the new arrivals were monitored. They couldn't be trusted.

In the 1600s, New York and Boston became the first two cities in colonial America to organize public police units to "control" immigrants. These so-called Watchmen were mostly volunteers, but some were paid by private citizens. Initially, they followed the English system with constables and sheriffs. Constables organized the Watchmen to patrol towns at night. They kept an eye out for "suspicious" individuals and activity. It was during the Jim Crow period, when state and local municipalities legalized segregation in response to the Fourteenth Amendment's grant of equal protections to Black people in 1868, that communities across the United States began to establish police departments to make sure residents followed local laws. Across the South, defeated Confederate soldiers became police and sheriff's deputies—and were used to brutally enforce segregation.

The Ku Klux Klan and other hate groups also arose during this period. They terrorized Black communities, carrying out lynchings and destroying Black schools. Many law enforcement and other government officials became KKK members. And when Black Americans protested against segregation and other racist laws, it was these same police officers who were often called in.

The racism of the time was endorsed at the top of the US government. President Woodrow Wilson, born in Virginia and raised in Georgia, had the influential 1915 film *Birth of a Nation* screened in the White House. Its villains were Black men—sometimes portrayed by white men in blackface—and its heroes were KKK members. The film led to the resurgence of the KKK, which had been moribund. By the mid-1920s, the hate group had millions of members. And in 1925, tens of thousands of Klansmen in white hoods and robes marched down Pennsylvania Avenue in Washington, DC.

During the civil rights era, images of police brutally suppressing peaceful activists, including with the use of dogs and fire hoses, helped usher in the Civil Rights Act of 1964, which outlawed discrimination on the basis of race, color, religion, and sex.

But as Black people gained more rights, lawmakers on both sides of the political aisle passed laws that only increased the incarceration of minority Americans. In 1971, the Nixon administration launched the "war on drugs," resulting in increased arrests and harsher prison sentences largely for Black people. Politicians in the late 1980s and early 1990s ratcheted up this pattern when they enacted tougher laws for possession of crack cocaine that jailed even more Black and Hispanic people. Meanwhile, the penalties for possession of cocaine in powder form—mostly used by white people—remained lower.

Against that historical backdrop, it's no wonder that Black and Hispanic people are proportionately more likely to be arrested and die in police encounters than white people.

It's important to remember, however, that police don't operate in a vacuum. Prosecutors and medical examiners also play critical roles in our flawed criminal justice system. Prosecutors are the ones who decide whether to investigate police custody deaths or to charge cops. And some medical examiners issue "natural," victim-blaming causes for these deaths, like excited delirium and sickle cell trait, making it easier for district attorneys to walk away from the matter.

When a medical examiner declares the manner of death in a police custody case to be accidental, natural, or undetermined, usually no criminal investigation ensues. No charges. No nothing. The police officer wasn't at fault. But if the forensic pathologist says the death was a homicide, that makes it harder for prosecutors to ignore the death. The district attorney will be more likely to launch an investigation or present the case to a grand jury for possible prosecution.

Even so, in the United States, there's little appetite for prosecuting a police officer. One reason is that law enforcement makes up a big, politically important voting bloc, and charging an officer could mean political suicide for ambitious prosecutors looking to run for higher office.

But there's another reason police are rarely prosecuted: America has no national system of death investigations and only has about 450 full-time forensic pathologists whose job it is to perform autopsies and determine cause and manner of death.

Not every jurisdiction uses medical examiners. Some rely on coroners, an elected position—and one for which, as I noted, many places only require US citizenship and being of voting age. That's it—not even any medical training. If an autopsy is needed, the coroner might use a hospital pathologist who is an expert in natural deaths, but who does not have the same level of training as a forensic pathologist in examining unnatural deaths. And in the end, regardless of the pathologist's findings, it's still the coroner who determines the cause and manner of death.

Medical examiners are physicians appointed on the basis of merit. Despite fulfilling a political position, they are supposed to be independent scientists— unswayed by outside pressure. But the reality is, many medical examiners say that in some cases, they have been pressured to change their findings to better support the prosecution. Others don't need to be pressured. They think of themselves as part of the prosecution team.

Since medical examiners are appointed, they have concerns that if they issue the "wrong ruling" in a police custody death, they may get political blowback from their superiors that could lead to being demoted, fired, or not reappointed.

When I began as a New York City medical examiner, I was proud and excited to be an essential part of the justice-seeking prosecution trinity along with the police and the district attorney. We were the good guys, working as a team against the defense as they tried to find loopholes for their "bad" clients. I spoke often and freely with prosecutors whenever they wished about the best ways to present my findings to the jury in support of the prosecutor's theory of the case. (In the early days, if my findings supported their theory, they'd go forward; otherwise, they would drop the case.)

My office was supposed to be an independent city agency. But if the defense wanted to discuss the autopsy findings with the medical examiner who performed the autopsy, a prosecutor had to be present or, we were told, the defense attorney would misstate what was said and it would be their word against ours. Defense attorneys thus rarely asked the medical examiner to discuss the autopsy findings prior to trial.

But I did occasionally experience political pressure myself and watched other MEs bend their findings to make prosecutors' cases stronger.

As a medical examiner, I was able to do research studies into heroin victims, alcoholism, child abuse, and suicide. But I could not do research into gunshot deaths (no research money available) or deaths caused by police (no one was interested, on the city, state, or federal level). The New York City Medical Examiner's Office did research into child toy deaths, falls from windows and fire escapes, and suicides in the elderly—but not into police-related deaths.

The conclusions of science and medicine do not necessarily coincide with political desires. Placing an independent physician-scientist like a medical examiner in a political position is like trying to put a square peg into a round hole. I learned this firsthand when, shortly after becoming New York City's chief medical examiner in 1978, I determined the cause of Black businessman Arthur Miller's death as restraint asphyxia—a homicide. In doing so, I broke the unspoken gentleman's agreement between medical examiners, police, and prosecutors to issue findings that minimize excessive use of force by police.

Miller had died in Brooklyn while being restrained by police. Witnesses said they heard him say, "I can't breathe." Other medical examiners might have attributed the cause of death to something other than the police officer's actions—something like psychosis with exhaustion, an earlier version of excited delirium. Something that meant the death was the decedent's fault. After all, the police officer hadn't intended to interfere with Miller's breathing. He was just trying to handcuff him from behind while he was being uncooperative. And after this case was over, the ME's office would need to continue to work with him and his fellow officers every day after.

My autopsy findings in the Miller case meant I was no longer a team player, and a year later Mayor Koch cited my declaration of Miller's cause of death when he demoted me from chief medical examiner. He stated that blaming the police for causing Miller's death could have started a riot—somehow forgetting that he had sent me a letter after I told the public my findings to congratulate me for being fully transparent and preventing a riot.

In 2020, on the forty-second anniversary of Miller's death, then–Brooklyn borough president Eric Adams described Miller as the nation's first *"I can't breathe* case"—or the first that was publicized, at least. Adams was a former New York City police captain, and in November 2021 would be elected mayor.

"If we had responded then, we'd be living in a different city and country today," said Adams.

Because decades later, there was George Floyd, uttering those same words. Nothing had really changed. The similarities were eerie, including how police officials in Minneapolis, just like in New York, initially tried to downplay the officers' role in the incident. The big difference was Floyd's death was caught on video. Seventeen-year-old Darnella Frazier's powerful video capturing how Floyd died, for which she was properly recognized with a Pulitzer Prize, was necessary for justice to be served.

Immediately after Floyd's initial autopsy, the prosecutor and medical examiner released a statement that the postmortem examination did not find any evidence that police restraint had caused his death. Instead, the prosecutor tried to shift the blame to Floyd's supposed drug use and heart disease, either of which, the prosecutor said, could have caused his death.

But the second autopsy, by me and forensic pathologist Allecia Wilson, quickly determined that Floyd's death was caused by how he was restrained, which prevented him from breathing.

In order to arrive at an accurate cause and manner of death, autopsy findings must be correlated with findings from the scene and the circumstances of the death. Unfortunately, today, many forensic pathologists do not independently examine the body at the scene of death and instead rely on whatever information police provide to them. And this police involvement with the death itself can severely compromise the information.

As I noted earlier, autopsies begin not on the autopsy table but at the scene of death. This is especially important when someone dies while being restrained by police. A lack of oxygen leaves little or no evidence (compression of the veins can cause petechial hemorrhages to develop in the face and eyes, but does not always). Obstruction of the nose or mouth usually leaves no marks. Neither do carotid artery lateral-neck-compression holds, which prevent blood from reaching the brain; or prone back pressure, which prevents the movement of the diaphragm and the expansion of the chest cavity necessary for inhaling air.

Ignoring the scene of death results in inaccurate diagnoses. In the case of restraint asphyxia that occurs during police altercations, it means medical examiners and coroners issue death certificates with causes that obscure the true cause and manner of death.

These inaccurate determinations include excited delirium, a junk science diagnosis, and sickle cell trait, a benign condition. Police-related deaths are attributed to a drug overdose even when the amount found is well below fatal levels. Other inaccurate diagnoses include blaming natural heart disease if any coronary arteriosclerosis is present and attributing death to pneumonia, which frequently develops after the injury that renders an individual comatose, while they are kept alive in a hospital before being pronounced dead.

Adoption of such unscientific junk diagnoses among medical examiners has increased since 2007—when smartphones and social media began documenting these incidents. These misdiagnoses require the belief that prone back pressure does not interfere with breathing and that victims saying "I can't breathe" is just a manipulation. They require the belief that victims—mostly Black males—acquire super strength while dying, so that police officers must use extreme force to subdue them.

Such misdiagnoses also lead to distrust in scientific experts and foster the community's impression that these experts are intentionally using bogus diagnoses to protect police officers from prosecution. Officers failing to turn on bodycams, as well as police departments hiding videos of scene activity from families and the public, adds to the sense that the system is stacked against communities of color.

Fortunately, public concerns raised about the racial inequities exposed by Floyd's death are now stimulating changes in our criminal justice system.

On June 14, 2021, the American Medical Association announced that "excited delirium" was a racist creation to justify excessive use of force by law enforcement—an instance of medical racism. The AMA also recognized racism as a public health problem and urged that medical and behavioral health specialists respond to calls involving "emotionally disturbed persons" alongside first responders.

On September 30, 2021, the internationally recognized *Lancet* medical journal published a report from the University of Washington that documented "massive underreporting" of deaths in police custody in the United States. The report showed that death certificate data in the National Vital Statistics system identified 17,000 police encounter deaths—by firearms and not by firearms—between 1980 and 2018, and found that 18,000 additional deaths were inaccurately "listed as another cause of death." The *New York Times*'s prominent front-page headline about the report was "Study's Stark Finding: Over Half of Police Killings Go Uncounted." The article concluded that the covering up of Black deaths in police encounters involves not just police, prosecutors, and judges, but also misleading information provided by medical examiners and coroners. The report specifically blamed "the system of medical examiners and the incentives that may exist for them to want to not classify a death as related to police violence . . . The system has long been criticized for fostering a cozy relationship with law enforcement . . . and in some jurisdictions they are directly employed by police agencies."

I agree that medical examiners and coroners are responsible for a major part of the bias that permeates the broken criminal justice system. Every time a medical examiner concludes that sickle cell trait or excited delirium caused the death of a Black person in a police encounter, they are contributing to the problem.

And so, the deaths continue.

When twenty-five-year-old Freddie Gray was restrained while laying prone by Baltimore police, a witness's video showed that he was already paralyzed and unable to move his legs because of injuries to his cervical spinal cord during the restraint, something that was apparent when he was lifted from the ground by police and carried to the police van. He was initially conscious but could not walk. The medical examiner, in ruling on cause of death, adopted the police information provided that he died of neck injuries caused by a fall while seated on a bench in a police van. The only police deficiency was a failure to seatbelt him properly—not having first damaged his neck and spinal cord by putting pressure on his neck while restraining him. This was the same medical examiner who testified in the Floyd trial that police restraints did not cause his death. No one was charged for Gray's death. The US Department of Justice investigated and announced it would not bring charges against any of the six police officers involved.

When Ronald Greene, a forty-nine-year-old Black barber, was chased by Louisiana State Police on May 10, 2019, and his car struck a tree, his family was told that he died immediately from injuries incurred in the crash. The autopsy described many separate blunt-force head lacerations, multiple facial bruises, lacerations of the aorta and liver, and neck hemorrhages. Toxicology found recreational levels of alcohol and cocaine in his blood, though not enough to cause death. The autopsy pathologist's opinion as to the cause of death was "cocaine induced agitated delirium . . . complicated by the motor vehicle collision, physical struggle, inflicted head injuries during restraint." The death certificate issued by the Union Parish Coroner only stated: "Automobile crash. Accident." End of investigation. The prosecution had no interest in pursuing the matter further.

Two years later, after much litigation by the family, the police body camera footage was released—and showed Greene fully conscious and alert after striking the tree. He apologized to the police for not stopping sooner as he got out of his car. However, he was immediately tased multiple times, pepper-sprayed, choked, struck many times in his face and on his head, and dragged on the ground while shackled. He lost consciousness, stopped calling for help, stopped breathing, became lifeless, and died after pressure was placed on his prone back—all evidence that he died of restraint asphyxia. A federal lawsuit brought by the family remains pending. The prosecution still hasn't brought any charges against the police officers.

Daniel Prude, a nude, obviously emotionally disturbed forty-one-year-old Black man, died in March 2020 after being physically restrained on the streets of Rochester, New York, by police who used prone back pressure and a spit hood over his head. This same type of spit hood was used by US forces in Iraq's infamous Abu Ghraib prison, allegedly to protect soldiers from being spit upon—but it also prevents breathing. The medical examiner determined that Prude had died of asphyxia during physical restraint and classified the death as a homicide. There were many witnesses and videos taken of his death. But the New York State attorney general called a well-known California expert, who testifies frequently on behalf of police officers that prone pressure restraints do not cause death, to give his opinion to the grand jury. No one was indicted.

So, the question is: How can we decrease police officer–involved deaths?

An important and necessary first step is to determine the extent of the problem, so that strategies can be developed to address it.

Right now, the federal government doesn't track police-related deaths. The US Department of Justice had tried to set up a system in the early 2000s but it didn't include a mandatory reporting requirement. As a result, most law enforcement departments didn't cooperate.

In 2018, the US Civil Rights Commission report on Modern Policing Practices in 2018 raised concerns about the issue. "No comprehensive national database exists that captures police use of force. The best available evidence reflects high rates of uses of force, with increased likelihood of police use of force against people of color, people with disabilities, LGBT people, people with mental health concerns, people with low incomes, and those at the intersection of these communities," the report said.

"A lack of accurate data, lack of transparency about policies and practices in place governing use of force, and lack of accountability for noncompliance foster a perception that police use of force in communities of color and the disability community is unchecked, unlawful, and unsafe," it continued.

Individual police departments have the data. It is only transparency that is necessary. We need an independent national body to which all police encounter deaths, whether during shootings or restraint, must be reported, so they can be evaluated and strategies developed to prevent them. If law enforcement refuses to cooperate, they should face penalties.

Shooting deaths are easily identified. According to newspaper reports—again, because there are no official national statistics—about a thousand police-shooting deaths occur each year. Right now, it's the job of police internal investigations and the prosecutor to determine whether each of these shootings was justified.

Deaths that occur during non-shooting altercations with police are, of course, more difficult to identify because of the many inaccurate causes listed on death certificates.

We don't need more data to know that better training is part of the solution—something else noted in the Civil Rights Commission report: "The lack of sufficient training—and funding for training—leaves the public at risk." When companies sell the latest generation of restraint equipment to police departments, they teach officers *how* to use the devices, but not *when*. Many police departments likewise provide no training on proper occasion of use. As a result, officers sometimes use Tasers or devices like hobble restraints (used to hogtie suspects) when they don't have to.

Officers also receive little training in de-escalation tactics—ways to defuse a situation rather than exacerbating it—especially when dealing with the mentally ill. The result is unnecessary in-custody deaths.

Responding to calls involving people with mental health issues requires specialized training that police officers do not currently receive, but should. Better yet, we could set up units of mental health professionals who can respond to some of the mental health calls, either with or without police by their side. We could also ensure that when police do need to respond to these calls, a mental health professional accompanies them, as is the case in some cities now.

And of course, we need to keep warning officers about the dangers of exerting prone back and neck pressure.

We should follow the lead of other nations that have banned grand jury secrecy. (We inherited the secret grand jury system from England during colonial days. England abolished secret grand juries in 1933.) The current approach leaves too much power in the prosecutors' hands. The public should be allowed to know how the district attorney prosecuted the case and to hold them accountable if needed. Did they present all the appropriate available evidence?

There are simple steps that can be taken immediately to reduce or eliminate deaths during arrest and in custody, including banning prone back pressure, choke holds, and spit hoods, as well as restraint chairs—all of which impair breathing and can cause death—and limiting qualified immunity so that bad cops can be charged and disciplined. We should also replace the anachronistic coroner system with medical examiners, especially in this day and age when medical knowledge and forensic science are so important in accurately determining cause of death. Medical examiners should be independent of police and prosecutors. Excited delirium, sickle cell trait, and similar junk diagnoses should not be valid causes of death. All deaths in police encounters should be reported to a central national database. And mental health counselors should be available to accompany police on all calls involving mentally disturbed persons.

Even with all these solutions in place, the problem won't end overnight. But slowly, over time, the culture in the law enforcement community will change. We just need the courage to admit that this is a problem and then do something about it. Otherwise, more innocent people will die.

Rudolf Virchow, the father of pathology, wrote 175 years ago that "it is the curse of humanity that it learns to tolerate the most horrible situations by habituation." Such is evident now: persistent racism, sexism, religious extremism, poverty. "The physicians," Virchow added, "are the natural attorneys of the poor, and social problems fall to a large extent within their jurisdiction."

If not us, who?

If not now, when?

· · ·

AFTERWORD

A *merican Autopsy*—Dr. Michael Baden's transformative journey from naïve but intellectually curious medical school graduate to one of forensic pathology's most accomplished and principled practitioners—is a deeply moving and timely narrative. I loved it. As cofounder and special counsel of the Innocence Project, a national litigation and public policy nonprofit dedicated to exonerating the wrongfully convicted through DNA testing and other scientific means, and reforming our criminal legal systems to prevent future injustice, I have spent decades toiling at the crossroads of science and law. For more than thirty years I have collaborated with lawyers, scientists, community activists, legislators, judges, and members of the executive branch to improve the validity, reliability, equity, and compassion of what the government unrealistically calls "criminal justice." Yet, I still learned a great deal from Michael's book about the alarming extent to which racism, politics, and cognitive biases have influenced many pathologists' conclusions and opinions regarding cause and manner of death.

Michael has delivered an inside-baseball account of many of the most important criminal cases of the last fifty years, having played a critical and often decisive role in each. Several made front-page headlines. Others, while lesser known, were just as important in shaping Michael's perspective on justice—and that of the nation. But he offers much more than just great storytelling. Michael also shares his initial reactions to events and cases (sometimes the products of his own bias or naiveté); how his thinking changed once he applied his skills to the facts; and how, over several decades, his understanding of the presence or absence of justice in our criminal legal systems has evolved.

American Autopsy arrives as our nation embarks on an unprecedented re-investigation into its legacy of slavery and racism: how history, and the psychology that history has produced, intrudes into every aspect of our individual beings and collective culture. While multiple studies have described and analyzed how explicit and implicit racism have infected policing and the prosecutorial function, *American Autopsy* is unprecedented in revealing (in the author's words) the critical role that forensic pathologists have been expected to play in helping convict the "bad guys" drawn into the crosshairs of the American criminal legal system—regardless of their actual guilt—while thwarting attempts to hold police accountable even where their misconduct is abundantly clear.

I have known Michael for as long as there has been an Innocence Project. Since the project's inception in 1992, Michael has repeatedly and unselfishly offered us hundreds of hours of his much-in-demand time, professional expertise, wisdom, unparalleled analytic skills, and extraordinary humanity to help us get to the truth in dozens of cases, all for free.

On September 15, 1990, a three-year-old girl was abducted from her home in rural Mississippi, sexually assaulted, and disposed of in a pond two blocks from her house. When her lifeless body was recovered, Dr. Stephen Hayne, the go-to pathologist for almost every prosecutor in Mississippi, concluded during autopsy that marks on the toddler's wrist looked like human bite marks. Hayne asked his friend, dentist Michael West, to confirm his finding. West not only confirmed they were human bite marks, but—after comparing the impressions to the dental molds of several suspects—concluded that the biter was Levon Brooks, a young Black man with a solid alibi who had dated the victim's mother. Brooks was convicted of capital murder and given a life sentence.

Just four months after Brooks's conviction, less than two miles from where the first victim was found, another three-year-old girl was abducted from her home, raped, and then submerged in a nearby creek. Again, Dr. Hayne claimed there were human bite marks on the body. This time, West concluded they matched the mother's Black boyfriend, Kennedy Brewer. Brewer was convicted of capital murder and sentenced to death. (None of the law enforcement involved appeared to have considered the possibility that the two almost identical crimes occurring in the same sparsely populated rural community might have been committed by the same person.)

Post-conviction DNA testing on the semen in the Brewer case eliminated him as the source. (DNA testing in the Brooks case failed due to poor storage, which allowed mold to consume the sample.) Even so, after the DNA profile excluded Brewer as a suspect, the local prosecutor produced a jailhouse informant with an outlandish story to explain away the significance of the DNA exclusion. According to the prosecutor's investigator, the informant had told him Brewer confessed that, while someone conspiring with Brewer had raped the victim, Brewer had nibbled on her arms and legs.

We asked Michael to examine all the evidence. He found, contrary to Dr. Hayne's conclusions, that none of the marks on either body were made while the victims were alive, thus refuting the opportunistic narrative attributed to the snitch. Had they been living while bitten, there would be evidence of blood or bleeding under the skin, since once the heart stops beating, blood ceases to circulate. There had been no bleeding beneath any of the marks on either victim. Michael further observed that the various groupings of two or three marks on the victims' bodies looked nothing like human bites, which invariably leave marks from both the upper and lower teeth. None of the impressions on either body displayed evidence of what could possibly be a lower bite. Instead, Michael noted, the postmortem impressions on the skin were very similar to those he had observed in many other cases of dead bodies retrieved from water. There had been no allegations of human biting in those cases, and the marks most likely had been caused by small aquatic creatures biting the submerged bodies.

Michael's affidavit led to another round of advanced DNA testing, which identified the single source of the semen as Albert Johnson, an early suspect in both cases given that he had lived at various times next to both victims and had a criminal history of sexual assault. After the DNA hit, Johnson confessed to both crimes and offered nonpublic details about the murders corroborated by contemporaneous documentation of the two crime scenes. He did not know either Brewer or Brooks, both of whom were exonerated. Johnson pleaded guilty and is serving a life sentence.

Michael also testified in the Philadelphia retrial of Tony Wright—the only retrial in the history of the Innocence Project. A nineteen-year-old Black man, Wright was framed in 1991 by homicide detectives for the rape and murder of an eighty-year-old widow. Post-conviction DNA testing proved that the crime had been committed by another man, Ronnie Byrd, a chronic crack user who lived in an abandoned house nearby. The DNA results bought Wright a retrial in 2016—twenty-five years later. But the Philadelphia prosecutor retried the case under the absurd theory that after Wright stabbed the woman and departed, Byrd snuck in and had sex with a corpse.

At the retrial, the homicide detectives falsely claimed, as they did at the first trial, that they recovered blue jeans, a sweatshirt, and a pair of sneakers with a few small smears of blood from beneath Wright's bed, and swore that Wright had admitted he wore those jeans, sweatshirt, and sneakers when committing both crimes. DNA testing proved the few blood stains did belong to the deceased. However, testing throughout the inside of the jeans, sweatshirt, and sneakers produced a consistent DNA profile of the wearer of the clothing that didn't match Wright's DNA.

Michael noticed details in the crime scene and autopsy photographs omitted from the report of the deputy medical examiner who conducted the original autopsy. That examiner had noted and photographed a "pattern injury" on the victim's cheek but surprisingly said nothing more about the pattern. Michael pointed out that the pattern was unmistakably the shape and dimensions of the heel of a shoe or boot. Moreover, the autopsy X-rays revealed a fractured cheek bone directly beneath the heel mark. The victim had been stomped by her assailant. Michael's testimony provided additional evidence that the sneaker had been planted, since the perpetrator had worn a shoe with a hard heel, not a sneaker with a flat rubber sole. The second jury acquitted Wright in less than an hour.

This case, like the ones in Mississippi, illustrates that when the pathologists get it wrong—either by commission or omission—and explicitly or implicitly bolster a prosecutor's theory of the case, not only are they complicit in securing wrongful convictions, but their misstatements also cut off investigation, enabling the real criminals to remain at liberty to commit other violent crimes.

Three years after the Wright acquittal, Michael provided evidence essential to another Philadelphia exoneration. In 2001, Termaine Hicks came to the aid of a screaming woman who had been beaten and dragged into an alley behind a hospital in South Philly to be raped. Her attacker fled before completing the rape, once her screams alerted the community. When the police arrived, they saw Hicks, a young Black man, standing next to a woman lying on the ground and reaching into his pocket for his cell phone to call 911. Rather than asking any questions, the police—erroneously suspecting that Hicks was the assailant and that he was reaching for a gun—shot him three times in the back, almost killing him.

The victim did not identify Hicks as her attacker, and the police quickly realized he was unarmed and merely reaching for his phone. To cover up having shot an innocent man, they planted a gun on Hicks and framed him for raping the woman he had been trying to help. (It was ultimately proven that the gun was an off-duty revolver registered to another Philly police officer.) The cops claimed that they had shot Hicks in the front of his body as he lunged toward them while pointing a gun. At trial, the emergency room doctor said he could not distinguish the entry wounds from the exit wounds, a critical detail to either supporting the police version of events or proving the cover-up. No other medical witnesses testified. Hicks was convicted and spent two decades imprisoned.

In 2019, while Hicks was still serving his sentence, Michael reviewed the 1991 X-rays taken of Hicks in the emergency room. Michael explained that the bone fragments from the ribs shattered by police bullets were all in front of the ribs, consistent with the bullets coming from the rear. He then examined the coat, slacks, and shirt Hicks had been wearing when he was brought into the operating room. The clothes had been removed by the doctors before operating and stored in the police evidence room for two decades. The two small holes in the back of the jacket and shirt, and the one hole in the rear of his underpants, were consistent with three bullets having been fired from behind Hicks. None of the clothing had holes in the front. The new Philadelphia medical examiner agreed with Michael's conclusions, and in December 2020, Philadelphia's district attorney agreed that the police had perjured themselves in the original prosecution and threw out Hicks' conviction.

These are just a few of the many cases in which Michael, without fee, helped the Innocence Project and other lawyers (including my wife, Adele Bernhard) secure freedom for the wrongly convicted, who were more often than not people of color.

Although Michael attributes many of the miscarriages of justice he's seen to implicit and explicit racism in policing, and sometimes calls out specific colleagues in this book who succumbed to political pressure, he also speaks broadly and favorably about the higher calling of his profession, declining to highlight the consequences of structural racism and systemic bias in forensic pathology and at every step in the criminal legal system more broadly. Other writers have thoroughly documented how the legacy of slavery molded modern-day policing and prosecution, and this brief afterword is not the place to summarize that work. But on the topic of forensic pathologists and medical examiners, Michael's revelatory firsthand experiences highlight some of the intrinsic and fundamental deficits of the practice of forensic pathology in this country—though Michael himself is too polite to criticize the individuals along with their work product. When his mentor and father figure, Dr. Milton Helpern, chief medical examiner of New York City, buries the truth to help law enforcement, Michael keeps his disappointment to himself. Indeed, as Michael says, Helpern had taught him that the pathologist was the third leg of a three-legged stool—the other legs being the police and the district attorney. Together, the three were the "good guys," expected to cooperate with one another by rounding up the "bad guys" and putting them away for a long time. Lessons like this, which Michael learned from his early days at the Office of the New York Medical Examiner, were imparted not only to him but broadly, to generations of young pathologists. Despite his personal evolution and resistance to political pressures in his commitment to following the science, there is not enough said about the catastrophic consequences of a profession with a worldview very different from his own.

Under the various state and federal rules of evidence, expert witnesses receive special privileges that are denied all other witnesses. Ordinary witnesses are generally limited to testifying to what they personally observed and are not permitted to give opinions about those observations. Experts, in contrast, are allowed to provide informed opinions about what they or others observed if those opinions arise from their specialized knowledge. However, they are given this extraordinary privilege only when the subject matter at issue in the trial is too technical or scientific for lay jurors to be expected to readily understand without the help of someone with specialized knowledge and credentials. Forensic pathologists are given leeway well beyond that enjoyed by other experts, particularly as to manner of death. They are permitted to provide opinions partly based on data that is neither scientific nor medical but that nonetheless will be easily understood by a nonspecialist jury.

In most courts, once the pathologist offers an opinion on cause of death, they are permitted to opine on *manner* of death, an issue that rightfully belongs to the jury, not the doctor. The five categories of manner of death are homicide, suicide, natural death, accident, and undetermined. To render an opinion, the pathologist often relies, in addition to the medical findings, on subjective police reports and police interviews with civilian witnesses, and other nonscientific evidence (e.g., an alleged suicide note, admissions police officers claim suspects made). Comprehension of nonmedical and nonscientific evidence, and the weight it should be given, is clearly not beyond the capacity of lay jurors, who are routinely asked to evaluate the credibility of such evidence when they hear testimony in open court, be it from a neighbor or a police officer. There is no reason to believe that doctors are better situated to assess the accuracy or reliability of ordinary evidence than judges and jurors. Almost one-half of the wrongful convictions for homicide cleared by DNA evidence relied on what turned out to be false confessions. Most of these confessions were shared with pathologists before they issued their final autopsy reports and certainly before they testified to their conclusion as to manner of death. In other words, the opinions in their reports and testimony rely not just on the medical science but also on alleged facts of a nonmedical nature. The basis of these opinions exceeds the scope of a doctor's specialized medical expertise and should not be given the mythic infallibility and deference they currently enjoy.

The pathologist's unique privilege and power has less to do with reason or logic and more to do with an artifact of history. As Michael points out, the coroner system originally emerged in England nearly a thousand years ago to protect the financial interests of the monarch whenever a subject died. The coroner was a political appointment with no medical background, expected to conduct inquests to confirm the identity of the deceased, determine "the cause and manner of death," and collect property and death duties to benefit the Crown. It was important for the political appointee to identify the manner of death because, for example, if he called the death a suicide, or "self murder," the decedent's entire estate would be taken away from the family and escheated to the crown.

It was not until the late nineteenth century that doctors were allowed, in a few jurisdictions, to assist the coroner in determining cause and manner of death. Today, in many counties and some states, coroners have been replaced by physician medical examiners, a subset of whom are board certified in forensic pathology. But by statute in many states, the coroner has the last word on cause and manner of death, either alone or in collaboration with a medical examiner. To answer the question of whether a death from the ingestion of poison was brought about by a volitional act of the deceased (and therefore a suicide) or at the hands of a third person (and therefore a homicide) does not require medical training. Instead, the question is best answered by a competent investigator. Thus, the common law delegation to doctors to determine "manner of death" is nothing more than a relic of our nation's colonial past and is perpetuated more out of tradition than any well-reasoned justification.

And what of the consequences? Determinations on cause and manner of death impact decisions by prosecutors, grand and trial juries, and judges over whether a crime was committed and, if so, what offense a defendant is charged with or convicted of. These determinations can lead to execution or lengthy imprisonment for the innocent and can help police avoid accountability where their actions have contributed to the death of a civilian. The innocence movement, which includes our project plus several dozen smaller projects across the country, has brought about more than one hundred exonerations since 1989 where, in the original wrongful prosecutions and convictions, forensic pathologists have erred in determining cause, manner, or time of death. Such investigations reveal cognitive biases and misplaced reliance on subjective nonmedical evidence, along with diagnoses that are ill defined and not based on rigorous scientific criteria.

These same deficiencies and biases are responsible for dismissing deaths in custody as nonhomicidal or undetermined when it is obvious that police use of restraints was the "but for" cause in the deaths of unarmed civilians. If not for the witness's smartphone video of officer Derek Chauvin's knee on George

Floyd's neck, it is doubtful Chauvin would have been prosecuted, much less convicted of murder. Just as DNA testing caused an unprecedented appreciation of the misapplication of forensic science (50 percent of DNA exonerations involve such misapplication in the original prosecution and trial), the modern prevalence of civilian smartphones and police body cameras have cast doubt on the validity of past and present death-in-custody determinations. For the first time, the public can compare a pathologist's findings with the visual record.

Chauvin's expert witness, Dr. David Fowler—for seventeen years the chief medical examiner of Maryland—and others like him have substituted "excited delirium" for Milton Helpern's old "death by psychosis and exhaustion." As a result of Fowler's unsuccessful effort at Chauvin's trial to gaslight the billions of people who watched the bystander's video into believing that Floyd's death was the result of drug use, a heart condition, or invisible fumes from an exhaust pipe of a parked police car (where there was no evidence the engine was running), dozens of Maryland death-in-custody cases are expected to be reinvestigated by an audit at the direction of the state's attorney general. Fowler is not an outlier and Floyd's murder is not a one-off. Many other forensic pathologists have characterized deaths in custody caused by police restraints as either natural, accidental, or undetermined where there is ample evidence to support a finding of asphyxiation and homicide. All too often, causes like excited delirium, a nonlethal dose of drugs, or a noncritical medical condition are cited incorrectly and unfairly as the cause of death.

A March 2022 Physicians on Human Rights report found that excited delirium diagnoses could not be disentangled from their racist and unscientific origins and are not guided by diagnostic standards. Excited delirium is not defined in the International Classification of Diseases or in the *Diagnostic and Statistical Manual of Mental Disorders*. The report concluded that excited delirium "is not a valid, independent medical or psychiatric diagnosis." Yet Black people have been represented disproportionately in excited delirium diagnoses for deaths occasioned by police intervention. In three-quarters of the cases the group studied, medical examiners, forensic pathologists, coroners, and autopsy reports were the source of the excited delirium claim. In addition to excited delirium, sickle cell trait—a benign condition that is present in one out of thirteen Black people living in the United States—is sometimes used to explain cause of death when a Black suspect dies during or shortly after an altercation with police.

Racial disparity is also prevalent in our exoneration data. Two-thirds of the men and women the Innocence Project have helped free or exonerate are people of color and 58 percent are Black. Black people are almost seven times more likely to be wrongfully convicted of murder than white people.

Generally, the only nonmedical witnesses permitted to be present during autopsies are police. Even for deaths-in-custody autopsies, the police are often present, which can influence the outcome. In autopsies for those who didn't die in custody but where foul play is one of several possibilities, cops in attendance may suggest their theory of the case to the pathologist, thus giving it undue weight. Medico-legal investigators, rather than increasing their proximity to clinical medicine, have all too frequently been influenced by law enforcement priorities, particularly in their treatment of deaths in custody.

Clinical medicine is highly regulated, thanks to research requirements, regulatory agencies like the US Food and Drug Administration, and federally enforced standards like the Clinical Laboratory Improvement Amendments. In contrast, forensic medicine (and in particular cause and manner of death determinations) are basically unregulated. As long as a prosecutor likes a pathologist's conclusion or judge permits its introduction into evidence, the jury hears it—no matter how scientifically and medically illiterate that prosecutor or judge might be. The constituency pushing to regulate clinical medicine includes all of us—we all want to remain healthy. By contrast, the constituency that historically has pressed for enhanced regulation and scrutiny of forensic medicine is much smaller: those accused or convicted of crimes and their advocates. The constituency lobbying for heightened standards in clinical medicine is powerful. The constituency for quality assurance in forensic medicine is not. But we in the innocence movement remain hopeful that the number of proven exonerations and publicized videos of deaths in custody will increase the pressure for more rigorous science in medico-legal death investigations.

A 2021 study on potential bias in forensic pathology diagnoses indicated that death investigators were more likely to call an infant's death a homicide if the baby was Black and the caregiver who brought them to the hospital was the mother's boyfriend, versus if the baby was white and brought to the hospital by their grandmother. Rather than welcoming the study as an opportunity for further research, however, many of the leaders of the National Association of Medical Examiners attempted to suppress publication of the article. And when their irrational attempt at censorship failed, the association filed bogus ethics complaints against the authors in the United States and Great Britain. Although the complaints were eventually dismissed on the merits, their chilling effect on future research and scholarship critical of the status quo cannot be underestimated.

Nevertheless, as Michael's book demonstrates, at least one forensic pathologist has done much in the span of fifty years to disrupt that status quo. But the core problem is not with just a few cases or a handful of bad actors; it is systemic and structural, far greater than any one medical examiner—even one as insightful as Michael—can solve. Much needs to be done in the field of medico-legal death investigation if we are to achieve greater accuracy, reliability, and justice in our criminal legal systems. I hope this book moves us in a more positive direction—that it inspires us all to further introspection and analysis, and to become forces for change.

Peter Neufeld
September 2022

Acknowledgments

• • •

With many thanks to ...

Attorneys Benjamin Crump, Barry Scheck, Peter Neufeld, Nina Morrison, Vanessa Potkin, Antonio Romanucci, Robert Bennett, Julia Sherwin, Sharon King, Stanley King, Bob Shapiro, Robert Delaughter, Ed Peters, Kym Worthy, James Behrenbrinker, Andrea Lyon, Lesley Reisinger, Michael Reisinger, Kent Henderson, and Bob Tanenbaum.

Forensic pathologists Allecia Wilson, Werner Spitz, Cyril Wecht, and James Lauridson.

New York State Police colleagues Lowell Levine, Timothy McAuliffe, Robert Horn, and Ira Titunik.

Criminalist Henry Lee.

Journalists Jerry Mitchell and Mitch Weiss.

Former president of HBO Documentary Films Sheila Nevins.

My agent, Frank Weimann.

BenBella Books's superb editor Leah Wilson.

My office manager and typist extraordinaire, Patricia Hulbert, and her daughter, Christina.

... and the many others who helped me create this book.

Index

◆ ◆ ◆